AGING AND THE
RELIGIOUS DIMENSION

AGING AND THE RELIGIOUS DIMENSION

Edited by
L. EUGENE THOMAS
and
SUSAN A. EISENHANDLER

Foreword by HARRY R. MOODY

AUBURN HOUSE

Westport, Connecticut • London

Library of Congress Cataloging-in-Publication Data

Aging and the religious dimension / edited by L. Eugene Thomas and
  Susan A. Eisenhandler.
     p. cm.
  Includes bibliographical references and index.
  ISBN 0–86569–210–6 (alk. paper)
   1. Aging—Religious aspects. I. Thomas, L. Eugene.
  II. Eisenhandler, Susan A.
  BL65.A46A55 1994
  261.8'3426—dc20   93–9018

British Library Cataloguing in Publication Data is available.

Library of Congress Catalog Card Number: 93–9018
ISBN: 0–86569–210–6

First published in 1994

Auburn House, 88 Post Road West, Westport, CT 06881
An imprint of Greenwood Publishing Group, Inc.

Printed in the United States of America

The paper used in this book complies with the
Permanent Paper Standard issued by the National
Information Standards Organization (Z39.48–1984).

10 9 8 7 6 5 4 3 2 1

Contents

Figures and Tables

Foreword: The Owl of Minerva

Harry R. Moody

It was Hegel who said that the owl of Minerva takes flight only as the shades of dusk are falling. Wisdom, Hegel believed, only comes when a particular epoch—whether in a civilization or an individual life—reaches its final limit so that its character at last becomes known. Today, in the closing decade of the twentieth century, we are conscious of approaching a limit and pondering the character of our epoch. At this moment it ought to be the beginning of wisdom to acknowledge, at last, the enduring power of religion in human affairs. We stand at the end of the most self-consciously secular century that the world has ever known. Yet it would astonish the secular philosophers of the Enlightenment to acknowledge the persistence of wars of religion, wars which rage on, whether in Bosnia or the Middle East or elsewhere on the planet. But we must acknowledge the facts. While the great secular ideologies—notably communism—have lost their allure, religion has lost none of its power. Intellectuals, including gerontologists and other social scientists, ignore this fact at their peril.

But they have ignored this fact or repeatedly denied it, and the deniers have included some of the greatest minds of the epoch. Freud warned about the "return of the repressed" but what he had in mind was the subterranean force of sex and aggression. Religion, in Freud's view, was merely the tool of repression and self-deception, a factor destined to disappear with the advance of self-consciousness and rationality. Today, nearing the end of the twentieth century, and far removed from Freud's Victorian childhood, we might take a very different view of the matter. Sex and aggression are everywhere on display, no matter what cable TV channel we turn to, while the subject of religion still remains a matter of contempt and repression among the intelligentsia. Yet as Daniel Bell suggested, we may now be in the midst of an unexpected return of the repressed where the power of religion is acknowledged at last.

Of course religion today is far from being repressed in the everyday lives of people in the United States. But the intellectual elite "still doesn't get it," as Eugene Thomas suggests when he notes that contemporary gerontologists are engaged in a "fantastic effort" not to face up to religion. In fact gerontology has been colossally blind to the religious dimension of human aging, and the present volume is a welcome contribution which should open the eyes of everyone, religious or not, who is concerned about sources of meaning in the last stage of life.

The religious dimension of gerontology is not something for which we need to apologize. One reason is that a purely secular analysis is inadequate to the facts we have to deal with. For example, a purely secular analysis of power will not enable us to grasp how religious figures exert their force in history, including even the present age. Once we acknowledge the validity of the religious interpretation of gerontological themes, a whole new world of interpretation opens up to us. Old questions become reopened in unexpected ways.

Nietzsche once wrote that we cannot even begin to imagine what historians in future generations will discover in the meaning of events that, for us, are already long in the past. The same point can be made about the unexplored meanings that lie hidden in that repository of myth, symbol, and ritual that we call "tradition." A good example is the hermeneutic approach to the stories of Oedipus and King David taken up by Bertman and Achenbaum in their chapter in this book. What stories are more familiar to us than these two from the Hebrew and Greek traditions? Yet these stories retain unexpected meanings for us. Bertman and Achenbaum take up a theme emphasized by David Guttman in his interrogation of the sources of "power" and "empowerment" among elders. This whole discussion reminds us of the tremendous power, for good or ill, that can becomes vested in certain figures who cross the boundary between religion and politics, whether Martin Luther King and Malcolm X on American soil or Ghandi and Khomeini in Asia.

A deep question that runs through all the chapters of this book is how to live on the boundary between religion and social science. After more than three decades of studying religion and aging, it seems clear enough that mainstream methods of social science run the risk of trivializing the importance of religion, a point made by Eugene Thomas. Yet Thomas, like other scholars represented in this book, remains largely faithful to the methods and the theoretical constructs of social science as they understand them. But there is a difference, and to understand that difference is to recognize what it means to live in the "no man's land" of that elusive boundary between religion and social science.

An illuminating example of the point is to be found in the repeated citation of the work of Erik Erikson, a figure who is justifiably central in our thinking about the meaning of the last stage of life. But once we adopt a more forthright acknowledgment of the religious dimension, Erikson takes on a different importance. In this "revisionist" version of religion and social science, even a celebrated prophet like Erik Erikson begins to take on the role of Moses, the prophet who could see the promised land but not enter into it. Erikson, with his evocation of the ego integrity and wisdom in old age, is by far the most cited source in this book. Erikson once even delicately alluded to a "psychology of ultimate concern." But, faithful to the dominant secular powers of the age, Erikson's own formulation never quite does justice to the religious dimension of aging. Nonetheless the Eriksonian account of the life course remains a helpful heuristic framework, as it is for Edward Quinnan as he tries to put order into the idiosyncratic details of the life stories of aging priests.

Erikson's evasiveness about the psychology of ultimate concern raises an inescapable question. Are religious accounts about the universe true, or do they merely correspond to human beings' intense "need" to find meaning in life? Does religion constitute an objective or subjective fact about the cosmos? It is perhaps annoying to put the question this baldly. But it can't be helped. Too much is at stake. Barbara Payne and Susan McFadden seem to incline toward the subjective side of this question: "Spirituality can be understood as the human need to construct a sense of meaning in life." They are anxious to emphasize the compatibility between the religious and psychological approach and to maintain continuity between Erikson's language and the language of tradition: thus, ego integrity becomes analogous to the "communion with the saints." Payne and McFadden's approach allows them to make an important distinction between loneliness and solitude, one that parallels the distinction between disengagement and gero-transcendence made by Lars Tornstam in his chapter. Allan Chinen's analysis of the symbolic language of aging in fairy tales from around the world shows how far we can expand the language of psychology until we find a vindication for traditional mystical claims for transcendence and ultimate meaning.

A term that occurs frequently in this book is "spirituality." But what is "spirituality" anyway? In this book there are probably as many definitions as there are authors. We ought to recognize that in the Christian tradition, at least, the practice of spirituality has its own distinctive meaning, one which is intertwined with the mystical tradition within the Church and which finds a parallel in the mystical currents of other faith traditions. The domain of the "spiritual" points to a relationship with religion much deeper than anything that can be measured by participation in congregational activity. For a generation gerontological researchers with a behavioral and quantitative cast of mind have looked for "activity" that would somehow be an index for spiritual. They have not found it, and they never will. The authors of this volume point investigators in a much more fruitful direction. The assumption of most authors in this book is that a more phenomenological or human science approach is more helpful in probing the depths of late-life spirituality. Indeed, most chapters in the book exemplify the methods of the human sciences.

At the same time, we should not overlook the fact that critical, phenomenological and hermeneutic methods can fruitfully be combined with more orthodox techniques of the behavioral sciences. The chapter by Tornstam is an illuminating example of such methodological complementarity, which opens up reconsideration of topics in gerontology such as a disengagement theory, often judged dead and buried. Again, Nietzsche's remark about the open-endedness of the past comes to mind. Along with disengagement, we need bring greater scrutiny to other concepts from the "value-free" social sciences. Once we adopt such scrutiny with the religious dimension in mind, we are likely to make unexpected discoveries. Indeed, our understanding of the meaning of the "spiritual" will come to take on a multivalent quality and, at the same time, permit a "transvaluation" of theoretical topics related to the study of the human life course, such as cognitive development, the power of the aged, and other issues that seem to belong entirely to the secular side of gerontology.

There is of course a much broader use of the term "spirituality," which we observe for instance in Susan Eisenhandler's essay, where she uses the word to describe all of the ways in which older adults consider and weigh the experiences of life. Unlike the purely psychological or subjective approach, this broader definition of spirituality points to the social milieu in which the search for self-transcending meaning can take place. What social, educational or cultural structures nurture, or inhibit, spiritual growth? Here we might pay heed to Tornstam's suggestion that the Western celebration of activity, both in gerontology and in the broader youth culture, may actually serve to obstruct the emergence of that "gerotranscendence" which Tornstam believes to be empirically visible in some significant segment of the aging population.

Tobin, Fullmer and Smith take a comparable stance when they go so far as to speak of "secular spirituality," which appears to mean interpretations of one's personal life and of the world. Like other contributors to this volume, they quite rightly argue that no simple behavioral approach to religion or subjective well-being in late life will suffice. Culture-specific instruments are essential to measuring what religiosity may mean to different groups of people and to disentangle the ambiguous relationship between well-being and spiritual maturity.

The distinction between sacred and secular is central to Rubinstein's exploration of "pragmatic spirituality." Rubinstein, like other writers in this book, wants to rethink this distinction, and he does it by focusing on generativity. Generativity becomes ever more essential yet at the same time ever more problematic in a world where secular culture prevails and, as Rubinstein puts it, "death clearly signifies the end." As a mechanism for coping with finitude, the crisis of generativity is part of the crisis of second half of life: "Will anything

I have accomplished outlive me?'' If ''symbolic immortality,'' in Robert Jay Lifton's phrase, is the sum of all that can be hoped for, then what happens to the self in a postmodern culture where all varieties of meaning are susceptible to being ''deconstructed'' and infinitely revised or discarded as new narratives evolve?

A major theme running through many chapters in this book is the importance of life narrative and of qualitative methods that can seek to capture lived experience in ways that positivist social science typically fails to do. An earlier collection of essays on the human science approach to gerontology exemplified this same methodological innovation.

Yet at just this point we must register a cautionary note. Are narrative and biographical approaches simply a matter of *method* or do they constitute a covert vehicle for redemption—a kind of ersatz spirituality in which the ''life-review'' comes to occupy, covertly perhaps, the role of the Last Judgment? The modern preoccupation with psychological ''identity'' as a life-long process or task testifies to the way in which, for the modern consciousness, psychology has tended to displace religion.

The new interest in narrative and story-telling is not merely a matter of methodology in the human sciences. It signifies a resurgent aspiration for human community and even a nostalgia for a measure of spiritual reintegration: ''In its new meaning, the term (identity) registers the waning of the old sense of a life as a life-history or narrative—a way of understanding identity that depended on the belief in a durable public world, reassuring in its solidity, which outlasts individual life and passes some sort of judgment on it.''[1]

The reassuring solidity of a durable public world is what a ''pragmatic spirituality'' seeks to nurture. But isolated individuals cannot by themselves create self-transcending structures that sustain meaning in later life. They can only participate in those institutions or, at best, become co-creators of something that outlives the self, in Kotre's phrase. ''Reassuring solidity'' may perhaps have been available in the institutions of the pre-Vatican II Roman Catholic Church. That durability is symbolized by the fact that still-living elderly members of religious orders spent years of their lives speaking fluently in Latin, a quaint fact Edward Quinnan notes in his fascinating collective biography of aged male members of a Catholic religious order. The first-person account of one such religious man is movingly recounted in Richard Griffin's chapter in this book. Griffin's memoir should be read with an ear for the cadences of the great spiritual autobiographies, like Augustine's or Thomas Merton's, always in the background. But note the difference in our current, ''postmodern'' cultural landscape. Whereas these earlier autobiographies led the reader from the secular to the sacred, Griffin's memoir moves in the opposite direction, insisting that ''spiritual freedom'' can indeed be found in the secular world, too.

Griffin may be right. But the larger question of social structure and identity persists. In light of Christopher Lasch's question, we must ask: does the secular world constitute an enduring structure in which late-life meaning can be sus-

tained? For example, one wonders how far the sense of identity exhibited by
the monastic brothers was related to the enduring social structure of the order,
with its "rigid boundary existing between those entering religious life and the
rest of society." This is a question that needs to be asked again and again as
we ponder the relationship between individual spirituality and its social milieu,
as Susan Eisenhandler puts it in her chapter.

To be sure, not all of the brothers went on the same spiritual journey; nor did
they arrive at the same destination. They began their religious life "having a
strong identification with traditional belief and formal ritual" but now have
expanded to a wider sense of spiritual affiliation. Some of these older men
achieved an impressive sense of integrity in their own life stories. But they could
do so, one suspects, only because "religious and spiritual traditions have preserved life narratives and offer themselves as templates for the construction of
contemporary life structures." What is perhaps most striking about these lives
is the way they demonstrate how the process Jung called individuation can take
place within the context of a premodern tradition, a tradition constantly recon-
structed and also modified from generation to generation.

In the Middle Ages scholastic philosophers had a saying that "Authority has
a nose of wax," suggesting that what we call "tradition" can be pushed in many
directions. That malleability of tradition is a subtext for Dena Shenk's depiction
of how in the Jewish tradition aging women make creative use of the cultural
resources to survive in contemporary America. Barbara Myerhoff was the first
great exemplar of this approach. But Myerhoff in *Number Our Days* depicted
survivors who had seceded into a cultural enclave: the senior center as *shtetl*
rather than as suburbia. Up to the end of her life Myerhoff wondered just how
far traditions needed to be retained or perhaps transformed in order to sustain
their healing power.

This is a question that a multicultural United States asks itself over and over
again. Whether in caregiving styles or in Jewish humor, we see how the United
States is forever a land where traditions are both dissolved and preserved in
unpredictable ways. Curiously enough, that same bewildering transformation of
tradition is found in India, in the story of Swami Tamananda as told by Eugene
Thomas. The Swami, like Mahatma Ghandi, is evidently a man perfectly prepared to adapt Hindu tradition in order to maintain its heart, which is the mystical
experience of nothingness and self-transcendence.

The American experience, then, is not so different from the world experience:
the inescapability of tradition and, at the same time, the impossibility of retaining
any cultural form in isolation from a present moment which dissolves and transforms our sense of who we are. This is not merely the postmodern moment. It
is also the experience of aging, as T. S. Eliot put it in the *Four Quartets,* where
each moment "is a new and shocking valuation of all that we have been." The
present book is a vindication of the religious dimension of gerontology. It is an
exploration of new territory but it is also a rediscovery of truths about our
condition that were always there.

NOTE

1. Christopher Lasch, *The Minimal Self: Psychic Survival in Troubled Times* (New York: Norton, 1984), 32.

Introduction: A Human Science Perspective on Aging and the Religious Dimension

L. Eugene Thomas and Susan A. Eisenhandler

E. F. Schumacher (1977), in the introduction to his book, *A Guide for the Perplexed,* uses an arresting anecdote to indicate the extent to which religion has been removed from official consciousness in the modern world. He tells of being lost in (then) Leningrad, and his confusion in consulting a Russian map of the city. What confused him was that he could see several enormous churches from where he was standing, but there was no trace of them on his map. When he later asked his interpreter why the churches were not shown on the map, the cryptic reply was, "We don't show churches on our maps."

Although this event occurred in then Communist Russia, it is arguable that in many ways the same mentality prevails throughout the Western world—that is, that the religious dimension fails to appear on most of our cultural maps. For a variety of historical and intellectual reasons, religion has received scant attention in Western social science. Kant's distinction between "is" and "ought" has led to the sharp distinction between fact and value. This distinction has served as the basis for the ideal in the social sciences that research should remain "value free," and that it should be conducted in as "objective" a manner as possible (Dumont 1979). This in turn has led to the strong emphasis on quantitative techniques in all fields of the social sciences, which seek to eliminate as much as possible the subjective element (see Polkinghorne 1983 for a historical overview). Further, social scientists have been influenced in their view of religion by Kant's stricture that such terms as "God" and "spiritual" are not proper objects of knowledge at all, since they contain no distinctive sense-content (James, 1902/1958).

GERONTOLOGY AND THE STUDY OF RELIGION

The tendency to "leave religion off the map" has been, if anything, more prevalent in gerontology than other areas of the social sciences. Johanne Philbrick (1991), in an analysis of all articles published in the *Journal of Gerontology* and the *Gerontologist* (the two major publications of the Gerontological Society of America), from their founding up to the present decade, found only twenty-three articles which focused centrally on religion and aging. This averages out to less than one article a year over the forty-four-year span of her analysis, suggesting the remarkable extent to which religion has been ignored in the field.

It is gratifying to note that there has been a growing awareness of the importance of religion in the field of aging in the last few years, and this is reflected in an increase in research and publications. In the past decade three journals have been founded that deal with religion and aging (Cole 1992), and several handbooks and surveys of the field have recently appeared (see the overview of publications noted by Levin & Tobin, in press). Much of this new interest has been focused on pastoral and service delivery concerns, however, and the research base still remains limited (e.g., only three of the twenty-four papers presented at the Claremont conference on spirituality and aging, which served as the basis of Seeber 1990, were based on research).

Much of the research which has been conducted on religion and aging is based on a positivist paradigm (Tornstam 1992), and has utilized the quantitative approach. What this has meant is that only those variables have been studied which lend themselves to quantitative measurement (see McClelland 1981 for an examination of how this has distorted anthropological research, and Polkinghorne 1983 for a broader discussion of this issue). As a result, most of the research we have in the field of aging and religion is based on easily quantified institutional beliefs and behaviors by sociologists (Payne 1982), and paper-and-pencil structured instruments by psychologists (Gorsuch 1984; Spilka 1991).

What has been largely ignored by the field is the place that religious beliefs and practices hold in the lives of the aging individual. Despite the pleas of Neugarten (1977) and others (e.g., Coleman 1990) that a more phenomenological approach be utilized, few researchers have followed this lead. This is due, in no small part, to the fact that this approach is antithetical to the positivist paradigm which informs most of the research and theory in the field, in which operationally defined and quantifiable constructs are demanded, as well as a "value-free," "objective" stand on the part of the researcher.

As has been argued elsewhere (Thomas 1989), the human science paradigm offers a more appropriate philosophy of science on which to base our efforts to understand aging. And the field of religion, in particular, would seem to require this more spacious paradigm, if we are to understand the personal meaning it has for the individual. In breaking the sharp distinction between social science and the humanities, the human science paradigm allows us to draw on the insights of history, philosophy, religion, and literature in understanding the human experience. Freed from the narrow strictures of positivism, new and exciting horizons are opened up to gerontology in understanding the latter part of the life cycle.

ORIENTATIONS AND METHODOLOGIES UTILIZED IN THIS VOLUME

The present volume grew out of interest generated by symposia presented at recent meetings of the Gerontological Society. In fact, the core of these chapters was presented at symposia dealing with qualitative research on aging. The present volume broadens the field to include quantitative studies, along with theoretical and historical papers, reflecting the inclusiveness of the human science paradigm.

Within the human science framework the only limitation placed upon the researcher is that the subject matter determine the methodology. The present volume illustrates this dictum in that it contains chapters utilizing a range of methodologies written from a variety of disciplinary orientations. The first two chapters (Thomas and Payne & McFadden) are theoretical formulations, pulling together psychological and sociological approaches to issues raised in the study of religion and aging. As will be noted below, however, in this volume theoretical formulations are not sharply distinguished from empirical findings, and other chapters, particularly the chapter by Tornstam, raise important theoretical issues as well.

The authors of the next two chapters make use of the case study approach. Griffin's chapter is actually an autobiographical case study, based on his personal experience as a former member of a religious order, in which he reflects on the impact of historical and personal changes over more than a quarter of a century of turbulent church history following Vatican II. Thomas makes use of both his own participant observation and Erikson's (1969) account of the life of Gandhi, in seeking to understand the sources of power and influence held by some elderly.

The following four chapters (Bertman & Achenbaum, Chinen, Harris, and Shenk) draw upon the humanities—literature, history and theology—to add to our understanding of the place that religion holds in the lives of older persons. Harris analyzes the source of spiritual well-being in several, less well-known Old Testament characters, juxtaposing current social science theory with the experience of biblical figures from another historical period. Bertman and Achenbaum examine aging and spiritual empowerment, utilizing the well-known Old Testament figure, King David, and Sophocles' King Oedipus. Also drawing upon the Western cultural history, Shenk examines the role of women in the Jewish tradition, noting how this tradition impinges on the role of contemporary

Jewish mothers. Chinen, on the other hand, utilizes fairy tales from a range of cultural traditions to examine the spiritual dimension of aging.

Following these historical studies, Eisenhandler's and Quinnan's chapters bring us to contemporary social science analysis. They both utilize participant observation, but their focus, as well as their samples, are widely divergent. Eisenhandler examines how aspects of spiritual inquiry present themselves in a "secular" setting, devoted to the study of contemporary literature, while Quinnan analyzes the life span development of spirituality among elderly male members of a Roman Catholic religious order.

The final three chapters utilize interview and survey methodology, but, again, differ widely in focus. Tobin, Fullmer, and Smith and Rubinstein base their chapters on interviews with atypical elderly women, that is, those with developmentally disabled children, and women without children. In both cases they examine evidence of spirituality and the role that religion plays in the lives of their respondents. Tornstam's chapter is based on survey research, which he uses as a means for examining evidence of developmental transcendence among a sample of elderly. As indicated above, Tornstam's chapter is unusual in that he combines quantitative survey research with a wide-ranging theoretical examination of the concept of transcendence in a sample of overtly secular Danish elderly respondents.

The range of methodologies utilized in this book reflects the varied disciplinary orientations of the authors. In addition to the usual social science disciplines of psychology, sociology, psychiatry and anthropology, the humanities are represented as well, including history, literature and biblical criticism. Perhaps of even more importance, the authors do not limit themselves to the disciplines in which they were trained. Thus a psychiatrist (Chinen) utilizes the methodology of folklore; a theologian (Quinnan) utilizes participant observation; an anthropologist (Shenk) makes use of theological investigation; and a sociologist (Tornstam) uses quantitative survey analysis to raise questions about the nature of spiritual development.

In sum, the chapters in this book seek to follow the thrust of the human science paradigm, in that the researchers eschew the usual strictures of "methodological orthodoxy," in which methodological rigor takes precedence over content; rather, they have allowed the topics of their investigation to determine the methodology they used. In seeking to understand a dimension of life so pervasive and so multifaceted, any other approach runs the risk of trivializing the study of aging and the religious dimension.

The religious dimension of aging, as will be argued throughout this book, encompasses the spiritual, the social and the developmental aspects of a person's life. In order to recognize and understand these aspects of an aged self, women and men must be open to and engage in the kinds of activities that stimulate the "ultimate concern" and ultimate awareness echoed in St. Augustine's entreaty, "May I know myself so that I may know Thee." We now turn to a collection of work which explores the human science perspective on aging and the religious dimension, and illustrates the diverse ways of knowing the sacred and the self.

REFERENCES

Cole, T. R. 1992. *The journey of life: A cultural history of aging in America*. New York: Cambridge.

Coleman, P. 1990. Adjustment in later life. In J. Bond and P. Coleman, eds., *Ageing in society*. London: Sage.

Dumont, L. 1979. The anthropological community and ideology. *Social Science Information* 18, 785–817.

Erikson, E. H. 1969. *Gandhi's truth*. New York: Norton.

Gorsuch, R. L. 1984. The boon and bane of investigating religion. *American Psychologist* 39, 228–236.

James, W. 1902/1958. *The varieties of religious experience*. New York: New American Library.

Levin, J. S., and S. S. Tobin. In press. Religion and psychological well-being. Forthcoming in M. A. Kimble, S. H. McFadden, J. W. Ellor and J. J. Seeber, Eds., *Handbook on religion, spirituality, and aging*. Minneapolis: Fortress.

McClelland, D. C. 1981. Child rearing versus ideology and social structure as factors in personality development. in R. Munroe, R. L. Munroe and B. B. Whiting, eds., *Handbook of cross-cultural human development*. New York: Garland.

Neugarten, B. L. 1977. Personality and aging. In J. E. Birren and K. W. Schaie, eds., *Handbook of the psychology of aging*. New York: Van Nostrand.

Payne, B. P. 1982. Religiosity. In D. J. Mangen and W. A. Patterson, eds., *Research instruments in social gerontology*. Vol. 2, *Social roles and social participation*. Minneapolis: University of Minnesota Press.

Philbrick, J. 1991. *Journals in gerontology: The art of a science*. Unpublished dissertation, University of Connecticut, Storrs, CT.

Polkinghorne, D. 1983. *Methodology for the human sciences*. Albany, NY: State University of New York Press.

Schumacher, E. F. 1977. *A guide for the perplexed*. New York: Harper.

Seeber, J. J. 1990. *Spiritual maturity in the later years*. New York: Haworth.

Spilka, B. 1991. At heart, the psychology of religion may be too psychological. Address at the convention of the American Psychological Association, San Fransisco.

Thomas, L. E. 1989. *Research on adulthood and aging: The human science approach*. Albany, NY: State University of New York Press.

Tornstam, L. 1992. The quo vadis of gerontology: On the scientific paradigm of gerontology. *The Gerontologist* 32, 318–326.

I Theoretical Perspectives

1 Values, Psychosocial Development, and the Religious Dimension

L. Eugene Thomas

> Religion in its broadest terms consists of the belief that there is an unseen order and that our supreme good lies in harmoniously adjusting ourselves thereto.
>
> —William James,
> *The Varieties of Religious Experience*

> Among all my patients in the second half of life—that is to say, over thirty-five—there has not been one whose problem in the last resort was not that of finding a religious outlook on life.
>
> —Carl G. Jung,
> *Modern Man in Search of a Soul*

For a social scientist, the attempt to survey the conceptual domain of religion is, as William James noted in his famous Gifford Lectures (1902/1958), intimidating. If anything, the field is more muddled now than in James's day. The standard dictionary definition of religion, for example, provides little conceptual clarification: "A set of beliefs concerning cause, purpose and the nature of the universe . . . usually involves devotional and ritual observances" (Random House 1969). Indeed, beliefs and institutional observance have been the dimensions typically measured by social scientists, with their noted meager payoff (Payne 1982).

Nor does one get much help from the conceptualizations of the field as they appear in the research literature. Lukoff, Turner and Lu (1992), in a recent review of the literature on religion and mental health, accept as their definition of religion one little different from the dictionary definition, quoted above: "adherence to the beliefs and practices of an organized church or religious institution" (p. 43). Gorsuch (1984), in making a distinction between religious and non-religious people, does little to clarify the field. Concerning the dimension which he identifies as central in making the distinction between religious and non-religious, he suggests that it "reflects an intrinsic commitment to a traditional Gospel-oriented interpretation of the Christian faith" (p. 232). (It should be noted that this definition did not appear in a sectarian religious publication but in one of the major journals of the American Psychological Association.) The fact that such a definition of religion excludes persons of other religious persuasion goes without saying, making it totally inadequate for use in a pluralistic society such as the United States, to say nothing of its inadequacy for cross-cultural research. Even worse, such a circumscribed definition of religion fails to go beyond a verbal statement of institutional beliefs, hardly adding to our understanding of the place of the religious dimension in an individual's life.

In seeking to circumscribe the domain of religion for his Gifford Lectures, William James despaired of arriving at a precise definition. He concluded that there is no one essence that defines religion. Rather, he saw religion as a "collective" sentiment, no easier to define than an equally complex concept like "government" (1902/1958, p. 42). In focusing on the psychology of religious experience he proposed a working definition of religious sentiment as "the feelings, acts, and experiences of individual men in their solitude, so far as they apprehend themselves to stand in relation to whatever they consider the divine" (p. 42). And by "divine" he meant "such a primal reality as the individual feels impelled to respond to solemnly and gravely" (p. 47).

This level of feeling and sentiment is clearly beyond the scope of the standard measures of religiosity found in the literature. Rather than focusing solely upon institutional beliefs and practices, James's definition suggests a dimension of religion not unlike Tillich's characterization of religion as "ultimate concern"— that which is "a matter of infinite passion and interest, making us its objects whenever we try to make it our object" (1951, p. 12). From this experiential point of view, James's definition of religion (and presumably Tillich's) could include everything from traditional Christianity to Buddhism, as well as New Age religions, in so far as they are of central importance in a person's life.

INTRINSIC-EXTRINSIC RELIGIOUSNESS

Allport's (1963) concept of an intrinsic-extrinsic religious dimension probably comes closest to tapping this depth dimension of religion than any other formulation suggested by social scientists. Reflecting James's and Tillich's defi- nitions, persons would be judged to be high on the intrinsic dimension who "find their master motive in religion," and for whom "other needs, strong as they may be, are regarded as of less ultimate significance," such that "they are brought into harmony with the religious beliefs" (Allport & Ross 1967, p. 434). Persons who "use religion for their own needs," and whose values are "in- strumental and utilitarian," would be low on the dimension.

Donahue (1985), in a meta-analysis of two decades of research on Allport's Religious Orientation Scale (ROS) concluded that the scale is not unidimensional as Allport originally suggested, with the opposite ends being intrinsic and ex- trinsic religious orientation. Rather, the extrinsic and intrinsic components have been found to be two independent or orthogonal dimensions, which show dif- ferent factor loadings and correlate differently with other religious and social- psychological variables. Scores on the intrinsic dimension of the ROS have been found to correlate positively with measures of religious commitment, as distinct from institutional affiliation and theological doctrines, while the reverse has been found to be true for scores on the extrinsic dimension. Significantly, extrinsic religiousness has been found to be positively correlated with prejudice, dog- matism and fear of death—"the sort of religion that gives religion a bad name," Donahue observes (p. 416).

These findings actually fit well with Allport's suggestion that the dimensions be juxtaposed orthogonally to form a two-by-two table (Figure 1.1), which provides a meaningful typology of religious orientations. Those persons who are high in intrinsic and low in extrinsic orientation (termed Extrinsic by Allport) would reflect Tillich's definition of true religion, or ultimate concern. Persons high on both the intrinsic and extrinsic dimension, Allport's Indiscriminate type, and those high on the extrinsic dimension and low on the intrinsic dimension, Allport's Extrinsic type, would not qualify as being religious in the sense sug- gested by Tillich. Their high orientation to the extrinsic dimension of religion indicates that for them religion is not a matter of ultimate concern. For this reason it is by and large Intrinsic religiousness that is meant when reference is made to the "religious dimension" in this chapter, and throughout the book.

RELIGION AND PSYCHOSOCIAL DEVELOPMENT

Allport suggests that mature religious sentiment is "fashioned in the workshop of doubt" (1950, p. 83). That is, the route to an Intrinsic religious orientation is by way of a "dark night of the soul" (the term used by Western mystics), in which original convictions are subjected to doubt and skepticism. The resulting faith is no longer made up of one's inherited religious beliefs and parental values, but consists of one's personally embraced beliefs and convictions, a basic com- ponent of one's "ego identity" (Erikson 1968).

It is instructive to note that in his discussion of identity formation, Erikson maintains that fashioning a personal ideology constitutes one of the major de-

Figure 1.1
Allport's Intrinsic-Extrinsic Religious Orientation Typology

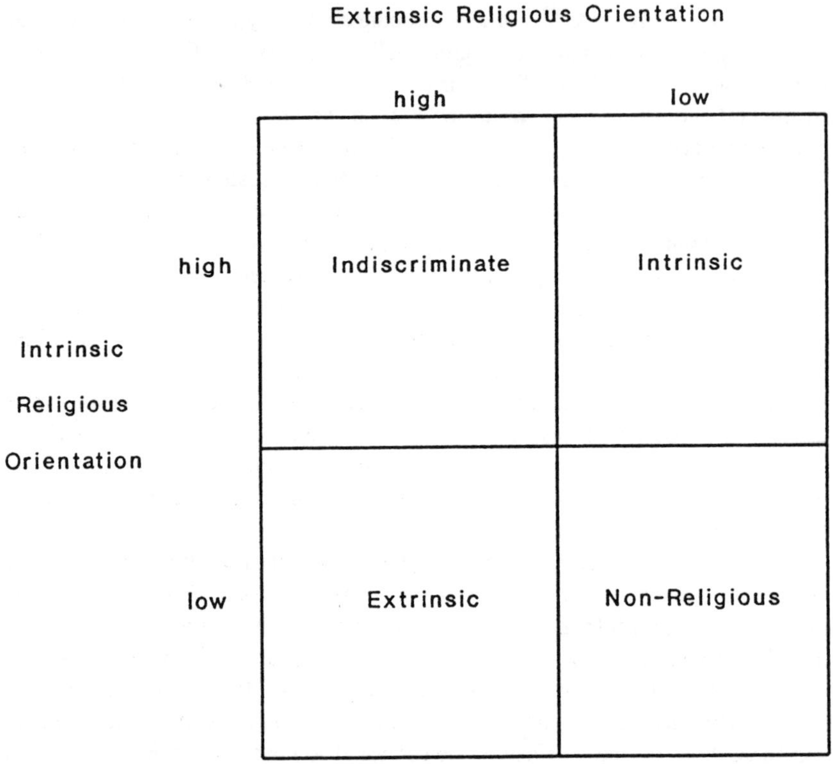

Extrinsic Religious Orientation

	high	low
high	Indiscriminate	Intrinsic
low	Extrinsic	Non-Religious

Intrinsic Religious Orientation

velopmental tasks of adolescence. Further, he argues that at this time the individual must give up the "introjected" beliefs of family and clan, and through questioning them, fashion his or her own. For most adolescents this is a time of critical self-examination, and in some cases, it constitutes a crisis. Those youth who never go through such a time of questioning, he suggests, fail to achieve a vigorous sense of personal identity. Rather, in accepting "received" values and beliefs, they are characterized as being in "Foreclosure."

Like Allport, Erikson originally conceived of the "identity/identity diffusion" construct as being unidimensional. Subsequent research led Marcia (1966) to conceptualize the two components as being orthogonal, creating a two-by-two typology of four meaningful identity statuses (Figure 1.2). The similarities to the Allport typology are striking. Those high on intrinsic religion, and identity achievement, are seen to have undergone a time of doubt (Marcia uses the term "crisis"). The outcome of the crisis leads in the one case to either Identity achievement or Moratorium (in which the individual is not committed to a personally binding ideology), or on the ROS to an Intrinsic religious orientation

Figure 1.2
Marcia's Typology of Erikson's Identity Statuses

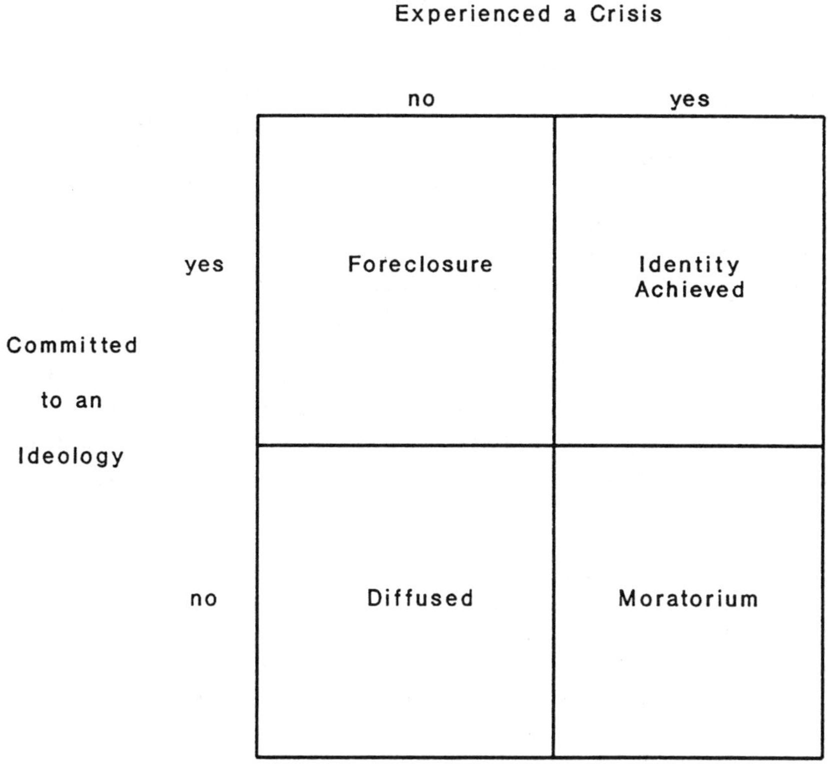

Experienced a Crisis

	no	yes
Committed to an Ideology — yes	Foreclosure	Identity Achieved
Committed to an Ideology — no	Diffused	Moratorium

or a Non-religious orientation (in which the individual is not committed to a personal religious orientation). Those who have not undergone doubt vary on the identity status typology by whether they are committed to a set of beliefs and values (Foreclosed) or not (Diffused), which are directly comparable to the Indiscriminate and Extrinsic quadrants of the ROS typology.

Research has indicated that the quadrants of the Erikson and Allport typologies show remarkably similar psychological correlates. Marcia (1966) found that those respondents in the Identity Achieved status showed low authoritarianism, and tended to be low in neuroticism, while individuals in the Foreclosure quadrant displayed high authoritarianism and those in the Diffusion status were high in neuroticism. Donahue (1985), in his review of research on Allport's ROS, reports consistent findings that those identified as Intrinsics displayed low levels of prejudice and fear of death, while those high on the extrinsic dimension (Indiscriminates and Extrinsics) were found to be high on measures of prejudice, trait anxiety and fear of death.

It will be remembered that Erikson's formulation of identity development was devised to describe adolescence as part of an overall sequence of developmental stages, while Allport's ROS of intrinsic-extrinsic religiousness was intended to describe religiousness in general. In other words, Allport's formulation is non-developmental; that is, he did not seek to chart change over time, and consequently did not make projections for change in his typology over time (although the concept that a time of doubt is necessary for a genuine Intrinsic orientation has developmental implications, as will be indicated shortly). Erikson's theory, on the other hand, seeks to chart the psychosocial tasks of the different stages of the life cycle, identifying three adult stages extending beyond that of the adolescent task of identity achievement. It will be useful, in seeking to understand the place of the religious dimension in the later part of the life cycle, to look at Erikson's formulation of the salient task of this period.

The last developmental task in Erikson's life span theory is that of achieving a sense of individual integrity, which he defines as "the ego's accrued assurance of its proclivity for order and meaning . . . the acceptance of one's one and only life cycle and of the people who have become significant to it as something that had to be" (1968, p. 139). Failure to achieve a sense of integrity is characterized by "disgust and despair," in which "fate is not accepted as the frame of life, death not as its finite boundary" (p. 140).

Faced with the physical insults to the body with age, and the loss of significant others, Erikson suggests that the aging individual is catapulted into "a new edition of an identity crisis" (p. 141). Referring back to the developmental task first faced in adolescence, Erikson suggests that persons who were on the "no-crisis" side of the identity typology in earlier life are likely to face new challenges which push them over to the "crisis" side in later life. In other words, inexorable changes in one's own body (the last push of the epigenetic principle, so to speak) and its similar effect on one's significant others would suggest a collapse of the fourfold typology of ego identities of adolescent, to a twofold typology of old age, as suggested in Figure 1.3.

As a social scientist, Erikson has been reluctant to deal with religion directly (for example, in an influential essay written in the early 1960s, Erikson noted, "I am not ready to discuss the psychology of 'ultimate concern,' " [1964, p. 133], and he has failed to do so explicitly in subsequent publications). But as a realist he is cognizant of the final existential boundary which defines the human condition. Identifying the unique strength associated with the last stage of the life cycle as "Wisdom," Erikson defines it as "detached concern with life itself, in the face of death itself" (1964, p. 133). In one of his last publications Erikson suggests that it may be necessary to add a ninth stage of development to the present eight, "a sense or premonition of immortality . . . as creatively given form in the world religions" (Erikson, Erikson & Kivnick, 1986, pp. 336–337).

The developmental collapse of Erikson's fourfold typology of identity into a twofold typology of later life, due to the fact that by the time of old age everyone has experienced crises, raises the question of whether Allport's fourfold typology

Figure 1.3
Conceptualization of the Collapse of Erikson's Statuses with Advancing Age

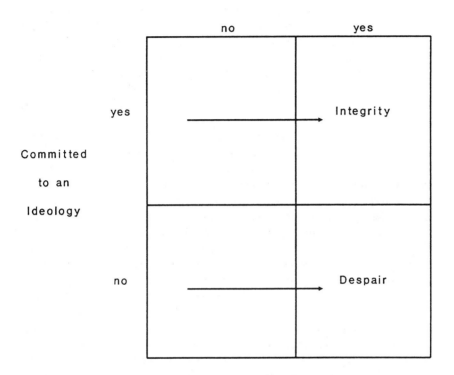

Experienced a Crisis

might not show a similar change with age. Allport's Intrinsic orientation would appear to approximate Erikson's late-life Integrity status, and would presumably remain stable (though conceivably their faith could be shaken by the subsequent trials, moving them into the Non-religious/Despair quadrant). Those who earlier were Indiscriminate in their religious orientation, in later years might be faced with sufficient existential crises to move them to the Intrinsic quadrant. Or, those persons high on the extrinsic dimension (both Indiscriminate and Extrinsics), lacking commitment to the intrinsic religious dimension, might well move to the Non-religious quadrant when faced with life's inevitable insults, the equivalent of Erikson's Despair category. Alternately, the "crucible of doubt" of later years might lead those high on the extrinsic dimension to rethink their level of intrinsic religious commitment, moving them into the Intrinsic quadrant. Just as the outcome of later psychosocial development in Erikson's theory is not predetermined by how earlier developmental tasks were negotiated, one would assume that the same might well be true in the religious realm as well, with the Indiscriminate and Extrinsic types moving to either the Intrinsic or Non-religious quadrant, depending on how they deal with issues of meaning and purpose in their later years.

Since Allport's theory of religious orientation is non-developmental, we can only speculate how individuals might change over time on the dimensions. James Fowler's theory of faith stages (1981), which is developmental, provides an interesting comparison for the typology that has been generated from the Allport and Erikson typologies. Fowler's lower faith stages, especially the Mythic-Literal (normative for late childhood), would seem to correspond to Allport's extrinsic orientation. At this stage the individual takes the religious symbols in a one-dimensional and literal sense. Ideas of religion and God are basically seen as external, or extrinsic to the self. This reliance on external authority continues into the Synthetic-Conventional faith stage, which is normative for adolescence.

It is not until the Individuative-Reflective faith stage, seldom reached before young adulthood, that reliance on external sources of authority diminishes. In Erikson's terms, at this time the individual's beliefs would cease to be secondhand ideology absorbed from parents and society, as the individual begins to take responsibility for his or her own commitments. At this stage an individual would be expected to be higher on Allport's intrinsic dimension. But it might well not be until Fowler's Conjunctive faith stage, characteristic of middle age, that Allport's true Intrinsic orientation would appear. Allport uses the imagery "workshop of doubt" to describe the route to this level, while Fowler suggests that the process of arriving at this "dialectical" or "dialogical" way of knowing may well entail a feeling of "vertigo." Finally, Fowler's stage of Universalizing faith would represent the solidification of Allport's Intrinsic religious orientation, and would doubtless display characteristics of Erikson's achieved ego Integrity.

There is some empirical support for Fowler's model of developmental change in faith stages with age. In a large-scale study of members of over 500 Protestant congregations, Benson and Elkin (1990) found that persons who were judged as having a mature faith, as defined in Fowler's theory, were likely to be older. They concluded: "Maturity of faith is strongly linked to age, increasing with each successive decade, and is most likely to be found among those over 70" (p. 3).

It should be noted that their findings suggest that spiritual development appears to be age-related, but not age determined. That is, it appears more frequently in older persons, but there is no guarantee that the faith of elderly persons will, in fact, reflect greater maturity. Indeed, Paul Pruyser, after devoting his professional career to the study of religion and psychology, observed that "there appears to be a bipolar distribution of religiousness in the aged and dying: some becoming more intensely or articulately religious than they were before, and others becoming less involved than they were" (1987, p. 179). Noting that there appear to be changes in the quality of religious attachment, as well, he suggests that what is most needed is a study of religion in the elderly, since "the psychology of religions [has] been skewed by disproportionate preoccupation with college students, children and early life stages" (p. 179).

CONCLUSION

In the article quoted above, Pruyser observes that persons who are bright and well educated often remain undeveloped in their religious ideas and beliefs. "These persons," he notes wryly, "appear to maintain a stylized stupidity, primitivity, naivete, or dull-wittedness in religious matters, much as a country may maintain a nature preserve or National Park area in an otherwise developed or industrialized region" (p. 179). He ends with the question that perhaps lies implicit in much of the antagonism toward religion among social scientists: "Is religion, even among the educated and intellectually ambitious, a favorite and socially sanctioned area of stagnation, fixation, or regression?" (p. 180).

Here Pruyser clearly raises the central issue that must be faced in a meaningful discussion on religion and aging: what is the nature of the religion that is being examined? As James reminded us (1902/1958), religion, like the term "government," is so broad that it defies easy definition. And just as there can be "good," "bad" and "indifferent" government, there surely can be the same in the religious realm.

Seen in this light, it isn't surprising that studies of aging and religious institutional affiliation, beliefs and behavior have been less than illuminating (Payne 1982). Such an indiscriminate lumping together of beliefs and behaviors under the rubric "religion" ignores the observation that Ramakrishna made a century ago: religion is like a cow that gives milk, but kicks. For social scientists to dismiss religion because it has been known to "kick" limits us unnecessarily, but to embrace it indiscriminately because of its positive features is hardly the answer, either.

The fact that the term "religion" carries so many different meanings and connotations suggests that we must be careful in our choice of terms in this field. Donahue (1985), in his extensive review of the literature on Allport's intrinsic-extrinsic religious concept, rejected the terminology of "intrinsic-extrinsic religiosity," which had developed around these concepts. He pointed out that " 'Religiosity' connotes an affected, artificial, or exaggerated religious interest," and noted that " 'religiousness' does not carry that conceptual baggage" (p. 400n). Such distinctions, it should be noted, are not mere "semantics," but have real consequences in setting the tone for theoretical formulation and subsequent research.

For those who are interested in understanding how persons handle the ultimate problems of life, the religious dimension can be seen as that aspect of mature faith and practice described by Allport and Tillich. It would seem desirable to reserve the terms "religion" and "religious dimension" for this higher level of development. If a word is needed for attachment to less mature religious beliefs and practices, characteristic of more extrinsic religion, perhaps it should be the more pejorative "religiosity."

The obvious problem of such an approach for the social sciences is that this involves value judgments: what one person sees as a religious dimension another might well see as religiosity. Here we face the limitation of the positivist "value-free" approach to the social sciences. In the spirit of the human sciences, perhaps it is time to confess that we have not been, and can't be value-free in discussion of matters of ultimate (or even proximate) concern. Rather than denying that we have such values, or pretending to conduct our work without them intruding, we might better acknowledge our value stance, and honestly state our conclusions within this context. Otherwise we run the risk of trivializing the importance of religion in the experience of aging, in the name of objectivity and scientism.

REFERENCES

Allport, G. W. 1950. *The individual and his religion: A psychological interpretation.* New York: Macmillan.

————. 1963. Behavioral science, religion, and mental health. *Journal of Religion and Health* 2, 187–97.

Allport, G. W., and J. M. Ross. 1967. Personal religious orientation and prejudice. *Journal of Personality and Social Psychology* 5, 432–43.

Benson, P., and C. Elkin. 1990. *Effective Christian education: A national study of Protestant denominations.* Minneapolis: Search Institute.

Donahue, M. J. 1985. Intrinsic and extrinsic religiousness: Review and meta-analysis. *Journal of Personality and Social Psychology* 48, 400–19.

Fowler, J. W. 1981. *Stages of faith.* New York: Harper.

Erikson, E. H. 1964. *Insight and responsibility.* New York: Norton.

————. 1968. *Identity, youth, and crisis.* New York: Norton.

Erikson, E. H., J. M. Erikson, and H. Q. Kivnick. 1986. *Vital involvement in old age.* New York: Norton.

Gorsuch, R. L. 1984. The boon and bane of investigating religion. *American Psychologist* 39, 228–36.

James, W. 1902/1958. *The varieties of religious experience.* New York: New American Library.

Jung, C. G. 1933. *Modern man in search of a soul.* New York: Harcourt, Brace.

Lukoff, D., R. Turner, and F. Lu. 1992. Transpersonal psychology research review: Psychoreligious dimensions of healing. *Journal of Transpersonal Psychology* 24, 41–60.

Marcia, J. 1966. Development and validation of ego stages. *Journal of Personality and Social Psychology* 3, 1551–58.

Payne, B. P. 1982. Religiosity. In D. J. Mangen and W. A. Patterson, eds., *Research instruments in social gerontology.* Vol. 2, *Social roles and social participation.* Minneapolis: University of Minnesota Press.

Pruyser, P. W. 1987. Where do we go from here? Scenarios for the psychology of religion. *Journal for the Scientific Study of Religion* 26, 173–81.

Tillich, P. 1951. *Systematic Theology.* Vol. 1. Chicago: University of Chicago Press.

2 From Loneliness to Solitude: Religious and Spiritual Journeys in Late Life

Barbara Pittard Payne and Susan H. McFadden

Loneliness is not a disease of old age. Persons of all ages experience the pain of loneliness; they also experience the pleasures of solitude. Beginning in infancy, human beings know both the terror of feeling abandoned and lonely and also the joy of contentedly being alone. Because of the many losses that accrue with the aging process, older persons may be particularly vulnerable to the lonely side of aloneness. Is it possible for aging adults to acquire the ability to transform the experience of being alone and lonely into the experience of being alone and relishing the solitude? This chapter will explore this and other questions because they so significantly affect not only how the idea of old age is socially constructed but also how older adults themselves manage to construe even their aloneness as positive and meaningful.

To begin, we will examine the psychological difference between loneliness and solitude. Next, we will survey the literature on aloneness, loneliness, and solitude as these conditions are experienced by older persons. This research tends to contradict the persistent social myth that defines older people as lonely because they live alone, are out of the work force, and are isolated and neglected by their families. Suggestions about the sources of such a stereotyped attitude about lonely older persons will be made.

Following our brief discussion of empirical studies of loneliness and solitude in later life, we will turn to the central focus of this paper, the religious and spiritual dimensions of loneliness and solitude. We will conclude by suggesting that an understanding of the dialectic of attachment and separateness can lead to a change in the ways older persons interpret their aloneness.

LONELINESS AND SOLITUDE

Paul Tillich, philosopher and theologian, attributes the universal and age irrelevant experience of aloneness to the human condition: being alive means being in a body—a body separated from all other bodies. And being separated means being alone (Tillich 1980). Tillich identifies two sides of being alone: loneliness and solitude. Like many social scientists who note the distressing and unpleasant nature of loneliness (see, e.g., Lopata 1987; Peplau & Perlman 1982), Tillich writes that loneliness is the pain of being alone. Solitude, on the other hand, is the glory of being alone.

Although the condition of physical embodiment inevitably produces a sense of separation from others, another, equally powerful, biologically based system produces attachment behavior. John Bowlby (1969, 1973, 1980) has shown how the behavioral system of attachment emerges in the infant and how at the same time, the adult caregiver is predisposed biologically to respond with care to the attachment behaviors of the young. When the attachment figure is absent, the child becomes distressed and behaves in a manner which often brings reunion with the caregiver. The longing of abandoned children for their primary care-givers has been poignantly documented by Bowlby, Spitz (1946) and others. This longing and the profound sense of disconnection form what Joseph Hartog (1980) has called the "skeletal frame" of loneliness, an experience encountered across the life span.

The tension between attachment and separateness becomes immediately clear: according to Bowlby, humans possess an instinctive system that predisposes them to seek out others and to overcome separateness, whereas Tillich and others note that separateness can never be wholly overcome because it is an essential component of the human condition. The existence of this tension between attachment and separateness does not mean that they occupy different poles on a continuum of positive to negative human experience. Rather, separateness as a part of the human condition is just as important for psychological—and spiritual—development as are attachment relations. It is the emotional salience of the experience of separation that determines whether it yields a sense of loneliness or of solitude.

People respond with a wide range of emotions to the condition of being alone; sadness, fear, anger, shame, guilt, interest, and joy can all be associated with being alone. Further, many different contexts can produce the felt condition of aloneness. One can feel alone on a crowded city street as well as on a mountaintop. Because the experiences of aloneness, loneliness, and solitude all depend upon the activity of consciousness to interpret the experience, the physical situation is not enough to determine whether a person will feel alone. One day a person might feel a sense of peace and solitude on that mountaintop; another time, that same person might feel an overpowering loneliness; still another day, perhaps when absorbed in an activity like painting or bird-watching, the individual may not notice the state of being alone at all. Aloneness should, therefore, be thought of as the subjective assessment of the individual's condition vis à vis the environment. When associated with positive emotions, this subjective assessment most likely signals solitude; negative emotions will elicit the subjective appraisal of loneliness.

Research has indicated that dispositional variables influence whether aloneness is acknowledged and whether it is experienced as loneliness or solitude. The individual who has persistently associated the condition of being alone with negative emotions may be more inclined to feel lonely than the individual whose personality structure shapes a less anxious response to aloneness. Pessimism and habits of social isolation in early life may also produce increased risk of depression and loneliness in later life (Solomon & Zinke 1991). Other personality factors, such as narcissism resulting from an overly intrusive relation with the mother (Andersson 1990), have been associated with a higher probability of loneliness in later life.

These efforts to identify personality factors related to loneliness in later life can be problematic for several reasons. First, this work on loneliness and solitude emerges from research conducted with older persons living in modern, Western societies founded upon individualistic ideals. The interpretations of the meaning of aloneness made by both researchers and elders themselves are influenced by cultural expectations about old age and loneliness. It is important to recognize that an understanding of the felt conditions of aloneness, loneliness, and solitude cannot derive solely from focus on dispositional factors in the individual. One needs to examine the root sources of the ways a culture interprets the fundamental human tension between the need for connection and the inevitable experience of disconnection or separateness, particularly in later life. For example, it may matter little whether or not an older adult possesses personality characteristics associated with loneliness if a society assumes that the old are "other" and thus isolates them with institutionalized ageism.

Another problem with stressing the personal variable without consideration of the sociocultural context derives from the description of modern, individualistic societies as reinforcing the fear of aloneness. This is somewhat paradoxical, because on the one hand, one of the major outcomes of modernism has been the explosion of personal encounters as the world has been opened up through technological advances in communication. We are, as Kenneth Gergen has stated, "engulfed" with one another (Gergen 1987). Beneath the engulfment of enforced sociability, however, may lie the fear that we really are lonely. In order to avoid facing up to this cauldron of emotions surrounding the condition of aloneness, aloneness itself—especially joyful aloneness—elicits social condemnation. The child who prefers to spend a summer afternoon "doing nothing" may have to resist the anxious inquiries of a mother concerned that he "call a friend" and "do something." Likewise, the elder who insists that she prefers to spend time alone may be viewed as socially deficient.

A third reason why excessive emphasis on specific personality variables associated with loneliness is problematic is that all persons feel lonely at various times in their lives. By focusing on the chronic feelings of loneliness often associated with depression, these studies can leave the impression that loneliness itself is pathological. Employing common mental health assumptions of our times, one would then assume that loneliness should be eliminated from human experience. This, however, is a naive hope, based on the limited view that expects all experience to be pleasant and free from conflict—the "high-noon" approach to mental health, as Robert Kastenbaum once wrote (1981). This paper will argue that although no one would want to impose loneliness on an older person, nevertheless the inescapable loneliness that all persons experience from time to time can be a source of growth in later life; the painful experience of loneliness can be transformed into a creative sense of solitude.

HOW LONELY ARE OLDER ADULTS?

Research shows that persons under fifty-five hold the view that most older people are lonely (Harris 1975), while in actuality, most older people report that they are seldom lonely. In addition, Shanas's (1979, 1980) work demonstrated that the majority of older people have regular contact with their families, and many live within ten to fifteen minutes from some family member. Living alone does not limit outside activities or the development of meaningful social networks. A person who lives alone is not by necessity socially or emotionally isolated. In fact, older people value their privacy like any other adult and consider living alone a sign of achievement, not a sign of rejection (Peplau, Bikson, Rook & Goodchilds 1982). Living alone can free an older person to discover facets of the self that are muted when one lives with another. Florida Scott-Maxwell expressed this by writing:

I wonder if living alone makes one more alive. No precious energy goes in disagreement or compromise. No need to augment others, there is just yourself, just truth—a morsel—and you. You went through those long years when it was pain to be alone, now you have come out on the good side of that severe discipline. Alone you have your own way all day long, and you become very natural. (1968, pp. 33–34)

Elsewhere, she wrote, "My kitchen linoleum is so black and shiny that I waltz while I wait for the kettle to boil. This pleasure is for the old who live alone" (1968, p. 28).

The robust findings in gerontological research regarding the high level of psychological well-being among older adults along with the association of that well-being with the availability of a confidant suggest that older persons are not overwhelmed by loneliness despite the assorted losses they may have experienced. Even those elders who have always been single (Gubrium 1975) or who never had children (Keith 1983) apparently do not experience any more loneliness than those with living children. Older adults with children may even find that interactions with persons other than their children are more important for morale (Arling 1976). Siblings, friends, neighbors and others who make up the "social convoy" across the life span can influence feelings of well-being while decreasing the probability of chronic loneliness (Antonucci 1985, 1990). Repeatedly, one finds in the literature on loneliness in late life that it is the quality of these relationships that makes the significant difference in whether people feel lonely, not the quantity of contacts. This is true for friends (Mellor & Edelmann 1988), spouse (Perlman, Gerson & Spinner 1978), siblings (Gold 1987; Gold, Woodbury & George 1990), and children (Arling 1976).

Although the research indicates that older persons do not suffer from as much loneliness as the general public might imagine, nevertheless the normative experiences of late life greatly challenge their ability to maintain "a sense of loving mutuality" (Erikson, Erikson & Kivnick 1986, p. 105). The trauma of widowhood produces a profound sense of loneliness in most older persons. Even those who did not enjoy a positive relation with the spouse when he or she was living, may engage in a kind of sanctification of the spouse after death and thus feel as lonely as the individual who had a close, intimate marriage (Erikson, Erikson & Kivnick 1986; Lopata 1979). Although some have suggested that men experience a greater degree of loneliness in widowhood than women (Glick, Weiss & Parkes 1974), widowhood for both men and women is likely to produce intense feelings of disconnection and longing. Both formal and informal supports can ameliorate these feelings of loneliness, though the extent to which they are relied upon depends upon their availability and the willingness of the widowed person to seek them out (Lopata, Heinemann & Baum 1982).

Caregiving can also produce feelings of loneliness because many of the losses of widowhood are experienced before the spouse dies. Caring for a spouse with Alzheimer's disease, a debilitating stroke, or some other kind of chronic illness, brings a change in the style of life and the loss of a companion not only for social encounters but also for sharing the daily activities of life in the home. One feels alone, even though the spouse still lives, because no longer is that individual able to share the joys and sorrows of everyday life. The physical demands of caregiving can be severe but as sources of stress they may be outweighed by the emotional pain of being responsible for the care of one with whom one had shared a lifelong partnership. In some situations, all sense of mutuality in the relationship may be lost, with every act of caregiving being a constant reminder of that loss of the very foundation of intimacy. Again, as with widowhood, both formal and informal support can make the difference in terms of how much loneliness is experienced. However, even the caregiver or widow with warm relations with friends and family and meaningful connections with formal organizations like religious institutions and service clubs still can feel the curtain of loneliness descend.

In addition to widowhood and caregiving, other experiences in late life make the maintenance of mutuality problematic. For example, visual impairment can rob a person of the pleasures of letter-writing; hearing impairment interferes with the mutuality of conversation; motor impairment may reduce social contact. The lifelong struggle that all humans experience to find a balance between intimacy and isolation becomes particularly acute in later life because of these kinds of difficulties.

In her studies of widowhood, Lopata has regularly found that one strategy widows employ in coping with their loneliness is to rely on their associations with religious organizations. She has also noted that the majority of widows, regardless of their social class, identify *themselves* as a resource for dealing with loneliness (Lopata 1979; Lopata, Heinemann & Baum 1982). These findings raise a number of questions pertinent to the central theme being explored here, namely, the way a sense of spiritual integration and participation in religious life may ameliorate the pain of aloneness. Is the elder's ability to retain a sense of meaning and purpose in life despite being assaulted by loss an indication of spirituality? Is it possible that religion for these elders represents the center from which the self draws strength in order to cope with loneliness? In other words, does religion do more for lonely elders than simply offer a building where social interactions can occur? It is to these questions and others, rarely asked by gerontologists, that we now turn.

SPIRITUALITY, LONELINESS, AND SOLITUDE

An old woman sits by her window in her third story apartment, looking out on a crowded city street. She has been widowed for six years. Her children, married now with children and grandchildren of their own, live in this city and visit her often. Yet, still, she experiences pangs of loneliness. She observes the activity below and feels apart from all that, isolated and alone. She says to herself, I wonder why I continue to live? What purpose has my life had? How can I continue living when so many of the people who gave my life meaning have died?

Psychology cannot answer these questions. A clinical profile of this woman indicating her emotional adjustment to old age would give scant information about the depths of her aloneness. Indeed, her questioning might even be interpreted as pathological rumination. Sociology, too, comes up short in its ability to address such issues. A diagram indicating this woman's social network and the frequency of her social contacts could tell little about this moment when she gazes out on life and asks herself these questions. Shrewd analysis of socioeconomic conditions affecting the experience of aloneness in later life would also obscure the fundamental existential moment that produces these questions.

The motivation to ask these questions springs from human spirituality, the basic drive to discern life's meaning and purpose (Frankl 1959). Spirituality can be understood outside a specifically religious context as the human need to construct a sense of meaning in life. However, because the origin of religious questioning lies in this need, religions have traditionally influenced how societies conceptualize spirituality. In response to the spiritual search for meaning and purpose, religions provide a language for the articulation of this need and they designate certain pathways in life toward meeting this need.

In the West, spirituality is usually associated with the human capacity to experience a transcendental sense of wholeness within the self, with other persons, the world, and with God (McFadden & Gerl 1990). In other words, Western notions of spirituality usually imply connection, integration, and wholeness. This conceptualization also points toward an understanding of the relation between spirituality, loneliness, and solitude.

When memories of the past, experiences of the present, and anticipation of the future are integrated, the individual feels a sense of meaningful connectedness within the self. In writing about the way persons experience this integration, or ego integrity, at the end of life, Erik Erikson noted that it conveys a "spiritual sense" (1963, p. 168) and he implied that not only does the individual recognize this, but the wider culture does as well. Object relations theorist Harry Guntrip (1969) has described this internal integration as including a "sense of inward peace and poise, of wholeness in depth and the security of inward unity" (p. 325). Presumably, the individual who senses this peace, wholeness, and security is better able to experience the joy of aloneness than the person who finds in aloneness a sense of self ridden with doubt, anxiety, and insecurity. One might propose a kind of positive feedback relation between this sense of integration and the ability to experience the glory of aloneness. Eugene Bianchi has noted that experiences of solitude evoke a "unitive or integrating perspective" wherein the individual feels not only a sense of connection within the self but also "with nature and other persons" (1982, p. 49).

This leads us to consider another aspect of spirituality—the transcendent sense of connection with other persons that conveys a sense of life's meaning and purpose. Older people do not have to be in actual physical contact with others in order to feel connected to them. Florida Scott-Maxwell described the way she populated her world with meaningful connections with others and implied that in so doing, she felt no pain of loneliness.

Although I am absorbed in myself, a large part of me is constantly occupied with other people. I carry the thought of some almost as a baby too poorly to be laid down. There are many whom I never cease cherishing. I dwell on their troubles, their qualities, their possibilities as though I kept them safe by so doing; as though by understanding them I simplified their lives for them. I live with them every minute. (p. 34)

This sense of relatedness to others that reinforces the conviction that life is meaningful despite occasions of being alone is an important component of spirituality. Erikson even suggested that this sense of relatedness might extend through time; he wrote that the individual who has achieved a measure of ego integrity feels a "comradeship" (1963, p. 168) with the ways, and presumably the people, of the past. This is not unlike the Christian notion of "communion with the saints."

Spiritual connections are also experienced with the world at large, whether in natural settings or in human environments. Older persons speak of their positive sense of relatedness to their homes, their gardens, the birds who visit their feeders. People experience pleasure in settings they define as meaningful, and often these settings incorporate nature in some way. Writing about the environmental psychology of people's relation to natural settings, Kaplan and Kaplan (1989) commented on the physical and mental health benefits deriving from the ways natural environments produce a feeling of restoration. They added that "on the spiritual side is the remarkable sense of feeling 'at one,' a feeling that often—but not exclusively—occurs in natural environments" (p. 197). One who feels lonely in such a setting would probably feel distanced from and threatened by it. Negative emotions would prevail instead of the positive sense of well-being depicted by Kaplan and Kaplan.

The last aspect of spiritual integration—and the first in importance for religious persons—is the sense of connection with God. Writing that religion is not to be found in the intellectual activity of theological discourse but rather in experience, Guntrip (1969) noted that religion is best understood as "our way of relating to the universe, the total reality which has, after all, evolved us with the intelligence and motivation to explore this problem: all that is meant by "experience of God." (p. 326) Guntrip believed that human beings have an "absolute need" for relatedness to others and that out of this need is born religious experience. To feel related to another person allows one to feel "at home" in the personal milieu; to feel related to God permits the sense of at-homeness in the universe. Both are necessary for mental health in Guntrip's view. We might also add that both are necessary conditions for the ability to feel joyful aloneness. Cosmic loneliness, on the other hand, originates in the sense of painful alienation in a "stark soulless mechanism which degrades and depersonalizes us to the level of meaningless accidents in an impersonal cosmic process" (Guntrip 1969, p. 328).

RELIGION ADDRESSES THE HUMAN DILEMMA OF ATTACHMENT AND SEPARATION

Traditionally, religion has addressed concerns that emerge from the tension between human needs for relatedness and the unavoidable experiences of separateness. A recent theoretical development in the psychology of religion has proposed that attachment theory provides a model for understanding this connection with the sacred realm (Kirkpatrick 1992). While it appears to have more relevance for understanding Western religions than the religions of the East,

Kirkpatrick's work strongly suggests that God represents a haven of safety for overcoming stress, much like the mother provides safe haven for the terrified infant. Additionally, in concordance with attachment theory, God also provides a secure base from which the believer can venture out to encounter the challenges of life.

Western notions of spirituality suggest, either implicitly or explicitly, that meaning and purpose are to be found in attachment or connection. Other approaches to spirituality, shaped primarily by Eastern religions, suggest that meaning in life will only be found when the spiritual seeker detaches from self, from others, from the world, and even from divinity. To the individual following this spiritual path, when specific attachments are overcome, confident serenity flows from the experience of unity with all. Thus, the drama of every human being's struggle between attachment and separateness is in some way central to the world's religions.

Whether Eastern or Western, religions define the fulfillment in human life that ultimately provides meaning (Courtney 1981). The Christian finds fulfillment in the loving relation between God and humanity mediated by Jesus Christ; Hindu fulfillment derives from the knowledge of unity of all things; fulfillment for the Jew derives from a covenantal relationship with God; Buddhists find fulfillment in being free from desire and overcoming the ego; Islam dictates the path to fulfillment through obedience to Allah in all things. However defined, this sense of fulfillment describes how the tension between attachment and separateness is ultimately resolved.

According to Berger and Luckmann (1966), religions represent socially constructed views of reality which then become a kind of "sacred canopy" over all human activity regardless of whether people understand themselves to be religious. This suggests that Western religion's emphasis on attachment, both in terms of the interpretation of spirituality and specific beliefs about the divine/human relationship, may affect the way aging and loneliness are understood and experienced in the West. If attachment is generally accorded a positive meaning while detachment or separateness is viewed negatively, then the elder who prefers to be alone rather than socially involved with others may be seen as odd or eccentric.

In a related way, attachment implies some kind of activity, a deliberate movement toward something or someone, while detachment is associated more with passivity. Christianity has struggled with the contrast between the active life of involvement with the world and the inactive life of contemplation. At various times in history, Christians have persecuted the cloistered contemplative and at other times they have devalued the active, prophetic individual immersed in the polis. Modern Christianity seems mostly to have rejected the contemplative life, favoring instead active involvement in the world.

We propose that this way of thinking has a significant effect upon the way elders are viewed within Western cultures. If an old person is not able to be actively engaged in social activities, or if by virtue of sensory limitations this person cannot fully appreciate the environment, then the assumption may be that he or she is detached and probably lonely. While this may or may not actually be true, still the cultural assumption about what constitutes the good life—activity and involvement rather than inactivity and disengagement—can shape the ways elders interpret their own experience.

A study comparing elderly Indian men and elderly British men supports this suggestion that elders in the West face a difficult challenge with regard to the dialectic of attachment and separateness. Although they did not specifically address the question of loneliness, Thomas and Chambers found important differences regarding their overall contentment with life. The Indian men were "more integrated into their families, and seem[ed] to feel themselves integrated with the larger cosmic order" (Thomas & Chambers 1989, p. 198). The Indian men appeared to be less affected by their condition of widowhood than the British men and thus one might presume that loneliness was less of a problem for them than for men living with a primarily Western worldview. They experienced their religion, Hinduism, as pervasive in their everyday lives while the British men, influenced by the individualism of the West, viewed religion as a personal choice to be made. Furthermore, the Hindu notion of the stages of human life legitimated detachment from the roles of earlier adulthood. Detachment for the Indian men was both socially and personally interpreted as a positive outcome of the aging process; detachment from earlier roles held by the British men left them bereft of their guideposts for how to continue to find meaning and purpose in life. For the Indian men, detachment could be viewed as part of the process of union with a higher order; for the British men, attachment and detachment were apparently irreconcilable.

With active involvement valued and inactive disengagement devalued, it is not hard to understand why the work of gerontologists Cumming and Henry (1961) created such an uproar. Older adults living in a modern, Western culture whose worldview has been largely shaped by Christianity cut off from its own rich tradition of mysticism may be highly susceptible to the self-perception that their inability to live active, independent, socially engaged lives represents some kind of monumental failure (Moody, in press).

ELDER LONELINESS AND RELIGIOUS INSTITUTIONS

Religion is highly important to older adults. Research has indicated that participation in a church or synagogue contributes to personal adjustment of older adults particularly if they continue to volunteer for church projects (Payne 1977, 1984). Payne found that membership and participation in a congregation is the single most pervasive community institution to which older adults belong. Participation provides older persons with continuity, social identity, and access to meaningful social roles. Even when other organizational memberships are dropped, the membership in a church or synagogue is retained (Payne 1988).

Clearly, older adults are attached to their religious institutions, and this attachment represents a significant source of meaning in their lives.

Although involvement with a church or synagogue has been found to be associated with less loneliness in older persons (Johnson & Mullins 1989), there is a negative side to this important relation between elders and religious institutions. This occurs when religious institutions separate themselves from older adults.

For example, churches and synagogues sometimes lose contact with their older members, particularly if these persons relocate at some distance from the religious institution. However, older people who have moved into a retirement center continue to feel an emotional attachment to the religious institution where they had invested so much of themselves even when that institution is many miles away and there is an active chaplaincy program and worship schedule at the retirement facility (McFadden 1987). The failure of the church to retain contact intensifies feelings of loneliness. This is true for homebound elders as well, who have not left the community yet can no longer participate in the activities of the religious institution. The elder who feels she has retained the contact in her heart while the church has broken its contact with her may experience loneliness amplified by the negative emotions of rejection. While she might be able to cope with not being able to attend regularly by maintaining private religious practices like prayer and by valuing both the memories and occasional contacts with visitors from the church, a sense of rejection can make that kind of adaptation problematic.

Sometimes, clergy and laity fail to recognize that even those elders able to attend religious services can still feel lonely because so many of their cohort have died. Older persons often state, "I just don't feel like this is my church anymore since I don't know anyone." Again, the expectation that one will be accepted, even welcomed in one's church or synagogue, coupled with the experience of being ignored can produce a profound sense of loneliness, especially when most of the attention seems to be directed toward young adults and their children. This situation could be so easily reversed given recognition on the part of clergy and lay leaders that even the oldest members of a congregation may need to be regularly reintroduced and invited to share in activities designed for an intergenerational group.

Many churches and synagogues actively seek to retain contact with their elderly members and devise innovative ways of keeping them involved in the life of the institution. Visitation programs, transportation services, contact via radio and television, and numerous other approaches are employed to maintain the connections between older persons and their religious organizations. Furthermore, even when participation in local congregations decreases, personal patterns of religious practice remain stable and contribute to happiness and life satisfaction (Payne 1988). In other words, the nonorganized aspects of religion that are maintained despite separation from the ongoing life of the church or synagogue can function to ameliorate loneliness. An accumulating literature on the way religious behaviors such as prayer represent an effective coping strategy for elders (Koenig, Smiley & Gonzales 1988; Pargament, Van Haitsma & Ensing, in press) suggests that religion provides much more for lonely older people than simply a building where other people meet. As further support for this idea, Gallup found that the two most significant experiences affecting religious practice for all adults are being lonely for a long period of time and change in work status, such as retirement.

FROM LONELINESS TO SOLITUDE

Despite the efforts of religious institutions to maintain contact with their members, and despite the comfort found in private religious practice, still older people will—like persons of all ages—feel lonely from time to time. For believers from theistic faiths that emphasize attachment relations between humanity and the divine, by far the most agonizing sense of loneliness results from feeling cut off from God. Issues of theodicy that weigh heavily on older persons can quickly turn aloneness into an overwhelming loneliness. The Psalmist cries out, "My God, my God, why has thou forsaken me? Why art thou so far from helping me, from the words of my groaning. O my God, I cry by day, but thou dost not answer; and by night, but find no rest" (Ps. 22:1–2, RSV). In the Psalms, the human experience of loneliness is never completely forgotten; nor is the terror of experiencing disconnection from God.

At the same time that the Psalms depict the agony of loneliness, they also contain much joyous affirmation of trust in God and God's mercy. Over and over again, one hears of the believer who felt separated from God and profoundly lonely. Yet, that loneliness is overcome and re-union occurs. Spiritual growth transforms the loneliness into a creative solitude imbued with the knowledge that even the aloneness of a venture into the valley of the shadow of death does not separate one from God. In the Christian testament, St. Paul writes that "neither death, nor life, nor angels, nor principalities, nor powers, nor things present, nor things to come, nor powers, nor height, nor depth, nor anything else in all creation, will be able to separate us from the love of God, in Christ Jesus our Lord" (Romans 8:38–39, RSV).

Therefore, the elder who has embraced a Western view of the world with all its conflict concerning attachment and separation, can, in Judaism and Christianity alike, find resources for the belief that one is never truly alone. Within both of these religions are traditions that emphasize the necessary interrelation of attachment and separation. For example, to be able to minister to others, Jesus had to first separate himself and go out to be alone in the desert. For the elder Christian or Jew, recovery of the mystical tradition would present numerous examples of the healing power of aloneness that can lead to union and love with all things. Out of separateness comes an attachment of a higher order that confers the meaning the human spirit seeks.

In the psychological language of Erikson, development does not proceed through the triumph of intimacy over isolation; the two are viewed as existing in some kind of ratio. Isolation can intensify intimacy and intimacy can moderate isolation. Clark Moustakas, who has written eloquently about the transformative power of loneliness, echoes this idea by stating: "The lonely experience gives a person back to himself, affirms his identity, and enables him to take steps toward new life. . . . Love has no meaning without loneliness; loneliness becomes real only as a response to love" (1972, p. 146).

Older persons who respond to questionnaires about loneliness by and large state that they are not lonely even though they may experience some social isolation. Although they may be influenced by their knowledge of the social desirability of denying the negative emotions associated with being alone, perhaps they have also found a way to tolerate being alone and to change the pain of loneliness into the glory of solitude. This change can be interpreted as the outcome of a spiritual journey that has included an encounter with the question of the meaning of an individual life, alone in embodiment and yet intertwined with other human lives, the world, and, for those who are religious, with God. Added to this spiritual journey can also be a religious journey into the paradoxes of human attachment and human aloneness as articulated in faith. Elders may find their religious commitments strengthened by discovering in the pain of loneliness the comforting presence of God. Aloneness provides the opportunity for growth through the kind of emptying practiced by mystics across the centuries. While the potential for this "growth through diminishment" (LaFarge 1963) should never be taken as an excuse to abandon old people to their aloneness, nevertheless there is much to be learned from older adults' ability to tolerate loneliness, to learn from it, and to transform its pain into the glory of solitude.

REFERENCES

Andersson, L. 1990. Narcissism and loneliness. *International Journal of Aging and Human Development* 30, 81–94.

Antonucci, T. C. 1985. Personal characteristics, social support, and social behavior. In R. H. Binstock and E. Shanas, eds., *Handbook of aging and the social sciences.* 2d ed. New York: Van Nostrand Reinhold.

————. 1990. Social supports and social relationships. In R. H. Binstock and L. K. George, eds., *Handbook of aging and the social sciences.* 3d ed. New York: Academic Press.

Arling, G. 1976. The elderly widow and her family, neighbors and friends. *Journal of Marriage and the Family* 38, 757–68.

Berger, P., and T. Luckmann. 1966. *The social construction of reality.* Garden City, NY: Doubleday.

Bianchi, E. C. 1982. *Aging as a spiritual journey.* New York: Crossroad.

Bowlby, J. 1969–1980. *Attachment and loss,* vols. 1–3. New York: Basic Books.

Courtney, C. 1981. Restructuring "the structure of religion." Unpublished manuscript.

Cumming, E., and W. Henry. 1961. *Growing old.* New York: Basic Books.

Erikson, E. H. 1963. *Childhood and society.* Rev. ed. New York: W. W. Norton.

Erikson, E. H., J. M. Erikson, and H. Q. Kivnick. 1986. *Vital involvement in old age.* New York: W. W. Norton.

Frankl, V. 1959. *Man's search for meaning.* Boston: Beacon Press.

Gergen, K. J. 1987. Self-discourse and the emergence of pan-cultural identity. Paper presented at the annual meeting of the American Psychological Association, New York, NY.

Glick, I. O., R. S. Weiss, and C. M. Parkes. 1974. *The first year of bereavement.* New York: John Wiley & Sons.

Gold, D. T. 1987. Siblings in old age: Something special. *Canadian Journal on Aging* 6, 199–215.

Gold, D. T., M. A. Woodbury, and L. K. George. 1990. Relationship classification using grade of membership analysis: A typology of sibling relationships in later life. *Journal of Gerontology: Social Sciences* 45, S43–51.

Gubrium, J. F. 1975. Being single in old age. *International Journal of Aging and Human Development* 6, 29–41.

Guntrip, H. 1969. Religion in relation to personal integration. *British Journal of Medical Psychology* 42, 323–33.

Harris, L., and Associates. 1975. *The myth and reality of aging in America.* Washington, DC: National Council on Aging.

Hartog, J. 1980. Introduction: The anatomization. In J. Hartog, R. Audy, and Y. A. Cohen, eds., *The anatomy of loneliness,* 1–12. New York: International Universities Press.

Johnson, D. P., and L. C. Mullins. 1989. Religiosity and loneliness among the elderly. *Journal of Applied Gerontology* 8, 110–31.

Kaplan, R., and S. Kaplan. 1989. *The experience of nature: A psychological perspective.* New York: Cambridge University Press.

Kastenbaum, R. 1981. . . . Gone tomorrow. In R. Kastenbaum, ed., *Old age on the new scene,* 318–26. New York: Springer.

Keith, P. M. 1983. A comparison of the resources of parents and childless men and women in very old age. *Journal of Applied Family and Child Studies* 32, 403–9.

Kirkpatrick, L. A. 1992. An attachment-theory approach to the psychology of religion. *International Journal for the Psychology of Religion* 2, 3–28.

Koenig, H. G., M. Smiley, and J. P. Gonzales. 1988. *Religion, health, and aging: A review and theoretical interpretation.* Westport, CT: Greenwood Press.

LaFarge, J. 1963. *Reflections on growing old.* Garden City, NY: Doubleday.

Lopata, H. Z. 1979. *Women as widows: Support systems.* New York: Elsevier.

———. 1987. Loneliness. In George Maddox, ed., *The encyclopedia of aging,* 408. New York: Springer Publishing Co.

Lopata, H. Z., G. D. Heinemann, and J. Baum. 1982. Loneliness: Antecedents and coping strategies in the lives of widows. In L. A. Peplau and D. Perlman, eds., *Loneliness: A sourcebook of current theory, research, and therapy,* 310–26. New York: John Wiley & Sons.

McFadden, S. H. 1987. The meaning of long time church membership to retirement community members. Paper presented at the meeting of the annual American Society on Aging.

McFadden, S. H., and R. Gerl. 1990. Approaches to understanding spirituality in the second half of life. *Generations* 14, 35–38.

Mellor, K. S., and R. J. Edelmann. 1988. Mobility, social support, loneliness, and well-being amongst two groups of older adults. *Personality and Individual Differences* 9, 1–5.

Moody, H. R. In press. Mysticism and aging. In M. Kimble, S. McFadden, J. Ellor, and J. Seeber, eds., *Aging, spirituality, and religion: A handbook*. Minneapolis: Fortress Press.

Moustakas, C. E. 1972. *Loneliness and love*. Englewood Cliffs, NJ: Prentice-Hall.

Pargament, K. I., K. Van Haitsma, and D. S. Ensing. In press. When age meets adversity: Religion and coping in the later years. In M. Kimble, S. McFadden, J. Ellor, and J. Seeber, eds., *Aging, spirituality, and religion: A handbook*. Minneapolis: Fortress Press.

Payne, B. P. 1977. The older volunteer: Social role continuity and development. *Gerontologist* 17, 335–61.

———. 1984. Protestants. In E. Palmore, ed., *Handbook of the aged in the United States*, pp. 181–88. Westport, CT: Greenwood Press.

———. 1988. Religious patterns and participation of older adults: A sociological perspective. *Educational Gerontology* 14, 255–67.

Perlman, D., A. C. Gerson, and B. Spinner. 1978. Loneliness among senior citizens: An empirical report. *Essence* 2, 239–48.

Peplau, L. A., T. K. Bikson, K. S. Rook, and J. D. Goodchilds. 1982. Being old and living alone. In L. A. Peplau and D. Perlman, eds., *Loneliness: A sourcebook of current theory, research, and therapy*, 327–47. New York: John Wiley & Sons.

Peplau, L. A., and D. Perlman, eds. 1982. *Loneliness: A sourcebook of current theory, research, and therapy*. New York: John Wiley & Sons.

Scott-Maxwell, F. 1968. *The measure of my days*. New York: A. A. Knopf.

Shanas, E. 1979. The family as a social support system in old age. *Gerontologist* 19, 169–74.

———. 1980. Older people and their families: The new pioneers. *Journal of Marriage and the Family* 42, 9–18.

Solomon, K., and M. Zinke. 1991. Group psychotherapy with the depressed elderly. *Journal of Gerontological Social Work* 17, 47–57.

Spitz, R. A. 1946. Anaclitic depression. *Psychoanalytic Study of the Child* 2, 313–42.

Thomas, L. E., and K. O. Chambers. 1989. ''Successful aging'' among elderly men in England and India: A phenomenological comparison. In L. E. Thomas, ed., *Research on adulthood and aging: The human science approach*, 183–203. Albany: State University of New York Press.

Tillich, P. 1980. Loneliness and solitude. In J. Hartog, J. R. Audy, and Y. A. Cohen, eds., *The anatomy of loneliness*, 543–47. New York: International Universities Press.

II Case Studies

3 From Sacred to Secular: Memoir of a Midlife Transition toward Spiritual Freedom

Richard B. Griffin

All seventy of us young men filed into the large dormitory. We each took a position standing at attention next to our bed. Then we stripped to the waist. When everyone looked ready, the leader flipped off the overhead lights, shook a small handbell, and we all started to beat ourselves as vigorously as possible. Using small whips made of knotted cords, we flailed away at our bare backs until the bell rang again some sixty seconds later.

This was to become a regular, three-times-a-week ritual in my life at Shadowbrook, the Jesuit novitiate in Lenox, Massachusetts.[1] The flagellation was one of the unforgettable elements in a new way of living which I entered upon in 1949 after having left Harvard College at age twenty-one. In looking back over my life from the vantage point of my middle sixties, I see my entrance to the Roman Catholic Church's official religious life as a pivotal event, one on which the whole rest of my life would turn.

Most critics no longer distinguish between secular and spiritual autobiography (Hawkins 1985). In agreement with Hawkins, however, I believe the differences significant. Spiritual autobiography focuses on the soul rather than the self, it aims at the ultimate meaning of the author's life, and it is written for God as well as human readers. This kind of autobiography also tries to persuade the reader of the value of a life lived for God.

This brief memoir shares in these characteristics except that it does not pretend to any hortatory aim. It also shows more preoccupation with self instead of an exclusive focus on the soul. The rhythm of this particular story also is very different from the classical pattern whereby in youth one is less religious, then, after entering into personal and often prolonged crisis, turns toward God and spiritual certainty. Finally, this narrative is set in the context of gerontological study and, in the words of a coeditor of this volume, "opens up to the researcher the whole realm of the subjective dimensions of life" (Thomas 1989, p. 6).

SPIRITUAL STIRRINGS

It is difficult to characterize the variety of religious experience which led to my entering the Jesuits. In any event, my fervent piety as a teenager does not accord with William James's assertion that "the religious age par excellence would seem to be old age." (James 1985/1901 p. 19n). Rather than any sudden illumination, I experienced a slow growth in a conviction within my inner self that the most important reality in my life was God. Increasingly I felt drawn to subject everything to Him. This inner attraction ultimately made me decide to seek God with an intensity not possible in the circumstances of ordinary life "in the world."

One might have expected my years as a Harvard undergraduate to have weakened my preoccupation with religion. (For precisely this expectation Catholic Church leaders had strongly discouraged enrollment at "secular" colleges.) However, my belief that Catholic identity was the most important value of my life intensified. In fact, my piety grew so strong that I would attend Mass every morning and take part in a weekly student prayer group. My worldview became eschatological: in a frequent interior image, I would ask myself what I, on my deathbed, would want to have done with my life.

The two spiritual books which had the biggest impact on me in those days were Augustine's *Confessions* and Thomas Merton's *The Seven Storey Mountain*. Augustine's search for God "in time and memory" confirmed for me the meaningfulness of a life spent seeking God. Though the rhythm of that seminal thinker's life was very different from my own, I identified with his turning away from the world toward divine reality and interpreting all events, historical as well as autobiographical, in the light of that reality (Augustine 1991).

Merton (1948) spoke to me as an intellectual and one who had been a fellow secular university student. His account of conversion away from the hollow rewards of the world gripped my imagination. Finding a pattern of God's search for him in the events of his life inspired me to look for my own vocation. Though I did not ever envision myself in a monastic life like his, I entered into his decision to leave the world and concentrate on what was most important.

So, against expectation, the Harvard experience reinforced my religious orientation. By allowing me to find nourishment for my youthful piety, it prepared me for entrance into the novitiate. Unfortunately, my college years did not lead to either the human or spiritual maturity which might have protected me against the distortions of the Jesuit training.

As noted, the image which accompanied my decision was of myself on my deathbed. I fantasized looking back upon my life and wanting to have spent it pursuing the supreme good. This image expressed an eschatological worldview presumably not characteristic of young people generally. To me the traditional "four last things" of Roman Catholic theology—death, judgment, heaven, and hell—were real and reference points for making decisions.

THE EARLY YEARS

This, in brief, was my worldview when I gave myself to the Jesuits. I fully accepted a new lifestyle, the details of which conformed to a pattern used in the training of Jesuits all over the world. It derived from a carefully devised plan which went back to the founding of the Society of Jesus in 1540. Ultimately, it reached back many centuries earlier to the development of monastic life within the Catholic Church.

During my two years of noviceship, almost nothing from the outside world was allowed to impinge on my attention. No radios, no television, no newspapers or magazines. The only books we were allowed to read were those written by Jesuits. No visitors could come to see us except for family members three times a year. Our letters in and out were subject to censorship.

The most important activity of each day was prayer. At ordinary times we meditated for one hour early each morning before participating in Mass. Each afternoon we meditated for a further half-hour. The rest of the day was to be marked by "recollection," that is, an interior disposition to prayer. Externally this was shown by silence, which we observed at all times except for periods of recreation.

At special times in the year we entered into "retreat." That meant stricter silence and four hours of meditation each day along with no periods of recreation. My first such experience was the so-called long retreat, which lasted for thirty days. Its inspiration came from the *Spiritual Exercises,* the classic book devised by the Jesuit founder St. Ignatius of Loyola. The exercises are not meant to be read; instead they are to be done. They took me through a carefully constructed sequence of ideas and experiences calculated to lay a firm basis for my life as a Jesuit.

The "Principle and Foundation" summarizes the worldview which St. Ignatius proposes for prayerful reflection:

Man is created to praise, reverence, and serve God our Lord, and by this means to save his soul. And the other things on the face of the earth are created for man and that they may help him in prosecuting the end for which he is created. From this it follows, that man is to use them as much as they help him on to his end, and ought to rid himself of them so far as they hinder him as to it.

For this it is necessary to make ourselves indifferent to all created things in all that is allowed to the choice of our free will and is not prohibited to it; so that, on our part, we want not health rather than sickness, riches rather than poverty, honor rather than dishonor, long rather than short life, and so in all the rest; desiring and choosing only what is most conducive for us to the end for which we are created. (Fleming 1978, p. 22)

How beautifully clear an approach to life Ignatius proposed! If only I could learn to live by this standard, then my life would be both simple and holy. At least this is the way I then saw it in the full fervor of my young manhood.

To live this way would require great self-denial. But at other points in the retreat I learned both negative and positive reasons for such mortification. After meditating on hell, I issued myself a stern warning and recorded it in my journal: "If I desire to gratify my senses, God in hell will give me such gratification for eternity as will be a torment for me." And after contemplating Christ carrying the cross on the way to his crucifixion, I made a radical resolution: "I want to keep this scene as the basis for choosing to do the hard thing always."

Thus did I enter upon a life dedicated to the pursuit of perfection. Inevitably that involved a regimen of what my colleagues called "beating it down." I became convinced that God wanted it of me, that it was my vocation. Following Christ as a Jesuit would mean systematic warfare against my natural inclinations. If I wanted to become a good Jesuit, then I had to subordinate everything else to the supernatural. If this involved my becoming a child again, subject to the commands and guardianship of others, then that is what I would do.

This way of life had the backing of the Roman Catholic Church and a tradition laden with authority. You could establish a chain of command that was unbreakable. Our superiors had behind them the authority of the Pope in Rome; the Pope was the latest in the line of the Apostle Peter; Peter had Christ's authority; and Christ had God the Father's.

At mid-twentieth century the Roman Catholic Church looked stable indeed. No significant challenges to its authority had emerged for a long time. While not high with intellectuals, its prestige on the world scene remained entrenched. The discipline of both right belief (orthodoxy) and right conduct (orthopraxis) as established by the Council of Trent in the mid-sixteenth century anchored the Church securely. No rebels within the Church could expect to get very far because the iron vigilance of the Papacy could be relied on to squash dissent.

At least this is how it looked to a young American Catholic like me. I had been brought up in a family which inculcated in me strong habits of piety and firm loyalty to Rome. A high point in my father's career as a journalist had been covering for a large metropolitan daily the accession to the throne of St. Peter of Pope Pius XII. Though very much a man of the world accustomed in his work to the seamy side of life, he was faithful to the Church and never missed Mass on Sundays.

For my mother, religion also loomed large as a source of value. However, for her it rarely brought inspiration or consolation, but largely obligation. This obligation she interpreted as narrowly as possible, the exact fulfillment of Church law. For years she suffered from scruples in a manner classically recognizable in the Catholic tradition. This had the effect of making the Church even more of an authority for her than for other observant Catholics.

The atmosphere in my home, though not untypical of middle class Catholics of the 1930s and 1940s, was marked by greater emotional constraint. There was rarely any mention of sex or, for that matter, of love or any of the more tender emotions. I felt a lot of life to be off limits. The code of morality I learned at home, in Church, and at school simply forbade all sexual activity. Catholic moral teaching was thunderingly clear: you were allowed absolutely no sexual activity before or outside of marriage.

Another important factor in my development was a physical defect. During birth my left arm was seriously damaged; surgery four years later followed by years of exercise in childhood enabled me to use it quite well for most purposes. However, this arm remained several inches shorter than my other one and it has always been a major fact in my consciousness of myself, with serious religious implications.

The Jesuit novitiate experience continued the emotionally constrained atmosphere of my home life and it heightened the psychological rigidity characteristic of my adolescence. Both theory and practice in the novitiate fed my native inclinations toward inflexibility. I held myself stiff and unbending so that no one could get me to break a rule almost no matter what the reason. Though I recognized that charity was supposed to be the most important reality of religious life, in practice I lived by the rule.

The end of my first Jesuit phase came after two years when I pronounced vows of poverty, chastity, and obedience. In the time-honored tradition of the Church, these vows would define my subsequent religious life. These promises were meant to free me from the classical threats to spiritual perfection: money, sex, and power.

In fact, I did experience many of the spiritual benefits associated with religious life. Peace of soul, satisfaction that my life was so meaningful, joy from the certainty that I was loved and appreciated by God and my brothers in religion— these and other deep personal realities made me happy. Sometimes I felt like bursting for sheer joy of soul.

Inside me a constant dialogue with God was taking place. I found it emotionally satisfying to talk with Him all the time. Thus I developed habits of interior prayer featuring repetition of a psalm verse or other line from scripture. It would become a refrain through the activities of the day. "Lord, be merciful to me a sinner," is one such prayer I remember using.

AFTER THE NOVITIATE

The years following my novitiate experience brought me further satisfactions, both spiritual and intellectual, along with severe trials of spirit. At first, I found the highly structured Jesuit approach to learning in accordance with the classical *ratio studiorum* a welcome change from the laissez-faire undergraduate experience at Harvard. A feature of my intellectual life became frequent sharp insights into truth which sometimes made study rewarding indeed.

At the end of my first year of studies, however, I developed what was known in the Jesuit environment as a "cracked head." It was as if an inner vise had seized me which I could not remove. It was not as palpable as a headache but had similar effects. Ignoring it was impossible; when it dissipated, usually after several hours, it left me thoroughly fatigued. This strange gripping within me was to plague me for the next nine years of my life.

My "cracked head" must have resulted from the unacknowledged but cumulative tension of the previous three years. Considering how rigid I had been all during that period, it cannot be surprising that something broke. The wonder is that it took so long. But I did not understand anything of this process at the time. All I knew was that some inner psychophysical event had happened, the dimensions of which remained mysterious.

I looked for help to my spiritual directors but they were among those least likely to be able to help. They had all been schooled in a tradition which put little value on human emotions. Theirs was a dichotomized view of human beings which placed sharp emphasis upon the superiority of the soul over the body. Relying upon the focal image of Ignatius in the *Spiritual Exercises,* they would have seen the soul as imprisoned within the body and oppressed by it.

It took a long time for me to develop enough freedom to learn how to dream. Years of prescribed course of studies in philosophy and theology, heavily rationalistic, tended to constrict inner freedom. My interior life, though not without its buoyant features, was inhibited by ideology; I was looking for a divinity tightly tied to the hierarchical Church. Those were the days when Catholic theologians knew altogether too much about God.

Gradually, however, a certain thawing of psychic life began to take place within me. Under the influence of psychotherapy and of Jung and other writers, I began to discover my own emotions and imaginative resources. The goal of priestly ordination helped center these efforts to develop a more vibrant and personal interior life.

Never did I feel closer to God than on the day of my ordination and in the ecstatic days that preceded and followed that event of June 1962. Whatever the struggles of the years previous, they could not deprive the day of ordination of a special place in my life history. It brought to fullest focus all that I had lived for during the previous decade. But it also expressed much of what I had been in high school and college. Indeed, it acted as summation of what I had been during my childhood, at home. Ordination thus marked completion of the first phase of my life, one that lasted from the beginning to the age of thirty-three.

It was not lost on me that, according to pious tradition, thirty-three was the age at which Jesus had died. But risen, too, as the Easter faith has it. Surely my own life would be different after ordination. It might not be all resurrection, but neither would it be all travail.

With ordination I acquired a special title to do ministry in the Church. Ministering to the People of God counted as spiritual experience providing me a sense of the divine presence in my own actions. Encounters with people who were poor, sick, or social outcasts were privileged moments of identification with Jesus. Gradually, I learned how to use the priestly authority of service.

VATICAN II—WINDS OF CHANGE

Further liberation would await astonishing changes within the Roman Catholic Church in the middle 1960s. An understanding of what happened in the Second Vatican Council (1962–1965) is vital for appreciating what happened in my own life both interiorly and outwardly as well. As just noted, my ordination took place just as the council began; as it proceeded, I was finishing theological studies at home and thereafter completing formal training as a Jesuit in Europe.

A distinguished Jesuit historian has judged this council as "a major turning point in the history of Catholicism" (O'Malley 1989, p. 24). Looking at its effects on members of the Church, the same writer affirms: "From the viewpoint of Church history, it can be asserted that never before in the history of Catholicism had so many and such sudden changes been legislated and implemented which immediately touched the lives of the faithful, and never before had such a radical adjustment of viewpoint been required of them" (p. 17).

In convening the Council, Pope John XXIII had called the Church to an *aggorniamento,* a bringing-up-to-date. That meant a dramatic break with an antimodern mentality which had become deeply ingrained within the Catholic Church. With an ideology and organizational discipline largely determined by the sixteenth-century Council of Trent, reinforced by the First Vatican Council in 1869–1870 and the teaching of the Popes, the Church had stubbornly resisted the onset of modernity with the latter's characteristic liberalism.

During my formal theological studies up through 1963, little change in the Church's outlook found expression. To look at the curriculum given me and the mentality of my teachers, one would never have guessed at the implosion that was about to happen. American Jesuits, for the most part, were still asleep and did not hear the giant stirring.

In Europe, however, theological and spiritual ferment had been felt for decades. Theologians and other scholars within the Church had undergone influences from which American Catholic leaders had been shielded. The German Bernard Häring, for example, who was one of the foremost moral theologians of the Church, once told me how imprisonment in Russia during the Second World War had led him to see the inadequacies of the old morality as taught by the Church. Biblical and liturgical scholars had seen the weaknesses of the Church in those areas and had been at work in preparing changes. In the United States, at least one theologian had elaborated thinking which was to have a great impact on the whole Church. John Courtney Murray, a New York Jesuit, had developed theories of religious liberty later enshrined in an influential document of Vatican II (Abbott 1966, pp. 675–696).

Vatican II changed my life in many different ways. First, it shifted my concept of Church. Instead of a vast hierarchical organization with a structure of divinely sanctioned authority, the Church became for me a community of the baptized, the People of God. This community was on pilgrimage, called by God to find its way to Him. All the members shared in priesthood and possessed a fundamental equality with one another. Though the Church lived by the Holy Spirit and could teach authoritatively, still this community had to search to understand the truth.

The official worship offered to God by the Church expressed this new understanding. In place of the Latin Mass with its inaccessibility, the new rite had the priest face the people, and use the vernacular language. The sacraments, instead of being seen as infallible instruments of grace, became favored encounters between Christians and Christ. They "worked" only to the extent that faith became operative.

Ordained ministers in the Church were also seen in a new light. Instead of being a separate caste with unique privileges and responsibilities, they were placed in the vital relationship with the entire People of God. Though set aside, the clergy still belonged to the community and could exercise ministry effectively only if the people worked with them.

Though such revisions in thinking and practice were revolutionary, many of them represented a return to earlier Christian tradition. It meant a peeling away of accretions grown in the Middle Ages and at other historical eras. Though resisted by conservatives, some, at least, of the changes should logically have been embraced because they so often recovered what had been standard long ago.

But not everything. The material on religious liberty represented distinctively modern ways of thinking. The idea that the Catholic Church would now respect different viewpoints, even if misguided, and not try to get the secular power to suppress "error," amounted to a major change. So did Council documents on other religious traditions, especially attitudes toward Judaism.

Underlying the entire approach of Vatican II was a shift from eschatology to incarnationalism. Instead of being oriented toward the next world, the Church recognized the concerns of this one as vital to its mission. This attitude found expression in many different ways—in Christology, in philosophical anthropology, and in the spiritual life.

In this latter area I felt an immediate and strong impact. I felt freer to find my own ways of maintaining contact with God. No longer did I have to restrict myself to the approaches which my Jesuit training had inculcated. And with the Jesuit tradition itself I felt freer to pick and choose what helped me.

Another major effect of the Council was to relativize what had previously seemed absolute. From the moment in the fall of 1964 when a Canadian cardinal had questioned the Church's wisdom in enshrining Scholasticism and the philosophy of Thomas Aquinas as normative for its teaching, I could feel the foundations shaking (Rynne 1968, pp. 396–397). The idea that other ways of thought could be as good or even better seemed almost blasphemous. And this was only one of many demonstrations of alternative worldviews which received the official stamp of approval.

BACK TO HARVARD

Three years after the end of the Council, I returned to Harvard to begin a campus ministry which would also prove a powerful influence upon me both in spiritual life and externally as well. This period coincided with a time of acute crisis in both university and church. Standing on the edge of both institutions, I was forced into a culture of radical questioning. Student unrest shook the foundations on which the university stood and went beyond to challenge the operating principles of American society.

A similar movement was occurring within the Church, especially the Church in two places where I was active—the university and the inner city. In both locales I experienced continual conflict with the religious establishment. Many Church leaders strongly resisted the changes of Vatican II and waged a sometimes bitter rear guard action. The impact of such warfare was to cause me both disillusionment with religious institutions and (surprisingly) greater interior freedom over them.

Developments like these helped convince me that God's love for me could find alternative forms in my life. Yes, I had been called to enter a religious order as a young man and later become ordained: that did not mean I must stay in that role forever. If I chose to return to the life of an ordinary Christian and regain the status of layman, God would not punish me. On the contrary, I could expect to find His love persist and even intensify. Like others, I too could lay hold of the spiritual freedom to leave some religious structures behind and yet, at the same time, remain favored by the God of love.

Not without hyperbole, perhaps, I also compared myself to Abram, the archetypal Hebrew patriarch who set out at God's command for a new land, guided only by faith. I was heading for my own land of Canaan.

At this time my psychic life found new freedom as well. I began to dream again and to recognize in my dreams patterns and motifs relevant to my spiritual situation. This phenomenon represented a return to an earlier time when I had become acquainted with the work of Jung. His autobiography, *Memories, Dreams, Reflections* (1989/1961) had become a key book for me and taught me to pay serious attention to the content of my dreams.

In one memorable dream, filled with significant details, I found myself on an airport runway in Detroit. There I came across a discarded clerical collar which I recognized as my own. There was a sign affixed to the collar which said: ''This was used in the filming of *Love Story*.'' In symbolic terms I thus realized that my leaving the clerical role was connected with love. Though, on later analysis, I felt embarrassed to have such an inferior work of literature express something of my spiritual life, still the meaning of the dream was clear.

Yet it was impossible to make such a life change without feelings of ambivalence. After all, my role as Jesuit priest was not merely one career among many. Nor was it only a career: it took in my whole life, private and public, all of the time. I was a sacred person, set aside from ordinary people and held in respect, even awe, by many. My life was invested with myths and symbols which made it something of unique significance.

Even though I felt liberated from literal readings of Scripture, various texts did run through my mind from time to time. Among them was the saying of Jesus about the man who put his hand to the plow then abandoned it. He called such persons "unworthy," a label which I shuddered to have applied to me. I also thought about the promises he made to disciples who left everything to follow him. Had I, by turning away from the call, forfeited the reward in heaven which helped motivate me to leave home in the first place?

But these scruples could not prevail over my deep and dominant spiritual conviction about God's personal love for me. That conviction was the driving force freeing me to pursue radical change. When at that time I came to write about my own life, I saw its deepest meaning as a progress toward freedom. If I never did anything else, it seemed to me, having laid hold of personal freedom would give my life significance.

For that freedom I was willing to take risks. Specifically, I would face the economic risk of perhaps being unemployable in the secular world. There was no assurance of my being able to support myself. I also thought it possible that I would be psychologically out of place, something of a misfit as a man who had spent all his adult life in an artificial world which had become almost connatural.

But in January 1975 I applied to Rome and in a few weeks was released from the priesthood and religious life. Definitively, at age forty-seven, I had stepped out of the sacred world and into the secular. Beginning the following year, an ecclesiastical iron curtain shut down against priests applying for their release, part of a new policy by Paul VI to keep clergy from leaving. I had escaped just in time.

Strangely, I had never felt better about the Jesuits than I did at the time of my departure. To me they were friends who belonged to an organization that had shown remarkable courage in making changes. The spirit of the Society of Jesus had become marvelously open in accordance with the teaching of the Second Vatican Council.[2] Jesuit officials could not have been more supportive and personally warm in their approach to me as I was about to turn away from their community.

My leaving was not traumatic because it came at the end of a long process of change, change resulting from a long and gradual evolution that affected the depths of my being. Leaving the priesthood and formal religious life only sealed events that had been taking place for decades. Midlife crisis had transformed my psyche. I was no longer the same illusioned and malleable person who had entered upon the Jesuit career more than twenty-five years previously.

Long before I had once dreamed that I had left the Jesuit Society, only to wake up in a sweat and with relief realize that it was not so. Now the dream had been fulfilled, except that I no longer felt any terror in it. Leaving had not been a horrible, irredeemable mistake but a deliberate action for which I felt no regret. Almost surely, I could never get back in but I did not care. I wanted to experience life without the structure which had supported me all my adult years.

If entering the Jesuit ranks had been an adventure in early manhood, leaving became one of the most crucial events of my middle life. The two—coming and going—had in common movement toward the unknown; both involved radical decision on my part. The going was definitive, however, as the coming turned out not to have been. And, given my middle-aged status, it was riskier as well. From the conventional religious point of view, my leaving seemed a devolution in allegiance to God and spiritual ideals. I did not look at it that way, however. I had become convinced that I might even be honoring God by leaving.

Was my original decision to enter religious life and then to stay with it so long a fundamental mistake? Or was it a decision that made sense even though it did not last? Sometimes it appeared a serious spiritual problem to decide between these two interpretations of my life course.

The first hypothesis, with its suggestion that I had made a bad decision which took almost thirty years to correct, was terribly threatening. If so much of my life had been wasted, bitter regret for the past seemed demanded. In the second scenario, however, I would have been delivered from the narrowness of my own immature self and given human opportunities open to very few other people. In being enabled to enter deeply into the world of the spirit and to develop a vibrant interior life, God had allowed me rare experience.

Probably this analysis was fundamentally wrongheaded because it ignored the circumstances of real life. The dichotomy applies the mentality of a later time to a situation which it does not fit. After wrestling with the issue for some years, I came to realize that only the present is available to me and I must find meaning there.

Life "in the world" lacked the mythic meaning characteristic of religious life. Most people did not realize how intensely imaginative was the environment I had lived in for so many years. One of my new challenges was to accept being "ordinary" and to get along without the props provided by a formally constituted religious community.

I had gone through the moral equivalent of a divorce, having left a pseudo-spouse—my religious family, with all of the intricate personal relationships built up over decades with members of that community. Drastic action had been required to define myself anew.

Many people assumed that I had left the Church too. But it was important for me to continue being a member of the Church in which I still believed. Rome had released me in accordance with canon law which defined me as a layman with the rights and privileges of that standing. I had become very critical of the official Church and had been chastened by its use of authority against me. Nonetheless, I kept my loyalty to the Church as the People of God, refusing to allow any break to occur because of office holders' actions.

With regard to Church laws, I took a much more flexible stance than when I had previously been a layperson. Though I generally kept the rules, I now tried to capture their inner spirit. Religious life among the Jesuits, post–Vatican II style, had taught me that mere external observance means little or nothing: the disposition of heart behind them is what counts. That gave me the freedom to exempt myself from the rules when appropriate.

NEW RELATIONSHIPS

My status in this new world changed notably when, a year after leaving the Jesuits, I married. Marriage in midlife meant for me social and emotional attachment to one other person in a way that went against the motif of my whole life up to that point. It embodied a radical break with the mystique of detachment which characterized my religious identity.

In the novitiate, personal relations were governed by rules. The prime rule which controlled choice among companions was *numquam duo* ("never two"). According to this time-honored regulation, you were never supposed to be alone with another person. Otherwise you would be running the danger of compromising your detachment. Even worse, you might develop a "particular friendship," a term applied to those who felt a special attraction to each other.[3]

Not surprisingly in that monosexual environment, certain novices would develop crushes on one another. Often this became generally known and joked about. I myself felt continually troubled by strong attraction for another fellow who seemed to me very feminine.

Homosexuality, though fear of it lurked in the background, was never explicitly mentioned, presumably because it was regarded as so evil. In any event, remedies for sexual temptation were readily available. Among the actions recommended in the rule book were: "fly the occasions, familiarities, books, etc.; fast and abstain from soft foods; use cold showers; vigorous manual labor; keep busy; cultivate a great love of God and His Blessed Mother."[4]

Loyalty to friends was always supposed to yield when it conflicted with obedience to the rules. For instance, I can remember replying in Latin to a question put to me by a fellow novice in English. By using the vernacular, he had clearly broken the rule and I was not going to condone that by breaking the rule myself.

In addition to these horizontal relationships, we also had to deal with authority figures of various ranks within the religious community. These vertical relationships were marked by inequality and a prescribed formality. Novice Master, Rector, Spiritual Father, and others were ordained priests who were both models for novices to imitate and sources of authoritative direction. It was hard to approach with relaxed confidence people who took themselves so seriously.

Obviously, this austere environment contained many elements inimical to the formation of close friendships. Its curbs on affectivity, especially as expressed in touch, make it easy to understand why some Jesuits had difficulty in developing close friendships. Even the sharing of spiritual ideals and experiences was rare for many men.

But for fear that this depiction mislead, it is important to add some correctives. First, the novitiate atmosphere was much stricter than that of other Jesuit communities. As one moved on to other houses, greater freedom characterized one's life in them. Secondly, even in the novitiate many people managed to lay the foundations of deep and lasting friendships. The fact of having shared such an intense experience, with elements both sublime and ridiculous, as the novitiate provided was often enough to provide a strong bond in itself.

I myself, despite personal rigidity, formed friendships which have proven sources of great value. One of my friends who left the Jesuits many years before I did was a major influence on my life. His intellectual range and esthetic insight were dazzling and helped my own development more than did my teachers. Significantly, however, there was little by way of overtly emotional components to our friendship.

So marriage and its intimacy became a way of life in dramatic contrast to what had been normative for me before. Spiritual development could no longer take place for me alone: whatever my religious strivings, they would involve another person as well.

And in fact my wife shared my religious aspirations fully. Spiritual development was equally important for her. An important part of our attraction for one another had been this sharing of values. Her religious education had been much like mine (though without the same intensity), and we hoped to grow together toward greater love, human and divine. This ideal found expression in the choice of biblical readings and music for the liturgical service at which we celebrated our marriage. We were committing ourselves to a life lived for ourselves and others in the sight of God and in the spirit of Christ.

Our dedication to one another and to the spiritual ideals of Christianity became enhanced four years later with the birth of our daughter. Like the child of Sarah and Abraham in Genesis, she brought special joy as the fruit of relatively old age. Her birth was an ecstatic event, producing in me intense euphoria. Sharing in the birth itself like a thoroughly modern father, I experienced a wide gamut of other emotions, including fear and suffering. What was happening to my wife and me provoked awe of a religious kind, though grounded in human realities from which my whole previous life had barred me. This was the way of attachment indeed.

So was the nurturing we provided to our child in succeeding years. Never before had I experienced another person being dependent upon me as was this daughter whom we had brought into the world. I learned a new kind of trust in divine providence: there was only so much I could do to ensure her well-being. The rest had to be left to God. Would the God of love protect the small person who was to me the most precious being in the world?

The issue had arisen even before our child's birth. As older parents, we faced greater risk that our child might incur a birth defect, possibly a devastating affliction like Down's syndrome. We decided not to use amniocentesis with its own risks, but instead to proceed in hope and accept whatever God gave us. Our reverence for the life of our child even before birth would have prevented us from violating it, in any event.

As it happened, our child was born perfect. This reality made me feel truly blessed by God. No matter what else happened, I had been given the altogether precious gift of a child and at an age when I did not expect it. There was indeed something providential in my search for freedom which had led me away from the celibate life toward marriage and fatherhood. Another human being owed her very existence to my pursuit of personal freedom.

Though I had known and appreciated spiritual fatherhood in my role as priest, it did not have the immediacy of this new experience. The former, after all, was merely analogical to the latter. One had to stretch the definition to make it fit the religious role. Physical fatherhood gave me a grounding in humanity which I did not find in the previous sphere. Daily bodily contact with my child expressed love as my disembodied spiritual strivings never could.

Being a father of a young child in my middle age did not carry with it any social problems. In fact, people expressed nothing but pleasure at my good fortune. Nor has it carried perceptible disadvantages for my daughter herself. Contrary to imaginings of some media types, older parenthood does not result in handicaps for children. I even argue the opposite: having middle-aged parents assures offspring of greater stability than other children may have. A strong case can be made for gerontological parenthood.

AGING AND RELIGION

The approach of old age has provoked changes in my spiritual life. Most of them are subtle requiring insight to discern and analyze. Yet I have had the advantage of having observed a great many elders up close; in the eight years I served in the Cambridge, Massachusetts, municipal government as director of elder services, I encountered people older than myself in all varieties. Dealing with them stimulated my thinking about old age, theirs and mine when it would come.

Ironically, I found myself at work in ministry again, ministry in a new guise. Somehow I had been unable to get away: God had fooled me into further service. But my new job ensured continuity in my life. Though I had not bargained for so much of it, this continuity carried with it spiritual value. It enabled me to maintain vigorously elements of character vital to my identity.

Observing Cambridge elders up close produced in me many reflections about the aging process. Many who dealt with me were financially marginal and educationally deprived. They formed something of an urban proletariat, victimized by hard economic times. Though in a city dominated by two great universities, these elders lived psychically at a far remove from these institutions. Their plight, that of people pushed to the edges of society, radicalized me as I thought about the fate of older Americans.

At the same time, it would often distress me that so many people in old age lacked self-knowledge and spiritual discernment. For inability to come to grips with their own lives, they lacked the peace of soul which could have made old age much more satisfying. Instead many would engage in a hurried round of activities designed, it seems, to distract them from the real issues provoked by the coming of age. Unfortunately, public services commonly encourage and support activities of this sort rather than education and other means of self-development.

Experience like this has convinced me that one of the most neglected aspects of old age in America is the need for spiritual development. It is good to find virtual confirmation of this view in the work of scholars like Harry Moody of the Brookdale Center at Hunter College, who stresses the potentialities of education in later life leading toward this development (Moody 1988).

Similarly, my experience as a professional in the field of applied gerontology makes me differ from the norm established by Sharon Kaufman. "The concept of aging appears too abstract, too impersonal to be an integral part of identity," she maintains (Kaufman 1986, p. 161). But for one who has been so involved with the subject, the concept is not so abstract or impersonal. Aging has become a constant focus of thinking for me and has taken on concrete reality in the observation of personal changes.

But Kaufman's views about continuity strike home. Old people, she holds, *"maintain a sense of continuity and meaning that helps them cope with change"* (Kaufman, p. 2, emphasis hers). Despite the dramatic changes in my life, awareness of personal continuity remains strong. Though to the casual observer I may seem a very different person from my Jesuit days, to me much remains the same. Basic values important to me then remain important now.

Nonetheless interior changes of great significance have taken hold. One of them is an increase in self-acceptance. This has always been an issue because of the earlier-mentioned physical defect. The issue has been heightened in later years by inability to gain access to professional employment consonant with my talents and education. Other failures, too, such as not getting elected when I ran for public office, have given bite to the question.

But through spiritual response to this painful situation I have reconciled myself to my place in the world. I have learned to accept not being successful, as the world judges it, in favor of other forms of success.

Similarly, I have become reconciled to the prospect of physical decline, something which has not yet occurred in any notable way. It will surprise me not to be tested through serious illness at some point. Perhaps, as classical doctrine would suggest, such a trial will be necessary for my spiritual growth.

On the basis of observation and personal experience, it seems to me that contemporary models of old age which eliminate suffering and death should be rejected as unreal. As Thomas Cole and other writers have demonstrated, the stereotypes of old age common in the late nineteenth and early twentieth centuries have been replaced by a new stereotype (Cole 1991; also Cole and Gadow 1986). This latter model constructs an old age which is relentlessly characterized by activity. It does not accept the afflictions which have classically been associated with growing old. Nor does it find any dignity in such sufferings or see them as part of spiritual development.

Work as an advocate for elders has brought me into intimate contact with this contemporary stereotype. Leaders of elder organizations whose rallying cry is "we wish to control our own destiny" have enlisted my support. But I cannot commit myself wholeheartedly to an ideology which devalues the experience of those to whom old age has brought disability. It is not only active elders able to advocate for themselves who deserve respect.

Though cultivating a mystique of suffering would represent an extreme response to the situation, to banish suffering from one's worldview strikes me as even more inhuman. Maybe "the compression of morbidity," whereby one dies in old age suddenly without much prior illness, ought to be a medical ideal (Fries 1989); how realistic it is for the individual to expect remains doubtful.

Though I am critical of the age liberation movement for its superficial activism, this movement has given me important values. It has shown me the importance of political action for winning civic respect for older citizens. It has demonstrated the possibilities of creativity and innovation in one's later years. By breaking stereotypes of old age and highlighting models of dynamic aging, age liberation leaders in both the political and scholarly arenas have provided some answers to Robert Butler's resounding question of 1975: *Why Survive?* (Butler 1975).

In any event, political concern is part of my spiritual life. A personal breakthrough of the 1960s was my realization of how closely they are connected. Reading Gandhi's autobiography, *The Story of My Experiments With Truth* (Gandhi 1982/1927), was the catalytic experience of this development, along with the lessons of the anti–Vietnam War movement. Gandhi's embodiment of spiritual/political life is one of the most valuable object lessons of world history and has had a strong impact on me. More recently, this ideal has found further inspiration in the writings of Vaclav Havel (Havel 1990).

The idea made explicit in Gandhi's title has also proven important. Earlier in my spiritual life, I used to accept truth as prefabricated. It was something readymade, to be accepted as handed down. An already tested scheme was the model for living. Eventually, however, I developed the courage to learn from trial and error. Instead of letting others determine the truth for me in advance, I began to experiment in order to find out personally what was true and what not. This idea, given such beautiful expression by Gandhi, now forms one of the major leitmotifs of my life.

TOWARD SPIRITUAL MATURITY

The Jesuit ideal, derived from Ignatius, of "finding God in all things" continues to inspire my spiritual life. But its application is more radical now that I no longer live in a religious setting. Instead of the facile reference to God provoked by statues, holy pictures, and so on, I look for the divine presence in the events of daily life in domestic and professional settings as well in the events of world history.

In practice I turn frequently to the Spirit within me in the course of each day. Sometimes using a phrase from one of the Psalms or another traditional source, sometimes simply praying wordlessly from the heart, I cultivate this contact. This dialogue buoys up my own spirit because it expresses personal relationship with the God of love.

In this dialogue I am conscious of myself as an aging person with a long history, physical and spiritual, for whom God is different now than formerly. My own vulnerability is a more palpable factor than earlier in life. For me the cliché turned out to be right: sometime in my forties, I began to measure my life not back to birth but forward to death. The prospect of this latter event forms a significant backdrop to my dialogue with God.

In preparation for this event God, in my view, has already called me to a certain letting-go. I have had to surrender hopes for more evident accomplishment than is actually mine. My place in the world has been much more circumscribed than I had dreamed. Nor have I published the books that I had envisioned. Maybe I will even suffer the awful fate of some gerontologists: never getting to experience their own old age.

Death, in prospect, seems to me the greatest of all adventures. Though I shrink from pain and enforced withdrawal from family, friends, and the pleasures of this world, I sometimes feel consumed by curiosity. Eternal life remains the bedrock of my belief about the after-death experience, but no more than anyone else do I know what shape that will take. But I do trust God to deal with me lovingly and have confidence deriving from my union with Christ. It remains to me incomprehensible, as it always has, that death could be the end of personal existence.

For fear this sound merely dour, I add that my life is characterized by joy and peace of heart. St. Paul's assurance that "all things work together for those who love God" has found verification in my life. My years of approach toward old age have been marked by myriad blessings. This does not induce complacency in me but makes me confident of continuing to enjoy God's favor.

It has been a peculiar spiritual development, however. Going from detachment to attachment, from being more religious to becoming less would be judged by the spiritual traditions of the great religions as dubious. To cite only the Christian tradition, St. Paul would say that by reason of marriage and parenthood I must be more occupied with the things of family rather than the things of God.

But I feel the hand of God in the unconventional turns my spiritual path has taken. The great realization of my middle years remains true: God's love for me as a person is so unshakeable that it does not make any difference what I do. That is, God will be pleased with me for having discovered human freedom and does not care that I left my first vocation. The Augustinian motto *ama, et quod vis fac* has validity in my own life. Loving and being loved, I can feel free to do what I wish.

But it would be unwise indeed to make assumptions about what the future will reveal. After all, my life up to now has upset all predictions. Events in human history may have an impact upon me the way Vatican II did. The Spirit at work in my heart may transform me further. I may be led along the paths of mystical union with the divine, even though that seems unlikely now.

Having rejected the trajectory view of aging whereby the first part of life shows ascent and all of later life decline, I see spiritual maturity as my goal. Instead of decline, the underlying model of the interior life is one of ascent. Not yet have I arrived at the heights.

In accordance with the motto of Cardinal Newman, *ex umbra et imaginibus in veritatem* (from shade and images into the truth), I am pressing ahead in search of reality. Thus far my grasp on truth remains tentative and incomplete. But I have confidence in guidance from the Spirit leading me toward fulfillment of my second vocation.

Though this process may sound individualistic, it is rooted in community. Spiritual development culminating in old age will find sustenance in other people and will in turn benefit them. Spiritual life is not for me alone; its ramifications touch many others.

This dimension of interior development has already found expression in a growing benevolence toward other people. With the advance of years I have discovered a much deeper sympathy with fellow human beings. Their trials and difficulties I can relate to with much more empathy than before. Perhaps this is the benignity and kindness which are listed classically as "fruits of the Holy Spirit." I even enter into the successes of others, something much more difficult than identifying with their failures.

So signs of spiritual movement toward maturity have appeared. But God is not done with me yet. I wish to remain open to continued divine action deep within. Long ago, I applied to myself the words of Kierkegaard: "What is it to be God's chosen? It is to be denied in youth the wishes of youth, so as with great pains to get them fulfilled in old age" (Kierkegaard 1954/1843, p. 32). Given my spiritual history, these words continue to hold great promise.

NOTES

1. In the Primum Ac Generale Examen, which serves as an introduction to St. Ignatius' *Constitutiones,* the following norm for corporal penances is given: "no customary pe-

nances or castigation of the body are to be undertaken by way of obligation, but anyone, with the approval of the Superior, can do those which seem good for his greater spiritual perfection along with those which Superiors may impose for the same purpose" (my translation from the official Latin version). The edition of the *Constitutiones* used was published in Rome (1949) by the Jesuit General's curia.

The instruction book used by New York novices before the middle 1960s made explicit the requirement that the "discipline" be used three times a week outside of liturgically festive days and seasons: "On Monday, Wednesday and Friday . . . the sign will be posted for the discipline to be taken. This penance is performed just before retiring and consists of twenty strokes." Custom Book for the Novices of Bellarmine College Novitiate, no date, mimeographed, p. 21. The Custom Book used by New England novices in the same period had a similar directive.

2. McDonough, cited in the references, covers only the period leading up to Vatican II, although he throws much light on the changes to come. In a review of McDonough, the Jesuit David Toolan (1992) incisively and frankly evaluates those changes.

Joseph M. Becker, S.J. (1992) provides a detailed account of the way the American Jesuits transformed themselves after Vatican II. The author, who promises a second volume, professes himself objective about the changes, though some elements of the book suggest disapproval.

3. C. Browning (1967) defines particular friendship as "an exclusive association between two persons based upon emotional satisfaction."

4. As transcribed from the novitiate "Custom Book" in the author's unpublished spiritual journal (1949).

REFERENCES

Abbott, W. 1966. *The Documents of Vatican II*. New York: Herder & Herder.

Augustine. 1991. *Confessions*. Translated with an introduction and notes by Henry Chadwick. New York: Oxford University Press.

Becker, J. M. 1992. In *The Re-Formed Jesuits: A History of Changes in Jesuit Formation During the Decade 1965–1975*. San Francisco: Ignatius Press.

Browning, C. 1967. "Particular Friendship." In *New Catholic Encyclopedia*, vol. 6, 205. New York: McGraw-Hill.

Butler, R. N. 1975. *Why Survive? Being Old in America*. New York: Harper & Row.

Cole, T. 1991. *The Journey of Life*. New York: Cambridge University Press.

Cole, T., and S. Gadow, eds. 1986. *What Does It Mean to Grow Old?* Durham: Duke University Press.

Fleming, D. L. 1978. *The Spiritual Exercises of St. Ignatius: A Literal Translation and A Contemporary Reading*. St. Louis: The Institute of Jesuit Sources.

Fries, J. F. 1989. "The Compression of Morbidity: Near or Far?" *The Milbank Quarterly* 67, no. 2: 208–25.

Gandhi, M. 1982/1927. *The Story of My Experiments with Truth: An Autobiography*. Translated from the original Gujurati by Mahadev Desai. Harmondsworth: Penguin.

Havel, V. 1990. *Disturbing the Peace: A Conversation with Karel Hvizdala*. Translated with an introduction by Paul Wilson. New York: Vintage Books.

Hawkins, A. H. 1985. *Archetypes of Conversion: The Autobiographies of Augustine, Bunyan, and Merton*. London: Associated University Presses.

James, W. 1985/1901. *The Varieties of Religious Experience*. Cambridge, Mass.: Harvard
        University Press.
Jung, C. G. 1989/1961. *Memories, Dreams, Reflections*. Rev. ed. Recorded and edited
        by Aniela Jaffé. Translated from German by Richard and Clara Winston. New
        York: Vintage Books.
Kaufman, S. R. 1986. *The Ageless Self: Sources of Meaning in Late Life*. Madison,
        Wis.: University of Wisconsin Press.
Kierkegaard, S. 1954/1843. *Fear and Trembling and the Sickness unto Death*. Translated
        with introductions and notes by Walter Lowrie. New York: Doubleday.
McDonough, P. 1992. *Men Astutely Trained: A History of the Jesuits in the American
        Century*. New York: Free Press.
Merton, T. 1948. *The Seven Storey Mountain*. New York: Harcourt, Brace & World.
Moody, H. R. 1988. *Abundance of Life*. New York: Columbia University Press.
O'Malley, J. W. 1989. *Tradition and Transition: Historical Perspectives on Vatican II*.
        Wilmington, Del.: Michael Glazier.
Rynne, X. 1968. *Vatican Council II*. New York: Farrar Straus.
Thomas, L. E., ed. 1989. *Research on Adulthood and Aging: The Human Science
        Approach*. Albany: State University of New York Press.
Toolan, D. 1992. "Learning to Die, Choosing to Live." *Commonweal* 119, no. 2: 31–
        34.

4 The Way of the Religious Renouncer: Power through Nothingness

L. Eugene Thomas

I have an inkling that our response to such a man (Gandhi) rests on the need of all men to find a few who plausibly take upon themselves—and seem to give meaning to—what others deny at all times but cannot really forget for a moment . . . that life is bounded by not-life.

The middle-aged need the occasional man who can afford to remember, and they will travel regularly and far to partake of his elusive power.
—E. H. Erikson,
Gandhi's Truth

This chapter will explore the issue of aging and religion by means of a case study of an elderly religious renunciate from India, along with a comparison of Gandhi's life in his later years. Utilizing this cross-cultural perspective, we will examine these two instances where aging has not led to a loss of prestige and personal authority. In the analysis we will take an in-depth look at the factors which contribute to this phenomenon, and explore the implications they might have for aging in Western society.

To place the analysis of this case study in perspective, and point toward the analysis that will be made later, the present crisis in aging in Western societies should be noted. As Cole (1992) observed, the displacement of the elderly from the workplace has led to their marginalization and segregation from the rest of society. Although an "aging industry" comprising caregiving, recreation, housing, and so on, has arisen to "meet the needs" of the elderly, this displacement has led to a loss of status and psychological well-being among the elderly that is seen (at least by social gerontologists, themselves part of the "aging industry") as having reached epidemic proportions. Butler's (1975) statement of the problem, "Why survive?," in which he deplores the plight of the elderly in modern society, has been amplified by numerous other scholars and social critics (e.g., Erikson, Erikson & Kivnick 1986; Moody 1988; Cole 1992).

In contrast, it is illuminating to note the role that the religious renunciate has traditionally played in Indian society. Dumont (1980) has argued that the religious renunciate plays a decisive role in Indian culture, providing for permeability and change in an otherwise static society. It is somewhat surprising that this role would be played by *sannyasi,* who are mostly elderly in India, in view of the fact that the elderly have typically been seen as committed to a traditional and conservative stance. This counterintuitive hypothesis is intriguing, and suggests that the Indian situation might be instructive in an understanding of the esteemed place that the elderly might occupy in Western society.

Before moving to the case study of an Indian religious renunciate, which constitutes the bulk of this chapter, note that the methodology utilized diverges from typical positivist social science research in that no attempt is being made to do hypothesis testing. Rather, in the human science tradition, the intention is to understand social phenomena (compare with Thomas 1989). In this particular instance, I am using the case study as an exemplar of a Weberian "ideal type." Such an ideal type is seen as an exemplar; it is not typical, any more than Luther was representative of late medieval Europe or Gandhi was representative of late colonial India. In times of rapid social change and uncertainty, an ideal type might well serve the purpose of helping us visualize alternate directions for solutions of problems that seem to have brought us to a dead end.

SWAMI TAMANANDA

When my interpreter and I inquired of members of the religious community in Varanasi, India, about the most spiritually mature persons they knew, several mentioned the name of a swami who lived alone in a Shiva temple at Gaya Ghat. Swami Tamananda is a tall, lean, vigorous man who does not look his seventy years. He wears the ocher robe and carries the distinct "Dandi" staff of the Dasnami order, one of the most respected and traditional of the Hindu religious orders (Tripathi 1978). His distinct Indian appearance stands in sharp contrast to his fluent English and friendly approachability.

Sw. Tamananda lives in a room at the top of a Shiva Temple, which commands a panoramic view of the Ganges River below. When I explained that I was interested in learning about the experience of aging in India, and wanted to talk with religious renunciates in particular, he assured me that I could ask him "anything." I explained that in particular I wanted to know his personal experience in becoming a renunciate. Although swamis are traditionally reluctant to talk about their personal lives (Tripathi 1978), Sw. Tamananda said that would be "no problem."

Sw. Tamananda has spent the last ten years of his life as a religious renunciate, joining the Dasnami order when his wife died. Prior to that he and his wife had lived in Varanasi from the time of his retirement from a government college in Bombay. "The day I left the chair and took the pension," he said, referring to the teaching position he had held for over twenty years, "we took the train to Varanasi." He continued, "Fortunately, my wife died ten years ago, and I was able to take *sannyas* (initiation)." I was somewhat surprised at this statement, and observed that he seemed to be a very satisfied man. He responded:

During my childhood my parents fed me on the very best food possible. I never drank milk without saffron. Now it is difficult to get—one of the delicacies. During my *bramacharya* [school days] I had the best of teachers. I am the luckiest man in the world, if you want to say it. Someone said "Is there a happy person in the world?" The question is put as if everyone is unhappy. I am the luckiest man in the world.

These were the essentials of his life that were readily forthcoming in our first interview. It would take long conversations in subsequent interviews (a total of fourteen audiotaped interviews were conducted over a seven-month period), as well as informal conversations with members of his family and friends and acquaintances to fill in the details of his life. Even more than chronicling the events that occurred in his life, it took focused effort over time (technically, utilizing the "constant comparative method," in which analysis and hypothesis formulation takes place while data are being collected; cf. Strauss & Corbin 1990) to determine the meaning that these events had for him.

As a young Brahmin boy he grew up with a religious mother and distant father (not atypical in India still today). His less traditional uncle started a trucking company with Tamananda's grandfather, and when it proved successful, Tamananda's father reluctantly joined the family business. Through the influence of his uncle, who was a follower of Gandhi in the independence movement, Tamananda studied science, and was sent to Banaras Hindu University to become an engineer.

At Banaras Hindu University Tamananda met a French scholar and musician, Alain Danielou, who was studying with the noted Sanskrit scholar and political activist, Sw. Kapatriji Maharaj. Danielou took Tamananda and his older brother into his circle of friends, and for the first time in his life Tamananda seriously engaged in religious studies. Today Tamananda identifies Danielou as the individual who had the most influence on his life, since he led him to return to his own tradition. "If he, a Frenchman, came to India to study and appreciate our Hindu scriptures, why should I remain ignorant of them?" he explained.

After four years of association with Danielou, and being swept up in Sw. Kapatriji's religious and political work, Tamananda abruptly broke with Danielou and his companion (later identified in Danielou's autobiography [1987] as Raymond Vernier, his lover), and went before the local Brahmin council to request that his childhood sacred thread initiation be redone. Thereupon Tamananda undertook intensive Sanskrit study. It wasn't until eight years later, when he became quite ill, that Tamananda was forced to give up his religious studies. His parents came from Bombay and took him home, where they nursed him back to health for the next three years.

Back home his mother was "very clever" in weaning him from his religious pursuits, he said, when she "managed to get me married." With a twinkle in his eye, he explained that in his life a man simply moves "from tit to tit"— from being cared for by his mother to attachment to his wife. But at that point it was necessary to make a living, and the practice of engineering was forbidden by the Vedic tradition, so he compromised and taught engineering for his livelihood. And he became a "householder" (the technical name for the third stage of life in the Hindu tradition), indeed, fathering thirteen children—seven daughters and six sons. In fact, his youngest son was born when Tamananda was fifty-three, and as a teenager is now studying the Vedas in the Sanskrit school next door to the Shiva temple where Sw. Tamananda lives. Not being allowed to receive money himself, Sw. Tamananda's retirement check now goes directly to the support of his son.

Throughout these years Tamananda continued the serious practice of his religious duties, carrying out the exacting religious rituals expected of the householder (but actually carried out fully by very few Hindus). In obedience to the Vedic tradition, and in defiance of the laws enacted by the modern Indian government, he married off each of his daughters before they reached puberty.

Two events happened when Tamananda was forty-five that show his tenacious dedication to the orthodox Hindu teaching—he broke with Sw. Kapatriji, and his eldest son committed suicide. Tamananda downplayed the importance of both events as having been turning points in his life. The information about his son's suicide was particularly startling, first, in how it was mentioned, and second, in its apparent lack of effect on him. In fact, from the first interview Sw. Tamananda had maintained that his life had been smooth, without any dramatic fluctuations. In a later interview, when I happened to ask him how his sons had turned out, he mentioned matter-of-factly that his eldest son had revolted against his religious strictness, and committed suicide. He added: "He was supposed to go to engineering college, and my injunction was that he should cook his own food. He found it too difficult. The second also left me, and took to doing the engineering. The younger two followed my way. They were young enough and I did not put them to school from the beginning. They had to learn the Vedas first."

At the same time Tamananda and other followers of Kapatriji became suspicious that their teacher was deviating from the traditional teachings of the Vedas. "I followed Kapatri for twenty-four years," Sw. Tamananda observed, noting that the time from twenty-one to forty-five he had been under Sw. Kapatriji's influence, "but after that I opposed him for twenty-four years." (It was significant that throughout the interviews Sw. Tamananda did not use the honorific and affectionate suffix "ji" on the end of his former mentor's name.) Interestingly, the day that Sw. Tamananda received his initiation as a Dandi Swami (by another teacher) was the day that Sw. Kapatriji died.

Today Sw. Tamananda devotes his time to teaching the Vedas to a small group of devotees, consulting with visitors and pilgrims who come his way, and meditating. Having taken initiation as a renunciate, he no longer handles money or prepares food. He mentioned that begging is the noblest of professions, once one has completed one's duties as a householder, but much of the time food is brought to him without his having to leave the temple where he lives.

As a further indication of the regard in which Sw. Tamananda is held, his family has clearly accepted his spiritual leadership. When his mother died, Tamananda was chosen to conduct the funeral rites instead of his elder brother, as tradition would dictate. Further, when I asked him about his family's response to his lack of emotional reaction when his son committed suicide, he said that at the time (when he was still living with his family) one of his sisters criticized him for not crying. He added: "That same sister later came to Varanasi, leaving her family. She said, 'you are the only one correct with me.' She did a lot of penance over here. She said finally, 'My job is done,' and died. She sat in a posture [indicating the *pad asana*] and just passed away. It was wonderful."

THE CULTURAL SETTING

The meaning that an individual's action has, for himself and others, is, of course, intimately tied up with the cultural context in which it occurs. In interpreting the social and religious events in Sw. Tamananda's life, one must place them within this cultural context. For instance, a Westerner is likely to see his reaction to the death of his son and his wife as bizarre, if not pathological, much as Gandhi's midlife vow of sexual abstinence was viewed by many Westerners (Erikson 1969). Yet, when viewed from within the cultural context in which they occurred, their meaning can be profoundly different.

The key component of Hindu tradition that impinges on the individual is that of *dharma,* which "comprises the whole context of religious and moral duties" (Creel 1977, p. 2). In its broader sense (*varnasrama dharma*), it relates to one's social group or caste, and for the individual it represents the ordering of life in terms of four life stages (*asramas*). To make sense of Sw. Tamananda's behavior, we have to view it within both of these contexts.

The concept of stages of life as defining the duties of one's life is pervasive in Indian culture (Tilak 1989). The young Hindu is initiated into the stage of student with the taking on of the sacred thread at an early age (ranging from eight to twelve, depending on his caste, with the earlier age holding for Brahmins and the later for lower castes [Klostermaeier 1989]). After completing his studies he is married and begins the "householder" stage, of raising a family and pursuing a career. "When a householder sees his skin wrinkled, and his hair white, and the sons of his sons, then he may resort to the forest" (Muller 1982).

The "forest" stage represents a retirement from family and societal responsibility, when the individual can devote himself to the study of sacred scriptures and the performance of the prescribed ritual (it should be noted that these stages are specified for men, although women can be implicated, for instance, in accompanying their husband). The final stage is that of the renunciate, which is described in the *Laws of Manu:* "Having studied the Vedas in accordance with the rule, having begot sons according to the sacred law, and having offered sacrifices according to his ability, he may direct his mind to the attainment of final liberation" (Muller 1982, p. 18).

At the time of initiation into the final, or *sannyasi,* stage, the aspirant is divested of the attributes of his former life, his hair is symbolically shorn, and he takes vows of poverty and chastity. The initiation symbolizes death of the old self, and this symbolism is underlined by the initiation rite in which the aspirant conducts his own funeral ceremonies, such that at the time of his actual death the renunciate is not cremated. Since he has already experienced a ritual death, the funeral pyre is seen as inappropriate, and instead the body is buried or placed in a holy river (Dumont 1980).

It should be noted that although these stages are widely accepted as having religious sanction throughout India even today, not all individuals go through all of them (Madan 1982). The last two stages are, in fact, considered optional, even in the Hindu scriptural tradition (Dumont 1980). This is made clear in the *Laws of Manu,* for example, where it is stated: "the housekeeper is declared to be superior to all of them; for he supports the other three" (Muller 1982, p. 23). Dumont (1980) notes that this disclaimer reflects a tension in the Hindu tradition between veneration and suspicion of the institution of renunciation (which will be discussed later).

Beyond prescribing the duties of the individual through the four *asramas,* or stages of life, *dharma* further determines an individual's place in society by his caste designation. Thus Tamananda's membership in the priestly Brahmin caste influenced his behavior in countless ways. Because of his caste position, he was eligible for admission into the Dandi order, with its traditional status among the religious hierarchy of India. But prior to that, his rejection of engineering as a career unsuitable for a Brahmin indicates the power of the *dharma* tradition in his life. So does his opposition to innovations brought by the British and institutionalized by Indians at the time of Independence. For example, Sw. Tamananda refers to progressive Indians such as Nehru and Gandhi, who were instrumental in bringing about a secular state in India, as "black British." It was in defiance of laws enacted under their influence that Tamananda married off his daughters before they had reached puberty, in obedience to what he perceived to be the higher laws of the Vedic tradition.

Beyond the influence of the religious tradition of Hinduism, Tamananda was influenced by the social and historical forces that swirled around him in his early years. Erikson (1969) has written perceptively about those influences in his biography of Gandhi, who was responsible for helping to unleash the forces that catapulted colonial India to independence from British rule. A consideration of these influences would be far beyond the scope of this paper, but suffice it to say that the forces that Gandhi unleashed in India reverberated in Tamananda's life, even though for him it led in a direction different from Gandhi's.

Born in 1919, exactly fifty years after Gandhi's birth in the same area of India, Tamananda could not help being influenced by the forces set in motion by Gandhi and his Congress Party. It is interesting that the activist stage of Gandhi's fight for Indian independence began with the incendiary speech he gave at the inauguration of Banaras Hindu University in 1916, the institution Tamananda would attend as a young engineering student a quarter of a century later.

But ultimately it would not be Gandhi who would most influence Tamananda, but the brilliant Sanskrit scholar and right-wing political activist in Varanasi, Sw. Kapatriji Maharaj. Rather than following Gandhi's Tolstoyian ideal of democratic reform, Sw. Kapatriji followed the path of Hindu Revivalism, with its call to turn from the blandishments of this dark age (*kali yuga*), and for the restitution of the Vedic tradition from the past. It was the influence of Sw. Kapatriji that led the brilliant engineering student to turn from Western science and a political career patterned after Gandhi to Vedic study and austere religious practices.

Ironically, it was a Western scholar, Alain Danielou, who finally diverted Tambananda away from his politically active uncle to the orthodox Brahmin path. Whereas a trader caste (*Vaishyas*) Indian like Gandhi, in rejecting a British identity, chose the traditional peasant mystique, Tamananda turned to the orthodox religious tradition of his Brahmin priestly caste. In both cases, the larger historical forces which led India to throw off three centuries of British domination impinged on their sense of personal identity. The further forces of caste and personal influences determined the different directions the lives these two men would take. But they have in common an interesting feature, in that both of them commanded respect and attracted followers. Let us turn to seek the source of this attraction, since it is of central interest in this paper.

POWER OF RENUNCIATION

As indicated above, Dumont (1980) has argued that the religious renunciate has played an important part in Indian society, serving as a source of social change and innovation in a tradition-dominated culture. And this in spite of the fact that the majority of renunciates are elderly (at least at the time of their greatest influence), when traditionally they might be expected to be sources of resistance to any form of change.

In order for the renunciate to have this much effect on society, he clearly must be seen as having qualities that command respect from society at large. Whether this should be termed "power" is problematic, since that implies the ability to use force and coercion, which is hardly the case with the religious renunciate. But that he commands respect and, to use the sociological term, "legitimization" cannot be doubted, if he plays so central a role in Indian society as Dumont suggests.

It should be noted that the "power," or at least "prestige," that Sw. Tamananda has, does not stem from a general societal respect for religious renunciates. Madan (1987) points out that historically there has been a general skepticism of religious renunciates in India, noting that "Individual men and women may command respect, and even a following, but most of them are dismissed as charlatans" (p. 41). That this skepticism has not lessened in modern times is indicated by an observation made by an Indian sociologist in the introduction to a recent large-scale study of Indian religious *Sadhus* (itinerant religious adherents): "It is now growingly felt among the educated circles that the *Sadhus* tend to become a parasite class. . . . They liken *Sadhus* to the overgrown fingernails, causing inconvenience to the body which maintains them" (Tripathi 1978, p. xiii).

In seeking the source of power held by certain renunciates, like Sw. Tamananda, it is interesting to turn to Erikson's analysis of the source of influence and power that Gandhi exercised with his countrymen. It was when Gandhi was weakest, Erikson noted, that he exercised the most power. In particular, when he fasted, sometimes almost to the point of death, the country held its collective breath, and was most ready to bend to his will. Erikson concluded that the key to this power was Gandhi's willingness to embrace weakness, even "nothingness," in the cause he believed in. He clung to the dictum, Erikson noted, "that only insofar as we can commit ourselves on selected occasions 'to the death' . . . can we be true to ourselves and to others" (Erikson 1969, p. 411).

This, for Gandhi, was more than political fanaticism. It was not by chance that the name suggested by Nehru became the name that the Mohandas Karmachand Gandhi came to be known to the world, that is, "Mahatma," or "Great Spirit." In the common imagination in India, and the eyes of the world, Gandhi assumed the role of a religious renunciate. And Gandhi himself, though insisting that he was only a servant of the people, did not discourage this association. Further, his communal base near Ahmedabad was called an "*ashram*," the name given a religious center in India.

It is not surprising that when Erikson discusses the nature of Gandhi's power, he titles the chapter *homo religiosus*. And the source of this power, this willingness to face death, he suggests, is indicated by the quote given at the beginning of this chapter. It was his willingness to face "what others deny at all times but cannot readily forget for a moment" (p. 397), namely, the fact of non-being, or death. Jack Kornfield, writing in quite another context, observes that people who are not afraid to die are a great power in the world: "These are people who have touched the very source of their being, who have looked into themselves in such a deep way that they understand and acknowledge and accept death, and, in a way, have already died" (1988, p. 140).

Herein, I think, lies the power of those unique religious renunciates, of whom Sw. Tamananda clearly is one, who command respect despite the low esteem in which most Indian *Sadhus* are held in India (Tripathi 1978). For the authentic *sannyasi*, their very initiation involves a symbolic death of the old self, such that they now live as one who has already passed through death. And those at other stages of life, who must turn from the specter of death to provide for the young and maintain the institutions of society, instinctively turn to such men.

Perhaps it is the hope that the renunciate will protect them from death—certainly much of the attention given religious personages is based on the magical desire for protection and benefits. But in Gandhi's case, and in Sw. Tamananda's, no miraculous promises were made or implied, and it would seem that more than stoic willingness to face death on the part of the renunciate is at work here. Eliade (1959) suggests that it is those qualities of *homo religiosus* that point to the sacred, to the transcendent dimension of reality, that nonreligious man hungers for. Nonreligious man, though consciously having turned from religion, "continues to be haunted by the realities he has refused and denied," Eliade suggests (1959, p. 204). And the person who can offer help to a nonreligious man, "enabling him to transcend personal situations and finally gain access to the world of the spirit" (Eliade 1959, p. 210), holds promise and power for his nonreligious counterpart. This, I would argue, is the power wielded by Gandhi and Sw. Tamananda, and those few others who, despite weakness or old age, hold a fascination for their fellow man.

DISCUSSION

I would now like to return to the issue raised at the beginning of this chapter, concerning the state of the elderly in modern society. Accepting the view that the increase in life expectancy has not been matched with a similar increase in quality of life, many gerontologists and social commentators have suggested ways of rectifying the situation, in order to answer Butler's challenging question, "why survive?"

Prior to Butler's book (1975), which focused national attention on the problems of the elderly in this country, the assumption was made that what was needed was legislation to care for the economic and physical needs of the elderly. But after the Older Americans Act and other legislation of the 1960s was enacted which by and large rectified the financial plight of the elderly (Cole 1992), the problems of the elderly in this country were not "fixed." Rather than ushering in the golden age that liberal theorists had predicted, the relative absence of financial and physical problems exposed another, more pervasive layer of problems, related to questions of meaning and purpose for the added years of the life span (Moody 1988).

By and large, the answer suggested by social gerontologists and developmental theorists has been that what is needed is the "re-inclusion" of the elderly into the fabric of the workaday life. Typical of this approach is the advice given by

Erikson, Erikson, and Kivnick in their recent valedictory book on aging, *Vital Involvement in Old Age* (1986). The title of the book indicates the nature of advice: that elders "become more integral coworkers in community life" (p. 294); that they "continue to provide services after retirement" (p. 296); "that they pursue vigorously art activities of all kinds" (p. 335). It should be noted that Erikson's emphasis on activity and social engagement as the key to "successful aging" is not unique—this is the predominant message of most academic and lay gerontic advice offered today. Erikson's position is only a slight modification of the current "activity theory" of aging, which Thomas Cole (1986) has dubbed "Victorian morality in a new key."

Missing from Erikson's later analysis of the elderly is a discussion of the power he identified in Gandhi's life that comes from facing "not-life." One might have expected Erikson to say more about this issue when writing about old age thirty years later, when he himself was in his ninth decade. Even more, one might have expected him to pick up the suggestive themes contained in his earlier writings, in which he spoke euphemistically of death as, "the ultimate test, namely man's existence at the entrance to the valley which he must cross alone" (1964, p. 133). Declining, as a psychologist, to go into detailed discussion of "ultimate concerns" (theologian Paul Tillich's [1951] term for the depth religious dimension of life), Erikson three decades earlier gave a tantalizing hint of the deeper issues involved, issues which he unfortunately did not pursue in his later work:

I cannot help feeling that the order depicted suggests an existential complementarity of the great Nothingness and the actuality of the cycle of generations. For if there is any responsibility in the cycle of life it must be that one generation owes to the next that strength by which it can come to face ultimate concerns in its own way.... *Wisdom, then, is detached concern with life itself, in the face of death itself* (1964, p. 133; Erikson's emphasis).

It is interesting to see how another major theorist, David Gutmann, dealt with the issue of power in old age in a book (1987) specifically devoted to that topic. Written in his seventh decade, the book pulls together the main strands of Gutmann's life-long work and, like Erikson's book, represents his mature judgment on these issues. Here we find a brilliant analysis of the nature of problems faced by the elderly in modern society. Moving beyond the surface explanations of most gerontologists and social theorists, Gutmann is critical of ideological answers in which "the existential and irreversible burdens of later life are interpreted politically (1987, p. ix).

Whereas the "aging industry" paints a picture of the "weak face" of aging in order to justify their political agendas and social programs to "fix" these problems (Moody 1988), Gutmann sees the issues as far more complex and systemic. The true "weak face" of aging is the result of "deculturation," which is associated with urbanization and modernization. Urban deculturation leads to the loss of community, and values become private and a subjective matter, where "narcissistic preference dictates the lines of affiliation" (p. 247). In such a setting, "Culture loses the power to convert strangers into familiars" (p. 247), and the elderly become strangers, even to their own families. As a result the elderly, particularly males, are robbed of their "power"—their place in an established order. Such deculturation leads to the erosion of the extended family and of culture itself, which no longer is able to protect the elderly, or, of equal concern to Gutmann, to provide for adequate protection and socialization of the young. He observes ominously: "While the crisis of meaning and civility that comes with deculturation has special consequence for the aged and perhaps touches them first, it is also very much a shared affliction. . . . We have brought down the fathers and humbled the aged. In so doing, we are also bringing down the culture that sustains us all" (p. 252).

The root cause of the plight of the elderly in the United States since the Civil War is not, he argues, so much industrialization or changed demography. Rather it is the secularization of society which has accompanied these changes, and has been the real source of loss of power and status and meaning for the elderly. Turning to cross-cultural data on primitive societies, Gutmann maintains that the power of the elderly (again, particularly men) lies in "their special association with the sacred systems of society" (p. 218). The power of the elderly derives not from material wealth, he argues, but rather material wealth is a by-product of sacred power. In such cultures, sacred power is the major "independent variable," in the status of elderly.

Gutmann's analysis thus far accords with the conclusions reached from the case study of Sw. Tamananda, and Erikson's analysis of Gandhi. That is, it is their willingness to face nothingness, to be "bridgeheads to the sacred" (a term Gutmann used in an earlier [1983] paper). When Gutmann turns to the question of the loss of power of the elderly in contemporary society, it is curious that he fails to focus upon the importance of the religious dimension. Indeed, he seems to be afraid that nativistic, fundamentalist religion will fill the gap left by culture—"The gurus, the Mansons, the Jim Joneses, the televangelists," who are "waiting to 'meet our needs' " (1987, p. 253). In his analysis of primitive cultures he notes that the elderly gain their power by living on the border between the mundane and the sacred, from which position they "create and serve the cultural reality" (p. 227). For modern society, rather than seeing the elderly as potentially serving such a sacred purpose, he, like Erikson, proposes a more Promethean and largely secular agenda, whereby the elderly are enlisted to "help and guide us in the vital processes of reversing deculturation and of crafting the new myths on which reculturation can be based" (p. 253).

Erikson and Gutmann are not alone among social scientists in minimizing the place that religion plays in the lives of the elderly. As indicated in the Introduction, this is a glaring lacuna in the gerontological literature that is only belatedly being addressed. It is obviously beyond the scope of this chapter to state definitively what religious dimensions are relevant to aging, and the status and psychological well-being of the elderly. But the source of power that Erikson found to emanate from Gandhi—his willingness to embrace nothingness—appears to be very relevant to our understanding of the situation of the elderly in modern society. That is, the importance of some persons to save others "from the fantastic effort *not* to see the most obvious of all facts: that life is bounded by not-life" (1969, p. 397). Apparently many contemporary gerontologists are still engaged in the "fantastic effort" not to face it either, and to this extent are hampered in their attempt to understand the importance of the religious dimension in human aging.

CONCLUSION

Erikson's analysis of the source of Gandhi's power as lying in his willingness to face nothingness—in his willingness to face "non-life" in devotion to a larger principle to which he had dedicated his life—is suggestive of a source of power and status that elderly can have which is not necessarily diminished by declining strength and activity level. On the contrary, Gandhi's power came from his very weakness, in that it was willingly taken on in the name of a higher, cultural purpose.

Likewise, an analysis of the life of Sw. Tamananda, who in renouncing former status and power is accorded respect and admiration by family and acquaintances, suggests that the losses of age don't necessarily lead to marginality and meaninglessness. Here, too, it is clear that it is not social activity, nor possessions which serve as the basis for the esteem accorded Sw. Tamananda. He, like Gandhi, has indicated by his actions and words that he is willing to face the margins of life—including the numinous, and death, itself. More important, by his words and actions he indicates to others that he is able to find greater meaning and purpose in doing this.

But to say that the source of Gandhi's power was his ability to face "nothingness" is only half true. More than stoic resignation was involved in conveying power to both Gandhi and Sw. Tamananda. Their power came from renunciation of the everyday world in the name of a higher, transcendent power. Both of these *homo religiosus* partake of power that comes from "their association with the sacred system of society" (Gutmann 1987, p. 218). It is not their ability to "stare unblinkingly at *nothingness*," but rather their ability to "leach the great terror out of nothingness and render it transcendent" (Gutmann, personal communication).

From the lives of Gandhi and Sw. Tamananda we can see the importance of the religious dimension in securing the place of the elderly in society, and in providing meaning and purpose to their lives. In turn, the respect and admiration accorded them by those about them attests to the fact that they serve the needs of their fellow man in helping to bring them into touch with the sacred dimension. And in the process they help others to face with courage and purpose threats that would otherwise be unnerving and disorienting.

Our society is, of course, far different from that of India. The fact that ours is a more secularized society is, as Gutmann suggests, probably the primary reason for the loss of power and status by the elderly. But Eliade (1959) reminds us that despite the degree of secularization of modern man, "he continues to be haunted by the realities he has refused and denied" (p. 204). Despite his protestations, his *homo religiosus* past cannot be wiped out, because, Eliade argues, "religion is the paradigmatic solution for every existential crisis" (p. 210). And the quintessential existential crisis for humankind, whether young or the aged, is the inevitable prospect of one's own death. If and when the elderly are able to help mankind face that crisis, the chances are that in this society, as in Indian society, they will be accorded respect and honor. Rather than being relegated to the fringes of society, they would be actively sought out and, as is the case of Sw. Tamananda, and was true for Gandhi, people "will travel regularly and far" to partake of their "elusive power" (Erikson 1969, p. 399).

NOTE

This chapter was originally a paper presented at the Annual Scientific Meeting of the Gerontological Society of America, Washington, D.C., November, 1992. Field work on which this chapter is based was supported by a Senior Fulbright Research Fellowship in India, 1989–1990. I would like to express my appreciation to Professor B. S. Gupta, former head of the Psychology Department at Banaras Hindu University, for making arrangements for my visit, and to Om Prakash Sharma for serving as a knowledgeable guide to the religious community of Varanasi.

REFERENCES

Butler, R. 1975. *Why survive? Being old in America.* New York: Harper & Row.
Cole, T. R. 1986. Victorian morality in a new key. In T. R. Cole and S. Gadow, eds., *What does it mean to grow old? Reflections from the humanities,* 115–130. Durham, NC: Duke University Press.
———. 1992. *The journey of life: A cultural history of aging in America.* New York: Cambridge University Press.
Creel, A. B. 1977. *Dharma in Hindu ethics.* Calcutta: Firma KLM.
Danielou, A. 1987. *The way of the labyrinth: Memories of East and West.* New York: New Directions.
Dumont, L. 1980. *Homo hierarchichus: The caste system and its implications.* Chicago: University of Chicago Press.
Eliade, M. 1959. *The sacred and the profane: The nature of religion.* New York: Harcourt, Brace & World.
Erikson, E. H. 1964. *Insight and responsibility.* New York: Norton.
———. 1969. *Gandhi's truth: The origins of militant nonviolence.* New York: Norton.
Erikson, E. H., J. Erikson, and H. Q. Kivnick. 1986. *Vital involvement in old age.* New York: Norton.
Gutmann, D. 1983. Observations on culture and mental health in later life. In J. E. Birren

and R. B. Sloane eds., *Handbook of mental health and aging*, 114–48. Englewood Cliffs, NJ: Prentice-Hall.

————. 1987. *Reclaimed powers: Toward a new psychology of men and women in later life*. New York: Basic Books.

Klostermaier, K. K. 1989. *A survey of Hinduism*. Albany: State University of New York Press.

Kornfield, J. 1988. The Buddhist path and social responsibility. In S. Grof, ed., *Human survival and consciousness evolution*, 135–43. Albany: State University of New York Press.

Madan, T. N. 1982. The ideology of the householder among the Kashmiri Pandits. In T. N. Madan, ed., *The way of life: King, householder, renouncer*, 223–50. New Delhi: Vikas.

————. 1987. *Non-renunciation: Themes and interpretations of Hindu culture*. New Delhi: Oxford.

Moody, H. R. 1988. *Abundance of life: Human development policies for an aging society*. New York: Columbia University Press.

Muller, M., trans. 1982. The Vedic way: Laws of Manu. In P. L. McKee, ed., *Philosophical foundations of gerontology*, 14–24. Albany: State University of New York Press.

Strauss, B., and J. Corbin. 1990. *Basics of qualitative research*. Newbury Park, CA: Sage.

Thomas, L. E. 1989. The human science approach to understanding adulthood and aging. In L. E. Thomas, ed., *Research on adulthood and aging: The human science approach*, 1–10. Albany: State University of New York Press.

Tilak, S. 1989. *Religion and aging in the Indian tradition*. Albany: State University of New York Press.

Tillich, P. 1951. *Systematic theology*, vol. 1. Chicago: University of Chicago Press.

Tripathi, B. D. 1978. *Sadhus of India: The sociological view*. Bombay: Popular Prakashan.

III Historical and Literary Studies

5 Aging and Spiritual Empowerment: The Stories of Oedipus and David

Stephen Bertman and W. Andrew Achenbaum

Ancient literature, both classical and biblical, presents us with a variety of models for studying the phenomena and processes of aging. At times, the elderly are portrayed as exemplars of strength. In Greek culture: while on trial for his life, Socrates dynamically defended, even at an advanced age, the idea of truth. In Hebrew Scripture: Moses at 120 remained a towering figure, a leader of his people. Nor were men the only ones capable of powerful heroics. In the Book of Ruth, the widow Naomi sets into motion relationships that will culminate in the Davidic dynasty. At other times, writers accentuate the weakness of age. Barzillai, a venerable advisor, willingly opts for retirement in old age. Similarly, the enfeebled Anchises has to be carried by his son, Aeneas, from the burning city of Troy.

In certain cases, however, ancient texts present a different type of model, which challenges stereotypic notions of senescence as a period of irreversible, inevitable decline. Biblical and classical authors sometimes described a transformation of character in which weakness is superseded by strength. Occasionally, the transformation is physical, as when postmenopausal, nonagenarian Sarah gave birth to Isaac, or in Luke's account of how ancient Elizabeth conceived John the Baptist. Other transformations are spiritual, as illustrated in the stories of two ancient kings, Oedipus and David. In addition to portraying important facts of aging, their archetypal stories raise modern questions concerning the empowerment of the elderly and the religious dimension of growing old. We believe that in both cases Oedipus and David managed to overcome their infirmities by seeing how they still had strength to influence the future: indeed, they in late life surpassed their contemporaries' expectations by establishing the spiritual foundations for their successors' future security.

KING OEDIPUS

Psychologists have always been attracted to Sophocles's play, *Oedipus the King,* but it is another of his dramas, *Oedipus at Colonus,* which deserves the attention of gerontologists. The longest of all extant Greek tragedies, *Oedipus at Colonus* contains the greatest number of elderly characters: not one, but two, aged protagonists, and a chorus of old men as well. Moreover, it features the only character in Greek drama who visibly ages from one play to another. The aging of Oedipus, in fact, parallels the aging of Sophocles himself, for twenty years intervened between the composition of the two plays: *Oedipus the King* was written about 429 B.C.E., when Sophocles was sixty-seven; *Oedipus at Colonus,* when he was eighty-seven, three years before his death.

Studying the Oedipus plays thus allows us to examine how a dramatic character is made to "age" and to explore how a playwright who has aged will portray a character he previously introduced twenty years before. Are the two Oedipuses different in significant ways? If so, can the differences be attributed to the insights and experiences of a playwright who has himself aged? Indeed, does Sophocles's decision to "re-activate" Oedipus suggest a deliberate attempt on his part to make a statement about what aging implies? And, if so, what *is* that statement?

The Story of Oedipus

The story of Oedipus begins even before the action of *Oedipus the King.* As a prince in the royal house of Corinth, Oedipus began to suspect that Corinth's king and queen were not his natural parents. In quest of his true identity, he traveled to Apollo's shrine at Delphi, where he was told he would end up killing his father and marrying his mother if he returned home. To avoid this, Oedipus headed in the opposite direction. Coming to a narrow section in the road, he met an old man traveling in a carriage. When the old man refused to yield and struck him, Oedipus slew him and his bodyguards. Then Oedipus continued on his way. At the outskirts of Thebes, he was confronted by a monster called the Sphinx. The Sphinx posed the same riddle to all who passed, killing those who could not solve it. Oedipus succeeded in answering the riddle, much to the consternation of the Sphinx, who then committed suicide. When he arrived in Thebes, Oedipus was greeted as a savior by the populace, who offered the noble stranger the hand of their recently widowed queen, and with it the throne. Oedipus then became king of Thebes, but soon a terrible plague befell the kingdom.

It is at this point in the story that the action of *Oedipus the King* begins. Oedipus is informed by the oracle of Apollo that the murderer of the previous king must be brought to justice in order for the plague to end. With characteristic persistence and determination, Oedipus proceeds to investigate the unsolved mystery. To his horror he eventually learns that he was originally born in Thebes and later raised as foundling by the king and queen of Corinth. Thus his natural parents were the king and queen of Thebes. The king, his true father, was the very man he met and killed in anger on the road to Thebes; the queen, his mother, the very woman he married when he came to Thebes after the death of the Sphinx. Queen Jocasta had borne him four children: two daughters (Antigone and Ismene) and two sons (Polyneices and Eteocles). Horrified at the realization that he had fulfilled Apollo's prophecy, Oedipus blinds himself so that he may never have to behold in Hades the face of his murdered father and of his mother, now dead of suicide. Appealing to the new regent, Creon, Oedipus asks that he be allowed to go into exile with his children. Thus *Oedipus the King* ends.

When the action of *Oedipus at Colonus* begins, some twenty years have passed. Led by his daughter Antigone, Oedipus—now blind and destitute—has come to the outskirts of Athens, to a sacred grove in the precinct of Colonus. As a suppliant, he appeals for refuge. Soon his other daughter, Ismene (who had remained in Thebes during Oedipus's exile to look out for his interests), arrives. Ismene informs Oedipus of a new prophecy from Apollo: for Thebes to be militarily secure, Oedipus will have to be brought home and, upon his death, buried at the city's edge. She says that civil war has broken out between Oedipus's two sons: Eteocles, who had seized the throne with Creon's help, and Polyneices, who had now allied himself with the city of Argos. Soon Creon arrives and, after failing to persuade Oedipus to return voluntarily, attempts to seize Ismene and Antigone as hostages to compel Oedipus's compliance. Only the arrival of Theseus, king of Athens, and his militia force Creon to desist. Next, Polyneices arrives and seeks his father's help, only to be vitriolically rebuked by Oedipus, who charges him with willful neglect. Oedipus then offers Theseus the gift of his presence for, if buried in Colonus, the body of Oedipus will act as a spiritual guardian protecting Athens' future. Summoned by the gods to join their company, Oedipus mystically vanishes and the play concludes.

In terms of character development, *Oedipus at Colonus* represents an inversion of *Oedipus the King*. In *Oedipus the King,* Oedipus begins confident and self-assured, seeing with his eyes but blind to his own inner fallibility. Yet, by the play's end he is psychologically shattered and morally humbled. Dependent upon others, he is led offstage by his young daughter, Antigone, in keeping with the divine pronouncement that he be banished for his sins. In *Oedipus at Colonus,* however, Oedipus begins as a humble figure dependent upon others, only to end up confident, self-assured, and morally justified. At the play's conclusion, he himself—though blind—leads Antigone to the grove where, purified, he will ultimately be welcomed into the company of the gods.

The Rehabilitation of Oedipus

What accounts for Oedipus's moral rehabilitation? And what may have motivated the playwright Sophocles to, in effect, pardon a criminal he had convicted on the stage twenty years earlier?

Oedipus himself provides the answer, for in the latter play he argues in his own defense. The murder of his father, Laius, was an act of self-defense. What would *you* have done, he asks, if you were violently attacked and outnumbered? The marriage to his mother, Jocasta, is similarly defended, but on the grounds of ignorance. How was *I* to know she was my mother? he asks. Besides, he argues, if something is destined to happen, how can one resist? And if one does wrong in such a case, how can it be argued that such wrong was committed by free choice?

To be sure, such arguments can be challenged. Why did Oedipus, only recently warned that he would murder his father and marry his mother, kill the first man he met who was his father's age and marry the first woman he met who was his mother's? And how can one so speciously and flippantly dismiss acts of both murder and incest?

These are arguments *we* can make. But they are not arguments that Sophocles makes. Instead, it is Sophocles who validates Oedipus's position by having the Olympic gods welcome him into heaven.

Likewise, we may well regard Oedipus's rebuke of his penitent son, Polyneices, as cruel and unforgiving. Polyneices, now an exile like Oedipus, pleads for his father's help, only to be reminded that when Oedipus needed *him,* Polyneices made no effort to win the repeal of Oedipus's exile. To paraphrase Oedipus's complaint: "Only when you and Eteocles need me for your own advantage do you show concern for my welfare. When I suffered through years of exile, you didn't care. But now that the oracle of Apollo has spoken, you suddenly miss me."

Witnessing this exchange, we long for reconciliation between alienated father and son. But no such reconciliation is to come. Indeed, once again its very opposite is confirmed by the thunderous reception given the unrepentant Oedipus by the gods.

In short, the wisdom we expect, the humane wisdom born of both suffering and introspection, is missing.[1] Why?

The Relationship between Oedipus and Sophocles

More than seventy five years ago, Carl Robert (1915) suggested that Oedipus's condemnation of his son Polyneices may have been inspired by Sophocles's own animosity toward his own sons. Sophocles's sons, tradition tells us, sought to have their father declared mentally incompetent in order that they might gain control over his estate.

Sophocles wrote tragedies up to extreme old age, and when this preoccupation was thought to impair his attention to business matters, his son brought him to court to prove imbecility, on a law similar to ours which deprives a householder of the management of his property if he has proved incompetent. The old poet is then said to have read to the jury the *Oedipus at Colonus* which he had lately written and was revising, and to have asked whether it seemed the work of an imbecile. After the reading he was acquitted (Cicero). The ode was marvelously admired, and Sophocles was escorted from the lawcourt as from the theater, amid the applause and shouts of all present (Plutarch; quoted and translated into English by Moses Hadas, 1954, p. 84).[2]

Despite those critics who refuse to admit a correlation between a writer's words and his life, Robert may have been correct. Through his play, *Oedipus at Colonus,* and through its protagonist, Oedipus, Sophocles may have sought to affirm and justify his own anger toward his sons. In fact, it is doubly significant that the action of the play takes place at Colonus, for it is not only a part of Athens, the city where the play was performed, but the very neighborhood where Sophocles himself was born. Thus the playwright chooses the very soil of his birthplace to stand upon in arguing for the rightness of his values.

But what of the rather shallow defense Sophocles constructs, the defense by which Oedipus argues his moral innocence? How can we understand Sophocles's willingness to allow such arguments to be his final word on the question of Oedipus's moral responsibility?

Here too perhaps we should look to Sophocles the man for the answer, the man who had experienced eighty-seven years of life. The wisdom of those years seems to be this: we are not in total control of our lives. Young Oedipus thought he was, but he was wrong. In life there are forces we cannot control, and things we cannot ever know until it is too late. Such a realization should humble us into an awareness of our own limitations. But it must also teach us the limitations of our own culpability as well. It is altogether too easy to blame ourselves for the things that have gone wrong with our lives, and, like Oedipus, blind ourselves for the sins we have committed. The wrongs we have done to others are not totally our fault.

Now such a vindication may seem less noble than what we would perhaps expect of a "great writer." In the same way, the unremitting hatred of a son may seem beneath the dignity of a "sage of the stage." But perhaps they are understandable for a human being, battered by long years of life and wounded by his very own kin. It may well be necessary for us to surrender "Sophocles the playwright" in order for us to discover "Sophocles the man."

Oedipus and the Meaning of Aging

For gerontologists, *Oedipus at Colonus* can also be fascinating because of its commentary upon the meaning of aging. In a poignant ode, the chorus of old men decries the sorrows of aging.

Who so craves the ampler length of life, not content to desire a modest span, him will I judge with no uncertain voice; he cleaves to folly.

For the long days lay up full many things nearer unto grief than joy; but as for thy delights, their place shall know them no more, when a man's life hath lapsed beyond the fitting term; and the Deliverer comes at the last to all alike,—when the doom of

Hades is suddenly revealed, without marriage-song, or lyre, or dance,—even Death at the last.

Not to be born is, past all prizing, best; but, when a man hath seen the light, this is next best by far, that with all speed he should go thither, whence he has come.

For when he hath seen youth go by, with its light follies, what troublous affliction is strange to his lot, what suffering is not therein?—envy, factions, strife, battles and slaughters; and, last of all, age claims him for her own, age, dispraised, infirm, unsociable, unfriended, with whom all woe of woe abides.

In such years is yon hapless one [Oedipus], not I alone: and as some cape that fronts the North is lashed on every side by the waves of winter, so he also is fiercely lashed evermore by the dread troubles that break on him like billows, some from the setting of the sun, some from the rising, some in the regions of the noon-tide beam, some from the gloom-wrapped hills of the North. (Translated by Jebb 1904, pp. 104–105).

Best, then, is not to be born at all. But being born, it is best to die as soon as possible before the sorrows of aging befall one, sings the chorus.

It is easy to take such sentiments as autobiographical. But do they truly reflect Sophocles's view of his own life or of life in general?

Once again Oedipus offers the answer. When he steps upon the stage in *Oedipus at Colonus,* Oedipus has become a hero reborn, as Bernard Knox (1964) has argued. But by what psychological mechanism was that rebirth achieved?

Thomas Van Nortwick (1989) has stated that Oedipus's transformation is one in which Oedipus moves from passivity to activity, in the process re-engaging himself with life. Oedipus is indeed powerless when he first appears on the stage, but early in the course of the play he learns through an oracle that he possesses an unexpected power: the power to curse or bless by his presence. It is the realization of this power that animates him. In fact, he learns that this power transcends death itself, because his very grave, by its location, will help to shape future history. Indeed, once Oedipus knew he mattered, once Oedipus realized others depended on his presence, he was reborn.

KING DAVID

Parallels in life histories—some superficial, some not—invite a comparison of Oedipus and David in their later years. We have texts that provide biographical details for both men from youth until their deaths decades later; their traits and actions in old age are shown to be prefigured by events that occurred earlier in their lives. That each defeated a monster prior to assuming regal powers is taken as evidence of their fitness for high office. Oedipus and David, respectively, were guided by figures (Teiresias and Nathan) with prophetic powers who played a prominent role in their moral and political development. Because they were far from blameless, neither had an easy life: In each instance, a god punished the protagonist for a sexual transgression with a woman (Oedipus-Jocasta/David-Bathsheba) whose husband he had killed (Laius/Uriah). Nor were interactions with intimates without tragedy. Each man had to deal with generational discord.

Both were estranged from a father figure (Laius and Saul) who eventually died because of their actions; both in turn had at least one son (Polyneices and Adonijah/ Absalom) whose defiance culminated in a serious challenge to their power.

Yet there are fundamental differences between these two figures and the worlds in which they lived. As Joseph Heller (1984, p. 18) has the hero of his fictional biography *God Knows* assert, "I am David, not Oedipus, and I would have broken destiny to bits." Oedipus, after all, is the creation of the fertile imagination of a single mind. What we know about David comes to us from five books of the Hebrew Bible (Ruth, 1 and 2 Samuel, 1 Kings, 1 Chronicles, and the Psalms), which were written over the course of at least three centuries. Composed under disparate circumstances, the historical memories recorded in these Hebrew texts are bound to emphasize different themes. In addition, "modern" readers bring their own set of assumptions to biblical exegesis, just as they do when they interpret the classics. Much that twentieth-century Americans think that they know about Oedipus, for instance, comes from Freud, not Sophocles. Messianic imagery colors ideas about the House of David in Christian commentaries on the Bible. In significant respects, therefore, the re-presentations of basic facts and themes in David's later years in Scripture do not wholly agree. Even so, there are fewer blatant contradictions in the Hebrew biblical accounts of David than are to be found in the birth and resurrection narratives of Jesus.

Accordingly, the analysis in this section divides into three parts. First, we examine the images of old King David, focusing on the portraits in 1 Kings and 1 Chronicles, since they are the richest in detail about this stage of life. Second, we describe similarities and differences in the texts concerning the activities that David performed before he died. Finally, by taking account of points of convergence as well as of divergence, we seek to infer from various clues in the Hebrew Bible how and why it was that David, like Oedipus, came to be empowered in new ways at an advanced age.

Portrait of David in Old Age

Internal evidence and scholarly analyses suggest that David lived his biblically allotted threescore and ten years from 1040–970 BCE. 1 Kings (1:1–4) opens with a description of a man well past his prime:

King David was old and advanced in years, and although they covered him with clothes, he could not get warm. So his servants said to him, "Let a young virgin be sought for my lord the king, and let her wait on the king, and be his attendant; let her lie in your bosom, so that my lord the king may be warm." So they searched for a beautiful girl throughout all the territory of Israel, and found Abishag the Shunammite, and brought her to the king. The girl was very beautiful. She became the king's attendant and served him, but the king did not know her sexually.[3]

Decrepitude was not always the fate of biblical heroes who lived long lives. Saul suffered from severe bouts of mental illness throughout adulthood, but he was strong enough at age seventy to fight to his death in the battle of Gilboa. Moses lived half a century longer than David, reaching the maximum human life span (Gen. 6:3). When Moses died, "his sight was unimpaired and his vigor had not abated" (Deut. 34:7). In contrast, according to the compilers of 2 Samuel, there were telltale signs that David was gradually declining even in his prime. In chapters 11, 13, and 14 of that book David has little difficulty disengaging from grief upon the death of his love-child with Bathsheba. He had already lost face due to his vacillation in dealing with Absalom's challenge to his authority. By the time David approached the end of his life, he hardly seemed the paragon of patrician manhood. David expressed his anguish poignantly in verse (Ps. 71:9–10, 12):

> Do not cast me off in the time of old age;
>> Do not forsake me when my strength is spent.
> For my enemies speak concerning me,
>> And those who watch for my life consult together . . .
> O God, do not be far from me;
>> O my God, make haste to help me!

The king was succored with remedies for prolonging life and warding off old age known throughout Mediterranean communities in ancient times. David was kept warm and offered a virgin because this therapeutic regimen was thought to restore vitality (Gruman 1966; Robinson 1972).

Unlike 1 Kings, the Chronicler describes the king's senectitude tersely: "David was now an old man, weighed down with years, and he appointed Solomon his son king over Israel" (1 Chron. 23:1). In spirit the sentence more closely parallels the matter-of-fact genealogical lists that constitute the first eleven chapters of 1 Chronicles than it resembles the next section. In the middle chapters of this "stained-glass view of history" (Tarr 1987), the author uses rich religious symbolism to animate the story of David's bringing and installing the Ark to Jerusalem (ch. 13–17) and to relate the details of the war waged, the census taken, and the threshing-floor purchased during his reign (ch. 18–21). The Chronicler uses materials from 2 Samuel in writing his version of these episodes, but there is no reference made in chapter 23 to David's impotence or to the ministrations of Abishag the Shunammite. Nor does it appear here that any heir except Solomon might have (been) expected to succeed his father on the throne. Yet David had nineteen sons (1 Chron. 3:1–9), most of whom were alive when the king reached old age. Surely there was some competition among the brothers for power.

Because 1 Chronicles ignores sibling rivalry, the work omits the palace intrigues that afford such human drama in the version of the same event reported in 1 Kings 1–2. The Chronicler tells us nothing about Adonijah's boast that he would rule or the ensuing victory banquet to celebrate his rise to power. Nor do we learn about Bathsheba's entreaty on behalf of her son, initiated and reinforced by David's ancient mentor, the prophet Nathan. Nevertheless, the two scriptural accounts of the king's later years are complementary. In a world in which the fertility of the land was bound up with regal virility, the explicit mention in 1 Kings that David had no intercourse with Abishag calls into question David's continued capacity for wielding power or commanding authority. Then thirty-three verses later David is reported to have uttered for the record that Solomon will "sit on my throne; for I have appointed him to be ruler over Israel and over Judah." Apparently the king recognizes that he is no longer able to govern without the support of his successor. The Chronicler concurs: because David was old, he had to appoint Solomon king. In both accounts, the story of David's old age begins by noting his impotence, political and otherwise.

Divergent Accounts of David's Last Years as King

Just as 1 Kings and 1 Chronicles present David's weakness in old age in very different terms, so too they emphasize quite distinctive aspects of the last years of his reign—without necessarily contradicting one another. Indeed, the Chronicler ends his first book observing that "the acts of King David, from first to last, are written in the records of the seer Samuel, and in the records of the prophet Nathan, and in the records of the seer Gad, with accounts of all his rule and his might and of the events that befell him and Israel and all the kingdoms of the earth" (1 Chron. 29:29–30). The story in 1 Kings is to be read as the baseline, with supplementary information drawn from 1 Chronicles.

To the author of 1 Kings, David's selection of the one son capable of preserving the royal household becomes the critical action of his old age. As Bathsheba puts it, "And now, your majesty, all Israel is looking to you to announce who is to succeed you on the throne" (1 Kings 1:20). Bathsheba understands that dynastic considerations have political importance. If Adonijah takes power, she and her son "will be counted offenders" (1 Kings 1:21) in a palace revolt. The choice of heir also has religious significance—"May my lord King David rule forever!" (1 Kings 1:31). David is equally aware of what is at stake, politically and religiously. He swears that Solomon will succeed him "as the Lord lives, who has saved my life from every adversity, as I swore to you by the Lord, the God of Israel" (1 Kings 1:29–30). In David's mind, the fledgling monarchy is theocratic. Because its survival also depends on the will of the people, David orchestrated a coronation ritual that leaves no doubt about the *gravitas* with which he exercised his prerogative. The king had Nathan and two priests, as well as officers and guards of his household, escort his son on a mule to a public place to have his appointment recognized and approved amidst blaring trumpets.[4] Secular and spiritual realms meet in the ritual of anointing Solomon.

Adonijah obviously was not happy with the turn of events. But he could hardly discount what had occurred. Adonijah knew that David, although bent with age, had spoken with authority. "The king bowed in worship on the bed and went on to pray thus, 'Blessed be the Lord, the God of Israel, who today has granted one of my offspring to sit on my throne and permitted me to witness it' " (1

Kings 1:47–48). Under the circumstances, Adonijah had little choice but to go to Solomon and make peace. "Go home," Solomon commanded, ordering his older brother to retire from public life. Why did David say nothing in this part of the tale? Was his reign over? Did his opinions no longer matter? Or, was David merely waiting for the best moment to signal his intentions and act?

1 Kings 2 indicates that in his dying days David took actions and exacted promises that would affect his kingdom long after his passing from the scene. In phrases dear to the Deuteronomist tradition, the king insisted that Solomon "keep the charge of the Lord your God, walking in his ways and keeping his statutes, his commandments, his ordinances and his testimonies, as it is written in the law of Moses, so that you may prosper in all that you do and wherever you turn" (1 Kings 2:2–3). Affairs of state (in the author's mind) mattered almost as much as obedience to God. The king declared that Barzillai was to get a pension. Then, to protect his heir's reputation, David took upon himself responsibility for setting into motion a series of actions that valued prudence over mercy. The king advised Solomon to "act within [his] wisdom" as he dealt with Joab and Shemei, two of his father's enemies. Joab was a threat to political stability since he lately had associated with Adonijah. A cultural taboo had kept David from murdering Shemei long ago. Were Solomon to spare Shemei's life, his inaction might be construed as weakness, not compassion.

1 Chronicles 23:2 complements the political-religious themes with which 1 Kings sets forth David's succession. Seeking to reinforce the sense of collective solidarity, the Chronicler reports that "all the leaders of Israel and the priests and the Levites" were gathered to hear the announcement. Later on it is written that God has chosen Solomon "to sit upon the throne of the kingdom of the Lord over Israel" (1 Chron. 28:5). The phrasing differs subtly from that found in 1 Kings. In the Chronicler's worldview the spiritual and political do not merely complement one another; they often are indistinguishable. Indeed, to emphasize the point that all parties are involved in affirming Solomon's right to succeed his father, the Chronicler asserts that "they made David's son Solomon king a second time" (1 Chron. 29:22–24). This ceremony took place in the presence of the community, the Chronicler pointedly declares, with all of David's sons (although Adonijah is not specifically mentioned), as well as mighty warriors, and other leaders paying obeisance. The version of David's farewell address presented in 1 Chronicles is much expanded from the version in 1 Kings, yet it conforms in main lines to the earlier rendition.

Yours, O Lord, are the greatness, the power, the glory, the victory, and the majesty; for all that is in the heavens and earth is yours; yours is the kingdom, O Lord, and you are exalted as head above all. Riches and honor come from you, and you rule over all. In your hand are power and might; and it is in your hand to make great and to give strength to all. And now, our God, we give thanks to you and praise your glorious name. But who am I, and what is my people, that we should be able to make this freewill offering? For all things come from you, and of your own have we given you. (1 Chron. 29:11–14)

This magnificent prayer of thanksgiving and humility illustrates the perdurance of David's extraordinary gift for poetic expression. In both 1 Chronicles and 1 Kings, we encounter a rehabilitated David, one risen from the impotence of being bedridden to new heights of inspired oratory and renewed leadership.

In addition, the Chronicler stresses an activity that the author of 1 Kings does not invoke. Between his abdication and his death David seems to have been busily engaged in administrative matters and drafting plans intended to ensure the socio-political stability and future religious health of the kingdom. Chapters 23 through 26 detail David's plans for the Levites, priests, and musicians; as well as for "doorkeepers," to whom the king apparently gave responsibility for financial affairs and for arbitrating disputes. Chapter 27 lays out the reorganization of tribal divisions, which will facilitate operations under military and civil jurisdictions. In the penultimate chapter of 1 Chronicles, David gives Solomon the designs for the vestibule of the temple and its furnishings. God had forbidden the ancient ruler to erect the edifice "for you are a warrior and have shed blood" (1 Chron. 28:3), but David was empowered to do all the planning: "All this, in writing at the Lord's direction, he made clear to me—the plan of all the works" (1 Chron. 28:19). Just as Moses received plans for the tabernacle (Ex. 25), so too David's enviable place in history is to be assured in late life by his roles as architect of the Lord's Temple and elder trustee of God's chosen people.

Making Sense of David's Late-Life Empowerment

"David is the engine for Israel's imagination and for Israel's public history," observes Walter Brueggemann. "In the case of David, the construction is partly deliberate, as a means of political propaganda. . . . But partly that construction is inevitable and unplanned, and takes on a force and authority of its own" (Brueggemann 1985, p. 14; also see Gunn 1975). To the extent that biblical sources blend the image of David with the image of Israel, the truths that inhere in David's life influence the historical memory of the children of Israel. Furthermore, the king's empowerment in old age, as indicated by the logic of the scriptural narrative, builds on events and traits manifest earlier, particularly in his mature years. Even before Samuel's death, Saul told David that "Now I know that you shall surely be king, and that the kingdom of Israel shall be established in your hand" (1 Sam. 24:20). Having conquered Jerusalem, defeated the Philistines, and brought up the Ark, David's royal house seems destined to survive:

Thus says the Lord of hosts: I took you from the pasture, from following the sheep to be prince over my people Israel; and I have been with you whenever you went, and have cut off all your enemies from before you; and I will make for you a great name, like the name of the great ones of the earth. And I will appoint a place for my people Israel and will plant them. . . . When your days are fulfilled and you lie down with your ancestors, I will raise up your offspring after you, who shall come forth from your body, and I will establish his kingdom. He will build a house for my name, and I will establish the throne

of his kingdom forever. I will be a father to him, and he shall be a son to me. (2 Sam.
7:8–14)

But God's anointed brought human flaws to his covenantal relationship with
God and to his people. Thus, when the prophet Nathan confronted him about
Uriah's murder, David quickly responded: "I have sinned against the Lord" (2
Sam. 12:13). With those six words he saved his kingdom. David accepted his
punishment—his firstborn with Bathsheba would die, and he would not be allowed to build the Temple. But all was not lost. The repentant king thereafter
acknowledged his place in a theocentric cosmos (2 Sam. 15:25–26; 2 Sam.
16:12), singing praises (note how part of Psalm 105 is inserted at 1 Chron.
16:8ff) and committing himself liturgically to cultic rituals and Hebrew worship.

The challenge of David's old age was to place securely a suitable heir on a
refitted throne. Given his own relationships with Saul, Absalom, and other rivals,
accomplishing this task was bound to be no mean feat. But toward the end of
life, David recognized more than ever before the importance of what long ago
had transpired in Hebron, when the tribes of Israel had made him king: "Look,
we are your bone and flesh. . . . The Lord said to you: It is you who shall be
shepherd of my people Israel, you who shall be ruler over Israel" (2 Sam. 5:1–
2). A revolution in religious practices occurred during David's reign, which
reflected the king's increasing awareness of his special mission. This recognition,
as it became more widely shared, in turn accorded greater eschatalogical import
to his dynastic dreams (Gelander 1991; Brueggemann 1968). David revived in
his declining years, because he could not afford to do otherwise. Looking to the
future, he envisioned a greater likelihood of God's wishes being fulfilled with
Solomon on the throne, if there was an organizational structure in place that was
capable of getting things done.

The facts about the administrative restructuring presented in 1 Chronicles thus
are a key part of the story. The countless details should not distract us from the
bottom line that David delivered to Solomon: "Here are the Levites for all the
service of the house of God; and with you in all work will be every volunteer
who has skill for any kind of service; also the offices and all the people will be
wholly at your command" (1 Chron. 28:21). All of God's people, claimed
David, have been commissioned to serve—lay, clergy, political, military. Because the venerable king reminded his subjects that their fortunes depended on
their fidelity to the Hebrew cult, some scholars suggest that David assumed a
prophetic posture in his later years. Others suggest that the Chronicler's presentation of David's involvement in planning for the Temple was intended to ov-
ershadow Moses's earlier contributions to Jewish history. In any case, David
clearly made provisions before his death to guarantee that "ordered, well-ad-
ministered human resources go along with the promise of God" (Brueggemann
1985, p. 106; also see Newsome 1975; Talmon 1987).

Not everybody exulted in David's recrudescent exercise of power. In a last-
ditch effort to usurp power, Adonijah asked Bathsheba to ask her son, Solomon,

for the hand of Abishag, David's last concubine, in marriage. The request not only violated the cultic practice of passing along royal property (including a harem) to the next king, but it dramatized Adonijah's contempt for his father's sexual impotence. Solomon's response, true to his father David's guidance, was swift: he ordered that Adonijah be put to death. The realm and the cult had become intimately connected. It was the new king's responsibility, as head of the House of David, to remain faithful to God's demands and promises.

Conclusions and Implications

Hence, both the classical and the biblical traditions recognized and affirmed the possibility of some transforming sort of empowerment in old age. Each tradition presents us with shining examples of how aging leaders received spiritual invigoration, an invigoration that ultimately served to fulfill divine will. The stories of Oedipus and David teach that senescence need not imply obsolescence. Neither infirmity, chronic illness, nor disability is viewed as the inescapable, "normal" consequence of living past seventy. Instead, we are offered dramatically powerful instances of just the opposite, prototypical individuals who, with divine encouragement and blessing, rose from passive senility to new life. In transforming their own lives, these ancient kings altered the course of the future. These examples from ancient literature should lead us to reconsider with renewed perspective issues surrounding the relationship between leadership and age, issues that ethicists and gerontologists confront today in the context of societal aging.

David and Oedipus, of course, were not the only older men who wielded great power in ancient times. Both the Hebrew Bible and the New Testament refer to councils of elders, though scholars doubt that all who served on these advisory bodies were in fact aged. Bellicose Sparta, presumably a country that celebrated young warriors, was governed by a *gerousia,* a body on which only men over sixty years of age could serve. And the Roman Senate is cognate for *senex,* literally "old," which suggests that mainly those of rank and experience in their advancing years were likely to serve.

Once we get beyond these Judaeo-Christian and Greco-Roman bases, compelling examples of nations ruled by senior citizens are harder to find. Though anthropologists have reported gerontocracies in east Africa, the term "gerontocracy" itself dates only from nineteenth-century France. David Hackett Fischer (1977) claims that in the early phases of the American Revolution older men were returned to office, to offer a measure of stability in a time of crisis. Yet this pattern did not extend to other places in roughly the same time period. David Troyansky (1989), for instance, stresses that younger men spearheaded the French Revolution, though in the latter phases of the turmoil, the aged were invoked as important symbols and allies in partisan causes. Far more must be done, in short, before political gerontologists can generalize with any confidence about long-term trends in the status of age in political offices.

Even if we limit ourself to the U.S. experience during the past 250 years, trends vary by office and particular circumstances. Not surprisingly, given gains in the median age (which has doubled since 1790) and adult longevity, the age at which politicians enter office has risen over the course of our nation's history. Seniority brings additional responsibility in Congress; incumbency has advantages. Hence people tend to have careers as lawmakers that last decades, well into old age. On the other hand, though colonial and antebellum state governorships, like seats on the highest state and federal courts, were once the preserve of men at the pinnacle of their careers, governorships have now become steppingstones for people with greater ambitions. Hence the peak age for serving as governor has fallen from sixty-five to sixty-nine on the eve of the Revolution to forty-three to forty-nine nowadays (Simonton 1987). Similarly, of the eight men inaugurated to the U.S. vice presidency after their sixty-fifth birthday, only four have served in this century. Veneration for age, moreover, does not seem to be the salient reason for selecting such senior citizens: more likely factors were the need to thwart a younger person's ambition or to reward a person for the right place with the right views (Kiser 1992). Indeed, at the presidential level, age at inauguration is a poor predictor of performance. Among military leaders and monarchs, leadership may peak in the early forties, but exceptional leaders have proven vigorous after attaining the Biblical three score and ten (Simonton 1988).

If we confine the focus on age and leadership to religious institutions, then an observation by G. Stanley Hall in *Senescence* remains accurate: "men in their prime conceived the great religions, the old made them prevail" (1922, p. 420). The papacy, for which the best prosopographic materials exist, has not become a gerontocracy. There has over the centuries been a modest increase in average age of election, but that may reflect the fact that *papabili* increasingly since the 1700s served as cardinals and in the inner bureaucracy, positions where it takes time to accrue service. The span in age at election, however, has ranged from the late thirties to early eighties. Age at election is not a good indication of how long one might serve or of the esteem accorded his stewardship (Achenbaum, in press). Similarly, the Mormon church, one of the fastest growing in the United States during the past 150 years, was established by relatively young men, while power today resides with octogenarians.

All of this suggests that historical, structural, and political factors will exercise considerable influence in determining an older person's likelihood of attaining power vis-à-vis younger competitors. Yet personality is also a critical ingredient. "Extraordinary" characteristics are expected of leaders (Blondi 1987). Regrettably, political gerontologists have not written much about the ways older people rule. It is not clear whether there is a distinctive style of leadership, as there appears to be in expressions of creativity among elderly artists. The stories of David and Oedipus do suggest the possibility that older leaders can *transform* circumstances, along the lines that J. MacGregor Burns hypothesizes: Transforming leadership "occurs when one or more persons *engage* in such a way that leaders and followers raise one another to higher levels of motivation and morality. . . . Transcending leadership is dynamic leadership in the sense that the leaders throw themselves into a relationship with followers who will feel elevated by it and often become more active themselves, thereby creating new cadres of leaders'' (1978, p. 20).

Widows over sixty in the early Jesus movement were accorded vital roles in the fledgling churches' social-welfare arena (1 Tim. 5:9–17).

Let a widow be put on a list if she is not less than sixty years old and has been married only once; she must be attested for her good works, as one who has brought up children, shown hospitality, washed the saints' feet, helped the afflicted, and devoted herself to doing good in every way. But refuse to put younger widows on the list . . . they learn to be idle, but also gossips and busybodies, saying what they should not say. . . . If any believing woman has relatives who are really widows, let her assist those who are real widows. Let the elders who rule well considered of double honor, especially those who labor in preaching and teaching; for the scripture says, ''You shall not muzzle an ox while it is treading out the grain,'' and, ''The laborer deserves to be paid.''

Notice that the categories of ''leader'' and ''follower'' collapse in this Pauline passage, just as they do in Burns's notion of a transforming leader. To get support from the early Christian community, older women had to have lived upright lives in support of the well-being of all. Like elderly men, they were expected to remain active, exercising their influence. Leaders are servants, and vice versa. Those who fritter away their middle age, in contrast, will not be entitled to support in later years. Nor will they be doubly honored for their example and their contribution.

More generally, the stories of Oedipus and David teach a gerontological lesson that transcends the purely political. The materialism that dominates contemporary American society places the highest value on the physical and tangible. As a consequence, the physiological deterioration of the elderly is taken—even by the elderly themselves—as a patent indication of their declining value as human beings. Indeed, even Oedipus and David seemed to believe, late in their lives, that they had little left to contribute except their obituaries.

What their stories teach, however, is that there is another, deeper dimension to human existence, a dimension whose potential abides undiminished despite the assaults of time upon the body. Because the effects of aging are conspicuous and palpable, they can obscure this invisible, inner source of spiritual strength and psychological renewal.

Like the dying father in Dylan Thomas's ''Do Not Go Gently Into That Good Night,'' the elderly we love—indeed, the elderly we will someday *become*— possess the power to bless or to curse, to bestow upon their kindred, and themselves, the gift of love or of hate. Either emotion can empower the aged. But if they are neglected, or treated only as the means to someone else's end, they will never be able to transmit the love that is theirs alone to bestow. Perhaps, in recognizing the finitude of their own lives, elders with religious sensibilities ultimately bear witness to the potential for transmitting wisdom from generation to generation. At the very least, in their present efforts to complete the main work of their lives, the elderly can envision a future that they helped to create. With T. S. Eliot (1962, p. 129), they can declare, "In the end is my beginning."

NOTES

1. An argument for Oedipus's psychological growth is advanced by Thomas R. Cole (1991).

2. In the light of these ancient anecdotes, *Oedipus at Colonus* constitutes a classic argument against the view that old age and creative vigor are incompatible. Indeed, as Bernard Knox stated in *The Heroic Temper*, "The play is a worthy last will and testament. All the great themes of the earlier plays recur; it is as if Sophocles were summing up a lifetime of thought and feeling in this demonic work of his old age" (1964, p. 144).

3. Unless otherwise noted, all biblical quotations come from the New Revised Standard Version. For the argument that David lived for seventy to seventy-two years, see 1 Kings 2:10–12 and 1 Chron. 29:26–28 as well as Juan Bosch, *David*.

4. It is worth nothing that the New English Bible translates King Solomon's title as "prince over Israel and Judah," which probably more characterizes his status as long as his father was alive.

REFERENCES

Achenbaum, W. S. 1993. Was the papacy a gerontocracy? In K. W. Schaie and W. A. Achenbaum, eds., *Social structures and aging: Historical perspectives*. New York: Springer.

Blondi, J. 1987. *Political leadership*. London: Sage.

Bosch, J. 1966. *David*. London: Chatto & Windus.

Brueggemann, W. 1968. David and his theologian. *Catholic Biblical Quarterly* 30, 156–81.

———. 1985. *David's truth in Israel's imagination and memory*. Philadelphia: Fortress Press.

Burns, J. M. 1978. *Leadership*. New York: Harper & Row.

Cole, T. R. 1991. Oedipus and the meaning of aging. In N. Jecker, ed., *Aging and ethics*. New York: Humana Press.

Eliot, T. S. 1962. Four Quartets. In T. S. Eliot, *Complete poems*. New York: Harcourt, Brace, World.

Fischer, D. H. 1977. *Growing old in America*. New York: Oxford University Press.

Gelander, S. 1991. *David and his God*. Jerusalem: Simor Ltd.

Gruman, G. 1966. *Toward a history of ideas about the prolongation of life*. Philadelphia: American Philosophical Society.

Gunn, D. 1975. David and the gift of the kingdom. *Semera* 3, 14–45.

Hadas, M. 1954. *Ancilla to classical reading*. New York: Columbia University Press.

Hall, G. S. 1992. *Senescence*. New York: D. Appleton.

Heller, J. 1984. *God knows*. New York: Alfred A. Knopf.

Jebb, R. C. 1904. *The tragedies of Sophocles translated into English prose*. Cambridge: Cambridge University Press.

Kiser, G. C. 1992. Selecting senior citizens for the American vice presidency. *Aging and Society* 12, 85–104.

Knox, B. 1964. *The heroic temper*. Berkeley: University of California Press.

Newsome, J. D. 1975. Toward a new understanding of the chronicler and his purposes. *Journal of Biblical Literature* 94, 201–17.

Robert, C. 1915. *Oidipus*. Berlin: Weidmannsche Buchhandlung.

Robinson, J. 1972. *The first book of Kings*. The Cambridge Bible Commentary. Cambridge.

Simonton, K. D. 1987. *Why presidents succeed*. New Haven: Yale University Press.

———. 1988. Age and outstanding achievement. *Psychological Bulletin* 104, 251–67.

Talmon, S. 1987. 1 and 2 Chronicles. In R. Alter and F. Kermode, eds., *The literary guide to the Bible*. Cambridge, MA: Harvard University Press.

Tarr, H. 1987. Chronicles. In D. Rosenberg, ed., *Congregation*. San Diego: Harcourt Brace Jovanovich.

Troyansky, D. 1989. *Old age in the ancient regime*. Ithaca, NY: Cornell University Press.

Van Nortwick, T. 1989. "Do not go gently . . . ": *Oedipus at Colonus* and the psychology of aging. In T. M. Falkner and J. de Luce, eds., *Old age in Greek and Latin literature*, 132–56. Albany: State University of New York Press.

6 Fairy Tales and the Spiritual Dimensions of Aging

Allan B. Chinen

Religious phenomena are notoriously difficult to capture in research. When the complexities of aging are added on, the task is even more daunting. Familiar research strategies, both quantitative or qualitative, often prove inadequate in investigating the religious dimension of aging. In this chapter I describe a novel approach to the subject, a systematic analysis of fairy tales about middle and late life (Chinen 1989, 1992, 1993) and set forth two theses.

First, fairy tales offer a serious source of information about spirituality and aging. The claim may seem odd, since we normally think of fairy tales as something for children. However, this has been true only in the last few centuries, when fairy tales were published specifically for the children of the emerging bourgeoisie (Rowe 1986; Tatar 1987; Zipes 1979, 1983). Previously, fairy tales, like other folk stories, were for adults and about them. Before widespread literacy or the invention of mass media, fairy tales were a popular vehicle of communication, information and entertainment. Storytellers put their reflections about human nature in their tales (Bettelheim 1976; Dieckmann 1986; Dundes 1986; Grolnick 1986; Heuscher 1974; Tatar 1987; von Franz 1977). Moreover, fairy tales, like other orally transmitted folklore, are told and retold to many audiences over the years. In the process, the stories undergo a strenuous selection process. Only tales that have enduring appeal survive. Fairy tales thus distill the values and experiences of countless individuals across different cultures, and in this respect are analogous to large-scale international survey studies. Yet fairy tales also address highly emotional issues and reveal deep unconscious symbolism, just like dreams. So the stories provide information similar to that obtained by in-depth interviews, clinical case studies, and projective psychological testing. Fairy tales offer a rich, if unorthodox, source of data on common human experiences, including that of aging and spirituality.

While most familiar fairy tales today, from "Cinderella" to "Snow White," focus on children or adolescents, an important group of tales feature mature adults as protagonists. These tales might be called "middle tales" or "elder tales" because they portray men and women in the middle and later years of life. Most important, middle and elder tales highlight the spiritual aspects of aging, confirming contemporary research in the area and suggesting new lines of inquiry.

Middle and elder tales are remarkably similar across cultures and historical epochs, and this is the second thesis of my chapter. The stories are ecumenical and nondenominational. They escape the dogmatism inherent in most religious traditions, which prompts many scholars and scientists to avoid research on religion. The neutral, cross-cultural perspective of middle and elder tales also makes them surprisingly relevant to modern, secular, pluralist culture. The tales adopt a transpersonal approach, emphasizing the common elements of diverse religious experiences and traditions. The transpersonal perspective, in turn, offers practical suggestions for today about the social applications of spirituality in the later years.

METHOD

For purposes of this study, I defined fairy tales as orally transmitted folktales not meant to be literally believed, dealing with ordinary human beings and ending happily (Bettelheim 1976; Heuscher 1974). This definition excludes literary fairy tales written by individual authors; myths and legends which claim to be true; ghost or horror stories, which have unhappy endings; and fables, which are about animals. I defined a story as a "youth tale" if it identified its protagonists as a child or adolescent; an "elder tale" if it explicitly called its protagonist "old"; and a "middle tale" if the protagonist was called neither young nor old, and if he or she was married or had a job. I located middle and elder tales by systematically searching through fairy tales anthologies from around the world, published in English, using the libraries of the University of California at Berkeley.

Of about 5,000 fairy tales reviewed, approximately 3 percent qualify as elder tales, and about 15 percent as middle tales. The remainder are youth tales. Elder tales are most common from Eastern cultures, like Japan, Arabia, India, and China, and least common from Western Europe. This may be partly due to the greater respect Eastern societies traditionally accord older adults. However, Western culture in the past also revered elders (Arnett 1985). A second reason for the geographical variation is that early collections of Western fairy tales, like the Grimms' anthology, were published specifically for children. Stories were deliberately revised to appeal to children (Rowe 1986; Tatar 1987; Zipes

1979, 1983), and the role of older protagonists was reduced or eliminated (Chinen 1989). Fairy tales from other cultures, however, were collected much later, often by anthropologists rather than book publishers. Youth-centered revisions were less common, and elder tales were preserved. The percentage of middle tales, significantly, varies little across cultures, probably reflecting the uniform importance of the middle-aged generation in most societies.

When middle and elder tales are identified and compared with each other, recurrent themes are readily identifiable, and the two genres differ dramatically. Only tales with similar versions from at least two distinct cultures were analyzed. This comparative method avoids the criticism commonly raised against psychoanalytic interpretations—that they overemphasize idiosyncratic details of a particular story, absent in other versions of the tale (Dundes 1986; Grolnick 1986; Schenda 1986; Tatar 1987; Zipes 1976, 1979). Folkloric studies, on the other hand, typically analyze large numbers of fairy tales (Aarne & Thompson 1961; Propp 1968; Thompson 1955). Folklorists avoid overinterpreting details, but they also tend to neglect the psychological symbolism of stories. Hence they frequently ignore the rich folk insights in fairy tales. In the present study, I focused specifically on the symbolic themes of the tales, while maintaining a comparative approach. This method hopefully threads a middle way between psychoanalytic and folkloric perspectives.

In this chapter, I will discuss a typical middle and elder tale, summarizing each story and then discussing its symbolism, relating story themes to the spiritual aspects of aging.

THE MORTAL KING: A TALE FROM CHINA

Once upon a time, a King went riding with his friends. They stopped atop a mountain to rest and the King surveyed his realm. He smiled, pleased with what he saw. His land was rich, his people prospered, and he felt justly proud of his realm. Then a terrible thought struck him. "I will die one day, and lose all this!" the King exclaimed.

His companions paused, and then echoed the King's lament. "Aye, dying is cruel!" they murmured, thinking of the families, estates and honors they, too, would lose. One lord among them said nothing.

"If only we could live forever!" the King exclaimed. "How wonderful that would be!"

His nobles nodded in agreement, but one lord laughed to himself.

The King went on. "If we lived forever, think of all the hunting and feasts we could enjoy!" The nobles sighed, picturing the delights of immortality. The bold lord laughed again.

His companions turned to him and demanded, "What is amusing about death? Do you mock immortality?" The laughing lord said nothing.

The King ignored the interruption. "To live forever as we are now, what greater boon could we have?" the King asked.

The lords nodded again, and murmured approval, but the odd noble chuckled once more.

The King turned to the laughing lord. "What is the reason for your humor?" the King demanded. "I see nothing comical about death and immortality!"

The noble bowed to his monarch. "I do not mean to offend you, my lord. But I thought of what life would be like if we all lived forever, as you suggested." The lord paused. "Why, then, all the heroes of history would still live among us, too, the King who first unified the land, the Law-giver who brought peace, the great Sage with all his wisdom, and the holy prophets of our people." The noble sighed pensively. "Compared to them we would be peasants, fit only to plough the fields!" The lord chuckled. "And you, my lord," he turned to the King, "would no doubt be a clerk in the provinces!"

The King stared at the impertinent lord, and all the other peers held their breaths tensely. Then the King laughed long and hard. "You are wise and brave, my friend," the King said. "But you speak the truth." The King turned to the other nobles. "For encouraging me in my vanity," he said to them, "I penalize you two draughts of wine each!" Then the King embraced the laughing lord. "As for you, my friend," the monarch said, "whenever I lament the thought of my own death, you must cry out, 'A clerk! A clerk!' "

COMMENT

Death appears prominently as a problem in middle tales like "The Mortal King," and is fairly specific to the genre. Tales of youth typically show heroes cheating or escaping death, while elder tales, surprising as it may seem, simply treat death as a fact of life, not a troubling issue. Only middle tales portray death as a problem and a source of concern. Fairy tales match reality here, because the specter of mortality appears to be most troublesome in midlife (Soddy 1967; Auchincloss & Michels 1989; Modell 1989). Aged parents begin dying at this time, pushing their middle-aged children to the head of the line. Death also starts to claim colleagues, and medical ailments become increasingly common. The issue of personal mortality is unavoidable at midlife. Neugarten (1966), in fact, defined middle age as the time when a person no longer measures years from birth, but years till death.

Death, of course, is a central concern of most traditional religions. Buddhism and Christianity, among many others, focus on personal mortality to inspire individuals to seek spiritual instruction. In fact, confrontation with death at midlife often triggers an existential crisis, (Jaques 1965; Levinson et al. 1978; Ciernia 1985) and many people respond with an increased interest in religion. Even in modern, secular culture, death is a spiritual instructor (Fowler 1981).

In the story, the King accepts his own death by realizing that he must yield his place to the next generation, just as his predecessors yielded their places to him. If his children are to have a chance at life, he must make room for them by dying. Three points are important about his insight. First, the King begins with an egocentric view, concerned only with what he will lose when he dies. Then he glimpses "the larger picture"—the succession of generations throughout history, and his small place in the cycle. He transcends his egocentric perspective. The story dramatizes the process of self-transcendence by specifically making its protagonist a King, someone used to being obeyed and having his way, with far greater license than most mortals to be egocentric. Despite his power and glory, the King is still humbled by death: like the lowest peasant, the King, too, must die. Kings and queens, I might add, are frequently the protagonists of middle tales, and they reflect the fact that in most cultures, the middle-aged are in charge of society, heading households, companies, institutions and governments. Ironically, at the peak of their authority, won after years of struggling, middle-aged individuals are forced to recognize something beyond themselves. Other tales repeat the theme of self-transcendence, and emphasize the cross-cultural nature of the motif. In "The King Who Would Be Stronger than Fate" from India (Lang 1914), for instance, a King hears a prophecy that his daughter will marry the newborn son of a slave woman. To prevent the humiliating union, the King kills the slave woman and abandons her baby boy to die in the desert. The child survives, and despite the King's continuing efforts over the years to kill him off, the boy grows up to be a brave young hero. Through strokes of luck and his own gallantry, the son of the slave wins the heart and hand of the princess. Furious and frustrated, the King finally realizes that he cannot fight fate. He accepts his new son-in-law and makes him his heir, along with his daughter. The monarch thus transcends his egocentric pride.

"Destiny" from Dalmatia (Laboulaye 1976) repeats the motif. In the story, two brothers live together, but the elder labors all day, while the younger revels with friends. The elder insists on a division of the property, and they each live separately. The younger continues to enjoy good fortune without working, while the elder is beset by disaster and descends into poverty. He finally seeks Destiny to find the reason for his misery. Advised by a hermit, the elder brother arrives at Destiny's residence and watches silently for several days. On the first day, Destiny lives in a magnificent palace and at midnight, he throws jewels to all the souls born that day. The next morning, Destiny lives in a smaller mansion and at night, he throws gold coins to newborn souls. The following morning, Destiny lives in an ordinary house and that evening, he strews silver coins to the people born on that day. Then Destiny lives in a hovel and offers pebbles to everyone who comes into the world. The elder brother finally asks Destiny the reason for his bad luck. Destiny explains to the poor man that he was born on a day of pebbles, but his rich young brother was born on a day of jewels. So everything the older brother does turns out badly, while the younger can live without working. Destiny suggests that the older brother marry the daughter of his brother, because the daughter was born on a day of jewels. Destiny warns, however, that the older brother must not claim any property as his own, because it will all be from his wife. The older brother follows Destiny's advice and lives happily. One day, however, he talks proudly about his property. Instantly, fire appears and threatens to destroy everything. The older brother remembers Destiny's warning and corrects himself, noting everything that he has is his wife's. The fire vanishes, and he lives happily with his wife. She serves as a constant reminder to him that he cannot revert back to his narrow, egocentric viewpoint, but must remember the greater power of Destiny. "The Stonecutter" from Japan (Lang 1903) repeats the theme in a different drama.

Self-transcendence and insight into "the big picture" like that depicted in these fairy tales are characteristic of traditional religions. The exhortation to transcend an egocentric viewpoint is common to Christianity, Judaism, Hinduism, Buddhism, Confucianism, and a host of other religions. Middle tales like "The Mortal King," "The Stonecutter" or "Destiny" thus highlight a psychological process central to religious experience. Self-transcendence is a common event at midlife, independent of the culture of origin.

Closely associated with self-transcendence is self-reformation. In "The Mortal King," the monarch starts off lamenting his death, and then changes his viewpoint. In "The King Who Would Be Stronger than Fate," the proud King finally gives up his pride and acknowledges the power of fate. The self-reformation theme is even clearer in the Jewish story, "The Miser" (Friedlander 1920). There a man is a terrible miser, never giving to the poor, until he accidentally encounters demons. Frightened by the experience, the miser changes his ways, just like Ebenezer Scrooge in Charles Dickens's "A Christmas Carol."

Similarly, in the Italian tale, "The Siren Wife" (Calvino 1978), self-reformation plays a key role. Angered by his wife's affair, a husband throws her into the ocean to drown. She is saved by mermaids and becomes one of them. Remorseful over his act, the husband searches for his wife, hoping she survived his rage. They meet and she forgives him, but she cannot return with him since she is now a mermaid. The husband then goes on a quest to find a way to change her back to her human form. After great sacrifices, he succeeds and the two are reconciled.

"Stubborn Husband, Stubborn Wife" (Mehdevi 1965) repeats the theme of self-reformation on a more mundane level. A husband and wife quarrel constantly, until they make a wager over who will talk first. The wife leaves the house to avoid talking with the husband, and he remains silent when a series of people chance by. Since he refuses to speak, the strangers think he is a deaf mute and steal everything from the house. For his part, he thinks the people were hired by his wife to make him talk. When the wife returns she is shocked to find everything gone so she speaks first. Outraged by his stubbornness, she leaves him and pursues the thieves. Through clever tricks she regains their belongings and returns home. Separated from each other, they both realize how much they mean to one another and when they meet again, they reconcile and stop quarreling.

Surprisingly, self-reformation like this is rarely present in tales of youth. There the good and the bad are clearly demarcated, and the wicked summarily punished. In the original Grimms' version of "Cinderella," for example, the virtuous young Cinderella marries the youthful Prince, while her wicked stepsisters and stepmother have their eyes plucked out by doves. Villains do not reform in youth tales. Indeed, when the young hero and heroine do something evil, their wickedness is typically blamed on an evil spell from another person (Luthi 1984), leaving the young protagonist blameless. (The villain who cast the spell, of course, is destroyed.)

Middle tales thus suggest, somewhat surprisingly, that self-reformation is the province of mature adults, not younger ones. This goes against common sense, which portrays older individuals as more rigid. Yet systematic research confirms folk insights. In a longitudinal study based in Berkeley, California (Brooks 1981; Haan 1981; Mussen & Haan 1981), investigators noted the steady decline from midlife onward in projection and "extra-punitiveness," the practice of blaming others for their own faults and difficulties. Similar results were obtained by Vaillant (1977) in his longitudinal study of Harvard students. Adolescents and young adults typically protect their tender sense of identity by denying their faults and shortcomings, and blaming other people (usually parents, teachers, and other authority figures). With greater maturity, and a more secure sense of identity, older individuals are able to face the unsavory elements within themselves. Such self-reformation, of course, is another traditional focus of religion. Judaism exhorts individuals to moral self-reflection; Christianity reminds the faithful of their sinfulness and their need for redemption; while Buddhism encourages men and women to give up their attachments to material desires. Middle tales thus bring up a traditional concern of most religions.

"The Mortal King" is significant for another point. The story makes no explicit reference to gods, an afterlife, or other traditional religious doctrines. The story emphasizes secular concerns instead. The King accepts his death because he recognizes that he received his power and wealth from his predecessors, and must pass it on to his successors. The "larger picture" the King arrives at involves human history, and the cycle of generations, rather than religious revelation or metaphysical insight. This secular spirit is the third important aspect about the King's acceptance of death. His self-transcendence involves practical, everyday realities, not sublime theology or divine revelation. The same practical emphasis applies to other middle tales. In "The King Who Would Be Stronger than Fate," the profound philosophical issue of free will and determinism is portrayed in terms of a family conflict—the father's desire that his daughter not marry the son of a slave. The issue is also resolved not by elevated insight but by the monarch finally accepting the son of a slave as his son-in-law and heir.

In "The Mortal King" the monarch specifically accepts his death by recognizing he must give up his place so his children and his children's children have their chance, just as his forefathers gave way for him. The King's concern with the next generation reflects a spirit of generativity, as Erikson defined the term, that is, a concern with the well-being of children, students, and apprentices who represent the next generation (Erikson, Erikson & Kivnick 1986; Erikson 1983). The story is deeply perceptive here, because generativity helps resolve anxieties over death (Woods & Witte 1981; Shulz 1977). The reason for this has to do with self-transcendence again. As long as an individual is wrapped up in his or her personal concerns, death can only be a catastrophe and a tragedy, because death cancels every personal project, and overrides all private concerns. If an individual, however, transcends his or her egocentricity, and is committed to something beyond private gain, to one's children, for instance, or to an institution or social movement, death becomes less of a threat. The individual must die, but the children, the institution, or the cause will live on. Generativity is a secular form of self-transcendence. "The King Who Would Be Stronger than Fate" reiterates the motif, because the monarch transcends his egocentric pride by making the son of a slave his heir and son-in-law: the King learns generativity.

Other middle tales portray different types of secular self-transcendence. "The Gazelle" (Bushnaq 1986) offers an even more dramatic example. In this Arabian tale, a man went hunting with his son, only to have his child killed by an ogre. The father carried his dead son home, wrapped in a cloth, and told his wife that he brought home a gazelle that was so special, it could only be cooked in a pot that had never been used for a "meal of sorrow." So his wife went to all her neighbors to borrow such a pot. No one had one. A relative explained that she had used her pots at her husband's funeral meal, a friend used hers for her son's, still a third, for a daughter's death. Finally the wife returned home and told her husband that there was no home that had not suffered sorrow. The father then unwrapped the cloth from his son's body and said that it was now their turn.

The bereaved father and mother in this story have only one consolation for losing their son—the fact that everyone else has suffered equal grief. The parents accept their son's death, not through divine insights, but by recognizing that every neighbor, friend and relative have also grieved for a loved one at some time. The parents transcend their egocentric perspective, by seeing the larger drama of the human condition.

The Japanese tale, "The Man Who Did Not Wish to Die" (Ozaki 1982) repeats the emphasis on practical, secular forms of self-transcendence. In the story, a middle-aged man, troubled by the thought of his inevitable death, journeys far and wide seeking the secret of immortality. After many magical adventures, the man finds the answer to his anxieties in a book of wisdom given to him by the god of hermits. But the book only tells him to raise his children well, treat his neighbors with respect, give to the poor, and so on. He does not find the elixir of eternal life as he hoped, or metaphysical secrets about the universe. He receives the exhortation to be practical and generative. The Italian tale, "Solomon's Advice" (Calvino 1978), repeats the motif.

The reason for the secular, pragmatic focus on self-transcendence is not hard to guess. Middle-aged individuals have too many responsibilities for the younger and older generation to withdraw from active life and pursue a contemplative path. The practical emphasis makes the spirituality of the middle years somewhat elusive. It cannot be simply measured by attendance at church or temple, or explicit religious experiences. To a mother or father working long hours at a job to give their children a better life, the effort is often of spiritual depth and intensity. The same can be said of individuals dedicated to their careers, from scientists to artists, who treat their work as part of a divine calling (Cochran 1990; Chinen 1993). Moreover, from middle age onward, individuals become more altruistic, donating more time and money to charity, and more philosophical or reflective (Haan 1981; Vaillant 1977; Heath 1983; Thurnher 1975; Vaillant & Milofsky 1980; Viney 1987; Mussen & Haan 1981). These changes reflect another secular form of self-transcendence.

The form of spirituality changes dramatically in elder tales. These stories portray "old" men and women abandoning practical considerations for explicitly sublime insights. Spirituality takes on more traditional forms in old age, as the following elder tale emphasizes.

THE SHINING FISH: A TALE FROM ITALY

Once upon a time, an old man and his wife lived in a house overlooking the sea. The man was a fisherman in his youth, but with old age, he could no longer fight the wind and tides and now earned his living by gathering fallen wood in a nearby forest and selling it for firewood in the village. Through the years, he and his wife gave birth to three sons, who became fishermen like their father. But all the sons drowned in storms at sea, leaving the couple alone and impoverished in old age.

One day while working in the wilderness, the old man met a stranger with a long white beard. "I know all about your troubles," the stranger said, "and I want to help." He gave the old man a small leather bag and when the old man looked in it, he stared in astonishment. The purse was filled with gold! By the time the old man looked up, the stranger was gone. The old man threw away his wood and rushed joyously home. But along the way, he began to think. "If I tell my wife about this money, she will waste it all, spending it on relatives and friends. She will squander a fortune on useless things." So when the old man arrived at home, he said nothing to his wife. Instead he hid the money under a pile of manure.

The next day, the old man awoke to find that his wife had cooked a wonderful breakfast, with sausages and bread. "Where did you find the money for this?" he asked his wife.

"You did not bring any wood to sell yesterday," she said, "so I sold the manure to the farmer down the road." The old man ran out, but sure enough, there was no manure, and no gold. He dared not tell his wife what happened, but glumly went to work in the forest.

Deep in the woods, he met the stranger again. The stranger laughed, "I know what you did with the money, but I still want to help." So he gave the old man another purse filled with gold. The old man rushed home, but along the way he started thinking again. "If I tell my wife, she will squander this fortune. . . . Well, maybe she won't." He went back and forth in his mind, and decided to think further before telling his wife about the fortune. So he hid the money under the ashes in the fireplace. The next day he awoke to find his wife had cooked another hearty breakfast. "You did not bring back any firewood," she explained, "so I sold the ashes to the farmer down the road."

The old man ran to look, but there were no ashes or gold coins in the fireplace. In deep misery, he went back into the forest, and met the stranger a third time. The man with the long beard smiled sadly. "It seems you are not destined to be rich," the stranger said. "But I still want to help." He offered the old man a large bag. "There are frogs in this sack. Sell them in the village. Then use the money to buy the largest fish you can find—not dried fish, shell fish, sausages, cakes or bread. Just the largest fish!" With that the stranger vanished.

The old man hurried to the village and sold his frogs. Once he had the money in hand, he saw many wonderful things he could buy at the market, and he thought the stranger's advice odd. But the old man heeded the stranger, went to the fishmonger's stall and bought the largest fish he could find. He returned home, carrying the fish on his back.

By then evening had arrived, and with it came a storm. Rain poured down, and waves pounded the beach. When the old man entered his house and gave his wife the fish, she said, "It's too late to clean the fish today. It will be dark soon." So the old man looked for a place to keep the fish. Finally, he hung it outside from the rafters. He and his wife went to bed, saying a prayer for any fishermen who might be caught at sea, like their own three sons.

In the middle of the night, someone pounded on the door. "Who could that be?" the old man and woman exclaimed, because the storm still raged outside. They opened the door and found a group of young fishermen dancing and singing. "Thank you for saving our lives!" they told the old man.

"What do you mean?" the old man asked. So the fishermen explained that they were caught at sea by the storm, and did not know which way to row until the old man put out a light for them. "A light?" he asked. So they pointed. And the old man saw his fish hanging from the rafters, shining with such a great light it could be seen for miles around.

From that day on, the old man hung out the shining fish each evening to guide the young fishermen home, and they in turn shared their catch with him. And so he and his wife lived in comfort and honor the rest of their days (Calvino 1978).

COMMENT

The drama of this tale begins when the old man meets a mysterious stranger who gives him a bag of gold. This is a major theme of elder tales. After years of practical labor and in the course of ordinary events, magic returns unexpectedly. The story gradually reveals the symbolic meaning of this magic.

After receiving the gold, the old man hides the treasure without telling his wife. He acts out of suspicion and greed, and the fact that the old man conceals the gold under *manure* emphasizes the odious nature of his motivations. When the old man's wife inadvertently sells the manure the next day, he is punished for his avarice. The story repeats the episode to emphasize its message, and other elder tales make the point clear: material reward is not the goal in elder tales. These stories contrast with tales of youth, where worldly benefits, such as finding a fortune or winning a kingdom, are the ultimate goals. The aim in elder tales is spiritual rather than material.

The stranger gives the old man a bag of frogs, along with the advice to sell the frogs and use the money to buy the largest fish available at the market. The old man is tempted to buy other things, but finally obeys the stranger. This is a crucial event. We might infer that the old man heeds the stranger's advice because he knows by now how poor his own judgment can be: he lost a fortune twice because of his greed. So the story repeats the two major themes from middle tales like "The Mortal King": self-reformation, and self-transcendence. Like the mortal monarch, the old man transcends his egocentric, greedy impulses, and changes his ways.

The old man's self-transcendence, however, differs from the middle-aged monarch. First of all, the stranger's advice is odd and almost irrational. Buying a single large fish is hardly practical, since it would spoil easily. Dried fish, sausages, or something less perishable would seem more useful. In heeding the stranger's advice, the old man does something impractical, and his actions contrast with the pragmatic, worldly insight of the mortal king. Similar impractical action appears repeatedly in other elder tales. In "The Old Man Who Lost His Wen" (Ozaki 1970), an old man suffers from a wen, a benign tumor, on his face. No matter what he did, he could not get rid of the deformity. While chopping wood in the forest, a storm arises and the old man takes shelter in a hollowed tree. He then watches in terror as demons come out to dance. The demons are terrible dancers and the Demon King asks out loud if anybody can teach his demons to dance. The old man loves to dance, and is tempted to step forth. But he knows the demons might eat him, so he hesitates. Finally, however, the old man throws caution to the wind and steps out to dance for the demons. They love his dancing, and reward him by removing his wen. His decision to dance for demons seems crazy and irrational, but it ultimately proved to be healing for him.

The Arabian tale, "The Fisherman and the Djinn," reiterates the theme. A djinn threatens to kill an old fisherman but the man tricks the spirit into a bottle and traps the djinn. The djinn pleads with the fisherman to release him, and after a lengthy conversation, in which the old man and the djinn exchange fairy tales, the fisherman finally decides to release the djinn. He does this even though the djinn had tried to kill him before, but the djinn then rewards the fisherman. Ultimately, the fisherman liberates an entire country that had been enchanted by an evil witch. The old man's seemingly crazy decision to release a murderous djinn led to the liberation of a whole people. Similarly "crazy" actions surface in another Arabian tale, "The Simple Grasscutter" (Lang 1914), the Cossack story, "The Straw Ox" (Bain 1895), the Japanese tale, "The Six Jizo" (Ohta 1955), and the Tibetan tale, "The Widow and the Frog" (Hyde-Chambers & Hyde-Chambers 1981). In the latter, a widow adopts a frog as her son, although she knows that it is a crazy thing to do. But the frog then turns out to be a great hero in disguise, who helps the whole land.

"The Shining Fish" elaborates on the theme of old people doing apparently crazy things. After buying the largest fish he can find, the old man returns home and hangs it outside from the rafters. Both actions seem strange, since it would be more practical for him to buy dried fish, or some other less perishable commodity. Moreover, hanging the fish outside invites the possibility that somebody, or some animal, will steal it. Yet that night, when a terrible storm breaks out and threatens the lives of several young fishermen, the fish becomes a magic lantern whose light guides the fishermen safely to harbor. The fish is a traditional Christian symbol for Christ, something that would presumably have been known to the Italian listeners of this story. The tale thus introduces an explicit religious theme and refers to a sublime dimension. The story implies that the old man had to do something seemingly crazy and impractical, namely, buying the largest fish and hanging it from his roof, in order for divine intervention to occur. Only after transcending his usual egocentric, rational and practical outlook, did the old man become open to a spiritual event.

The message is emphasized in traditional religions (Nisker 1990). Christianity stresses the irrationality of its faith; Buddhism teaches that the practical, material order is an illusion, while Zen Buddhism adds that spiritual illumination requires "crazy wisdom." Abandoning pragmatic secular concerns, in fact, is a major task for later life, according to most religions. In Hinduism, the last half of life was a time for surrendering worldly concerns, leaving one's home, and seeking spiritual enlightenment in the wilderness (Kakar 1979; Rhadakrishnan and Moore 1957). In Confucianism, at around fifty years of age, the individual was to turn from worldly affairs to the "mandate of heaven" (Wei-Ming 1978). In Jewish tradition, the final years were often likened to the Sabbath, devoted to the contemplation of God, rather than worldly ambitions (Katz 1975).

The Christian symbolism is clear in "The Shining Fish." But other elder tales are surprisingly nondenominational. "The Fisherman and the Djinn," as mentioned before, is Arabian and reflects Islamic tradition. Yet by simply changing a few phrases, like the old man's appeals to Allah, the story could easily come from a Buddhist or Christian culture. The same holds in the Japanese tale, "The Six Jizo." There a poor old man tries to sell six straw hats, but no one buys any. Without money for food, the old man decides to give away his hats to six statues of Jizo, a Japanese deity. After this seemingly crazy action, the statues come alive, bringing food and gifts to the old man. Jizo, of course, is specifically Japanese, but other cultures have similar stories, in which individuals give food to statues of saints, Jesus, or other divine beings, and the statues come alive.

The German, Christian story of "The Aged Mother" (Grimm & Grimm 1944), provides another example of a story easily altered to fit other cultures. In the story, an old woman bitterly laments the death of her two young children, and her husband years before. In the midst of her sorrow, however, she has a divine vision, revealing why her children and husband died early: their early deaths prevented them from falling into sin and suffering horribly in life, saving their immortal souls. With this transcendent understanding, the old woman gives up her egocentric sorrow and finds inner peace. Coming from a Christian culture, the woman's vision is attributed to God, but it could come as well from Buddhist bodhisattvas, or the Islamic Kdir.

Other elder tales reflect magical beliefs common to many cultures, and independent of religious tradition, like "The Cat and the Dog" from Korea (In-Sob 1979), and "Princess Moonlight" from Japan (Ozaki 1970). "The Widow and the Frog" from Tibet is particularly clear here: the story portrays a magic frog turning into a human hero and the theme reflects magical animistic beliefs found around the world, independent of formal religious institutions.

Common to elder tales from different religious traditions is a focus on a general process of spiritual self-transcendence, the shift from practical, worldly, and egocentric concerns to numinous revelation. The drama is expressed in specific religious terms in some tales, or in general magical beliefs. But the process of spiritual transcendence cuts across religious traditions.

Self-transcendence is not the final event in "The Shining Fish." After the old man saves the lives of the fishermen, they come to an agreement. Each evening the old man hangs out his shining fish to guide the young men to harbor in safety, and they share their catch with him. The story thus introduces another major theme in elder tales: the old man brings divine magic into the world to help the next generation. He mediates between this realm and the next, benefiting society. The same theme can be seen in the Tibetan story, "The Widow and Frog" (Hyde-Chambers & Hyde-Chambers 1981). Only after the widow adopts him as a son can the frog assume a human form, become a great hero and help all the people. The Arabian story, "The Enchanted Head" (Lang 1914) repeats the drama. Only when an old woman is brave enough to deal with a terrifying apparition—a human head without a body—does the head turn into a great hero, who helps all the people. In the Croatian tale, "Stribor's Forest" (Berlic-Mazuranic 1924), similarly, an old woman refuses to live in a happy fantasy world and bravely confronts painful truths. Her decision breaks a magic spell on a whole country, freeing her son from an evil enchantment and helping all the people in her land.

Elder tales emphasize that the goal in later life is not simply self-transcendence and encountering the divine, but bringing the transcendent wisdom back for the benefit of young men and women. Transcendence must be tempered with generativity. In portraying older adults mediating between a supernatural realm and the human order, elder tales reflect the traditional religious role of elders in preindustrial societies. Elders act, as David Gutmann (1983, 1987) observed, as "bridgeheads to the sacred," linking their people to the gods or the ancestors. This sacred role has been much diminished in today's secular society, where things divine are questioned or outright disbelieved. Skeptical modern culture thus deprives older adults of opportunities for a meaningful old age (Shahrani 1981).

Nevertheless, the role of spiritual mentor is still possible, and some cases are dramatic, like that of Alfred North Whitehead (Chinen 1989; Lawrence 1968; Lowe 1985; Whitehead 1941). After years of highly successful work as a mathematician and educator, Whitehead embarked upon an entirely new area of work in his sixties, focusing on theology and metaphysics, two fields held in ill repute among scholars. Ignoring the risk to his reputation, Whitehead developed an original philosophy (Whitehead 1925, 1926, 1938), and profoundly influenced a new generation of theologians. Whitehead transcended egocentric concerns about status and success to pursue his spiritual interests, and then brought back his insights to the next generation.

Emmanuel Swedenborg offers another dramatic example. An eminent seventeenth-century Swedish scientist, at the age of fifty-five, Swedenborg began having dramatic dreams and visions focused on religious themes (Sigstedt 1952). Swedenborg initially feared he was going insane, but he recorded his experiences (Swedenborg 1977, 1979) and soon concluded they were part of a new religious vocation. He abandoned his numerous scientific and administrative posts and devoted his life to mystical, theological writings.

Other individuals exemplify the process of transcendence and mediation in more secular ways (Pruyser 1975; McLeish 1976). Benjamin Spock, for instance, late in life, risked his reputation as America's premier child-care authority to protest the Vietnam War. Unconcerned about losing the respect and honor he had earned from his many years as a physician, Spock committed himself to social reformation as a transcendent value. A similar situation occurred with the French philosopher Voltaire (de Beauvoir 1972). Moreover, transcendence and spiritual generativity are not the province of famous people. Grandparents often take this role with grandchildren, and senior mentors with their apprentices (Kotre 1984).

REFLECTIONS

Middle and elder tales present a view of spirituality and aging not bound to any particular faith and emphasizing cross-cultural similarities. There are several reasons for this. First of all, the tales are aimed at adults rather than children. Youth tales, as many folklorists have pointed out, seek to socialize children and adolescents in prevailing social mores (Degh 1982; Rumnley 1983; Tatar 1987; Zipes 1983). Middle and elder tales speak to adults who have presumably already been socialized. The stories therefore abandon their socializing role. Moreover, fairy tales for adults are explicitly not meant to be believed. The stories begin with a familiar phrase, different with each culture, which tells the audience to suspend belief. In Western tradition, the warning is "Once upon a time." In Arabian cultures, it is "There was, there was not," and in African tales, it is simply "Hoy," signifying "believe if you wish!" Fairy tales are therefore free to deviate from orthodox religious dogmas. They contrast with myths and legends which are meant to be believed. (The myths of today are the religious truths of yesteryear.) If an ecclesiastical authority found a story heretical, the fairy tale teller could simply say, "It's only a fairy tale. Why are you taking it so seriously?" Fairy tales were also told in intimate, informal gatherings, far from the control of religious or secular authorities. Furthermore, the stories were commonly recounted after much drinking, and such altered states of consciousness encourage the spontaneous emergence of unconscious material, normally repressed by social sanctions (Chinen 1992).

The cross-cultural perspective of middle and elder tales matches the outlook of modern transpersonal psychology, the systematic study of religious experiences and phenomena, independent of any particular religious faith. This viewpoint is uniquely suited to a modern, secular, pluralistic society, and to the future of aging in such a culture. Members of the baby-boom generation, for instance, often find it difficult to embrace traditional religions. Yet as they age, this generation, like others before them, will struggle with questions about death and the ultimate meaning of life. Without a religious framework for these timeless issues, many individuals will flounder in confusion. The transpersonal spirit of middle and elder tales offers a nondogmatic spiritual framework. At the same time, the stories emphasize the need for a social context in which to develop the spirituality of later life. For today's society, this means restoring the traditional, spiritual role of elders in society. Such a spiritual role, I think, offers aging individuals a more deeply satisfying alternative to the current image of the senior citizen, enjoying his or her leisurely "golden years" as a consummate consumer.

REFERENCES

Aarne A., and S. Thompson. 1961. *The types of the folktale: A classification and bibliography.* Helsinki: Academia Scientarium Finnica.

Arnett, W. S. 1985. Only the bad died young in the ancient Middle East. *International Journal of Aging and Human Development* 21, 155–60.

Auchincloss, E., and R. Michels. 1989. The impact of middle age on ambitions and ideals. In J. Oldham and R. Liebert, eds., *The middle years: New psychoanalytic perspectives,* 40–57. New Haven: Yale University Press.

Bain, R. N. 1895. *Cossack fairy tales and folk tales.* New York: Stokes.

Beauvoir, S. de. 1972. *The coming of age.* Translated by P. O'Brian. New York: G. P. Putnam's Sons.

Berlic-Mazuranic, I. 1924. *Croatian tales of long ago.* London: Allen and Unwin.

Bettelheim, B. 1976. *The uses of enchantment: The meaning and importance of fairy tales.* New York: Knopf.

Bottigheimer, R., ed. 1986. *Fairy tales and society: Illusion, allusion, and paradigm.* Philadelphia: University of Pennsylvania Press.

Brooks, J. B. 1981. Social maturity in middle age and its developmental antecedents. In

D. Eichorn, J. Clausen, N. Haan, M. Honzik, and P. Mussen, eds., *Past and present in middle life,* 244–69. New York: Academic Press.

Burton, R. F., trans. 1978. *Tales from the Arabian nights.* New York: Avenel.

Bushnaq, I. 1986. *Arab folktales.* New York: Pantheon.

Calvino, I. 1978. *Italian folktales.* Translated by G. Martin. New York: Pantheon.

Chinen, A. 1989. *In the ever after: Fairy tales and the second half of life.* Wilmette, Ill.: Chiron.

——. 1992. *Once upon a midlife: Classic stories and mythic tales to illuminate the middle years.* Los Angeles: Tarcher.

——. 1993. *Beyond the hero: Mythic tales and the quest for men's souls.* Los Angeles: Tarcher.

Ciernia, J. 1985. Death concern and businessmen's mid-life crisis. *Psychological Reports* 56:83–87.

Cochran, L. 1990. *The sense of vocation: A study of career and life development.* Albany: State University Press of New York.

Degh, L. 1982. Grimm's *household tales* and its place in the household: The social relevance of a controversial classic. In M. M. Metzger and K. Mommsen, eds., *Fairy tales as ways of knowing: Essays on Marchen in psychology, society and literature,* 21–53. Bern: Lang.

Dieckmann, H. 1986. *Twice-told tales: The psychological use of fairy tales.* Translated by B. Matthews. Wilmette, Ill.: Chiron.

Dundes, A. 1986. Fairy tales from a folkloristic perspective. In R. Bottigheimer, ed., *Fairy tales and society: Illusion, allusion and paradigm,* 259–70. Philadelphia: University of Pennsylvania Press.

Eichorn, D., J. Clausen, N. Haan, M. Honzik, and P. Mussen, eds. 1981. *Present and past in middle life.* New York: Academic Press.

Erikson, E. 1959. *Identity and the life cycle.* New York: International Universities Press.

——. 1983. *The life cycle completed.* New York: Norton.

Erikson, E., J. M. Erikson, and H. Q. Kivnick. 1986. *Vital involvement in old age.* New York: Norton.

Fowler, J. 1981. *The stages of faith: The psychology of human development and the quest for meaning.* San Francisco: Harper & Row.

Friedlander, G. 1920. *The Jewish fairy book.* New York: Stokes.

Grimm, J., and W. Grimm. 1944. *The complete Grimms' fairy tales.* Translated by Margaret Hunt. New York: Pantheon.

Grolnick, S. 1986. Fairy tales and psychotherapy. In R. Bottigheimer, ed., *Fairy tales and society: Illusion, allusion and paradigm,* 203–17. Philadelphia: University of Pennsylvania Press.

Gutmann, D. 1983. Observations on culture and mental health in later life. In J. E. Birren and R. B. Sloane, eds., *Handbook of Mental Health and Aging,* 114–48. Englewood Cliffs, NJ: Prentice-Hall.

——. 1987. *Reclaimed powers: Toward a new psychology of men and women in later life.* New York: Basic Books.

Haan, N. 1981. Common dimensions of personality: Early adolescence to middle life. In D. Eichorn, J. Clausen, N. Haan, M. Honzik, and P. Mussen, eds., *Past and present in middle life,* 17–154. New York: Academic Press.

Heath, D. 1983. The maturing person. In R. Walsh and D. Shapiro, eds. *Beyond health and normality: Explorations of exceptional well-being,* 152–206. New York: Van Nostrand Reinhold.

Heuscher, J. 1974. *A psychiatric study of myths and fairy tales: Their origin, meaning and usefulness.* Springfield, Ill.: Charles C. Thomas.

Hyde-Chambers, F., and A. Hyde-Chambers. 1981. *Tibetan folk tales.* Boulder, Colo.: Shambhala.

In-Sob, Z. 1979. *Folk tales from Korea.* New York: Grove Press.

Jaques, E. 1965. Death and the mid-life crisis. *International Journal of Psychoanalysis* 46, 502–14.

Kakar, S. 1979. Setting the stage: The traditional Hindu view and the psychology of Erik H. Erikson. In S. Kakar, ed., *Identity and adulthood,* 2–12. Delhi: Oxford University Press.

Katz, R. L. 1975. Jewish values and socio-psychological perspectives on aging. In S. Hiltner, ed., *Toward a theology of aging,* 135–50. New York: Human Sciences Press.

Kotre, J. 1984. *Outliving the self: Generativity and the interpretation of lives.* Baltimore: Johns Hopkins University Press.

Laboulaye, E. 1976. *Laboulaye's fairy book: Fairy tales of all nations.* Translated by Mary Booth. Great Neck, N.Y.: Core Collection Books.

Lang, A. 1903. *The crimson fairy book.* New York: Longmans, Green.

———. 1914. *The brown fairy book.* London: Longmans, Green.

Lawrence, N. 1968. *Whitehead's philosophical development: A critical history of the background of process and reality.* Westport, Conn.: Greenwood.

Levinson, D., C. Darrow, E. Klein, M. Levinson, and B. McKee. 1978. *The season of a man's life.* New York: Ballantine.

Lowe, V. 1985. *Understanding Whitehead: The man and his work.* Baltimore: Johns Hopkins University Press.

Luthi, Max. 1984. *The fairytale as art form and portrait of man.* Translated by Jon Erickson. Bloomington: Indiana University Press.

McLeish, J. 1976. *The Ulyssean adult: Creativity in the middle and later years.* New York: McGraw-Hill Ryerson.

Mehdevi, A. S. 1965. *Persian folk and fairy tales.* New York: Knopf.

Modell, A. 1989. Object relations theory: Psychic aliveness in the middle years. In J. Oldham and R. Liebert, eds., *The middle years: New psychoanalytical perspectives,* 17–25. New Haven: Yale University Press.

Mussen, P., and N. Haan. 1981. A longitudinal study of patterns of personality and political ideologies. In D. Eichorn, J. Clausen, N. Haan, M. Honzik, and P. Mussen, eds., *Past and present in middle life,* 393–414. New York: Academic Press.

Neugarten, B. 1966. Adult personality: A developmental view. *Human Development* 9, 61–73.

Nisker, W. 1990. *Crazy wisdom.* Berkeley, Calif.: Ten Speed Press.

Ohta, M. 1955. *Japanese folklore in English.* Tokyo: Tuttle.

Oldham, J., and R. Liebert, eds. 1989. *The middle years: New psychoanalytic perspectives.* New Haven: Yale University Press.

Ozaki, T. 1970. *The Japanese fairy book.* New York: Charles Tuttle.

Propp, Vladimir. 1968. *Morphology of the fairy tale.* Translated by Laurence Scott. Austin: University of Texas Press.

Pruyser, P. 1975. Aging: Downward, upward or forward? *Pastoral Psychology* 24, 102–18.

Rhadakrishnan, S., and C. Moore. 1957. *A sourcebook in Indian philosophy.* Princeton: Princeton University Press.

Rowe, K. 1986. To spin a yarn: The female voice in folklore and fairy tale. In R. Bottigheimer, ed. *Fairy tales and society: Illusion, allusion and paradigm,* 53–74. Philadelphia: University of Pennsylvania Press.

Rumnley, D. B., and E. Bergman. 1983. Enchantment and alchemy: The story of Rumpelstiltskin. *Bulletin of the Menninger Clinic* 47, 1–14.

Schenda, R. 1986. Telling tales—Spreading tales: Change in the communicative forms of a popular genre. In R. Bottigheimer, ed., *Fairy tales and society: Illusion, allusion and paradigm,* 75–94. Philadelphia: University of Pennsylvania Press.

Shahrani, M. N. 1981. Growing in respect: Aging among the Kirghiz of Afghanistan. In P. Amoss and S. Harrell, eds., *Other ways of growing old,* 175–92. Stanford: Stanford University Press.

Shulz, S. 1977. Death anxiety and the structuring of a death concerns cognitive domain. *Essence* 1, 171–88.

Sigstedt, C. 1952. *The Swedenborg epic: The life and works of Emanuel Swedenborg.* New York: Bookman Associates.

Soddy, K. 1967. *Men in middle life.* Philadelphia: Lippincott.

Swedenborg, E. 1977. *Swedenborg's journal of dreams.* Edited by G. E. Klemming and W. Ross Woofenden. Translated by J.J.G. Wilkinson. New York: Swedenborg Foundation.

———. 1979. *Heaven and hell.* Translated by G. F. Dole. New York: Swedenborg Foundation.

Tatar, M. 1987. *The hard facts of the Grimms' fairy tales.* Princeton: Princeton University Press.

Thompson, S. 1955–1958. Motif-index of folk literature. Bloomington: Indiana University Press.

Thurnher, M. 1975. Continuities and discontinuities in value orientations. In M. F. Lowenthal, M. Thurnher, and D. Chiriboga, eds., *Four stages of life,* 176–200. San Francisco: Jossey-Bass.

Vaillant, G. 1977. *Adaptation to life: How the best and the brightest came of age.* Boston: Little, Brown.

Vaillant, G., and E. Milofsky. 1980. Natural history of male psychological health. Pt. 9: Empirical evidence for Erikson's model of the life cycle. *American Journal of Psychiatry* 137, 1348–59.

Viney, L. 1987. A sociophenomenological approach to life-span development complementing Erikson's sociodynamic approach. *Human Development* 30, 125–36.

von Franz, M. L. 1977. *Individuation in fairy tales.* Dallas: Spring.

———. 1980. *The psychological meaning of redemption motifs in fairy tales.* Toronto: Inner City Book.

Wei-Ming, T. 1978. The Confucian perception of adulthood. In E. Erickson, ed., *Adulthood,* 113–20. New York: Norton.

Whitehead, A. N. 1917. *The organization of thought, educational and scientific.* London: Williams and Norgate.

———. 1919. *An enquiry concerning the principles of natural knowledge.* Cambridge: Cambridge University Press.

———. 1920. *The concept of nature*. Cambridge: Cambridge University Press.

———. 1925. *Science and the modern world*. New York: Macmillan.

———. 1926. *Religion in the making*. New York: Macmillan.

———. 1938. *Modes of thought*. New York: Macmillan.

———. 1941. Autobiographical notes. In P. A. Schilpp, ed., *The philosophy of Alfred North Whitehead*, 1–14. New York: Tudor.

Woods, N., and K. Witte. 1981. Life satisfaction, fear of death, and ego identity in elderly adults. *Bulletin of the Psychonomic Society* 18:165–68.

Zipes, J. 1976. *Don't bet on the prince: Contemporary feminist fairy tales in North America and England*. New York: Methuen.

———. 1979. *Breaking the magic spell: Radical theories of folk and fairy tales*. Austin: University of Texas Press.

———. 1983. *Fairy tales and the art of subversion: The classical genre for children and the process of civilization*. New York: Heinemann.

7   Spiritual Well-being, Maturity, and Aging: Biblical Illustrations

J. Gordon Harris

What does the Bible teach on spirituality in old age that human science professionals cannot find through research? Another way to ask that question would
be, how do biblical teachings reinforce or add to what human sciences discover
about spirituality in the latter years of life? Even in an age of specialization,
human science professionals recognize the Bible as a primary source for deci-
phering the complex nature of spirituality. For example, the Bible frequently
mentions examples of spirituality. Some of its characters are old. So these stories
of elders could be used as illustrations of and valuable sources for understanding
spirituality in old age. Identifying the characteristics of spirituality within the
Bible, however, remains a challenging endeavor. Such an enterprise demands a
carefully worked out synthesis of insights and methods from human sciences
and biblical studies.

First of all, identifying spirituality in biblical stories begins with examining
human behavior and the characteristics of spirituality. Defining spirituality in
human science terms is difficult. Early studies in religion and aging assessed
spirituality as participation in activities of a church or synagogue. Increasingly,
that approach has come under scrutiny. Activity participation, while quantifiable,
is particularly inadequate as a criterion for spirituality in the later years of life.

Recent essays on religion and aging focus more on spiritual characteristics
found in elders (Thibault, Ellor & Netting 1991).[1] Researchers interview older
persons as case studies of spirituality. These interviews produce qualitative in-

formation researchers assess and organize as experiences of spirituality in old age.

David O. Moberg makes some strides in this area by presenting a wholistic approach to research into old age. He identifies spiritual well-being with symptoms and signs of mental health, personality integration, meaning in life and functional social relationships. In his opinion, spiritual well-being is not the same as maturity. Moberg points out that well-being is based on feelings of personal integration, meaning in life, or wholeness. He adds that spiritual maturity is a lifelong developmental goal achieved by "relational interdependence between God, self and others" (Moberg 1990, p. 19).

Moberg's approach elevates spirituality beyond psychological subjectivism of mere "feelings of well-being." He defines the shape of spirituality in old age as a person in community who experiences peace with God, others, and self. Moberg's wholistic approach to human science provides at least a working definition of spirituality. Though ambiguous, Moberg's categories point out the variety of forms spirituality takes in the elderly.

Next, a researcher can examine how the Bible identifies spirituality. It does not define it or describe its characteristics any more specifically than the human sciences. The Bible records examples of spiritual well-being and maturity but does not promote one model. A reader finds that biographical sketches of older persons illustrate a diversity of spiritual behaviors within the people of faith. Biblical Christian teachings describe spirituality as a diversity of gifts (1 Cor. 12–14; Eph. 4:11–12), fruit (Gal. 5:22) and experiences (Acts 1:4, 8; 9:17; 11:16). Since no one source or method adequately defines spirituality in old age, a "co-exploration" as envisioned by Eisner (1981, Chenail 1992) provides a more fruitful discussion of the topic.

Biblical study provides data compatible with qualitative research when a reader uses narrative criticism. Narrative criticism can structure biographical sketches to roughly resemble case studies. This method is important because biblical narratives differ considerably from autobiographical case studies. For instance, biblical narratives contain several points of view and use a variety of narrative devices. For example, in a story from Kings, a narrator evaluates the actions of an older prophet who "lies" to a young prophet from Judah (1 Kings 13:18). In another example, Genesis includes a narrative about Jacob's blessing of his grandsons. The passage simply tells the story without comment (Gen. 48:17–19). This narrative leaves evaluation of the characters to readers. Another Genesis narrative has an angel who evaluates the spirituality shown in Abraham's near sacrifice of his son, Isaac (Gen. 22:15–18). Complex illustrations from the Bible need to be analyzed thoroughly before these narratives can be compared with data from autobiographical case studies.

Narrative criticism examines how biblical narratives are shaped to teach a point. A narrative tells a story assuming an ideology of spiritual well-being or maturity. Admittedly that happens in modern autobiographical storytelling. Memory remains a selective vehicle guided by certain assumptions. An interviewer also shapes interview questions through assumptions. The Bible, however, goes beyond that. Biblical narratives shape reminiscing to achieve goals which only by implication may be applied to understand spirituality in old age. Interpreting biblical narratives, therefore, begins with determining what assumptions shape the stories.

In summary, this essay combines insights from qualitative analysis with those from narrative criticism by applying criteria and distinctions from Moberg to three Biblical narratives. The elders described in these narratives are Caleb (Numbers, Joshua), Barzillai (2 Samuel), and Naomi (Ruth) (Harris 1987). The three stories are chosen for the following reasons. These elders successfully negotiate the journey to old age and spiritual well-being or maturity. The three are not the most important elderly in the Bible. As local heroes they perform some noteworthy task that is memorialized by the recording of their story. Their relative obscurity guards against reading preconceived notions about their spirituality into the narratives. The stories are not full biographies or autobiographies but descriptions of brief incidents within their pilgrimages. However, the stories tell enough about elders and their pilgrimages to allow a researcher to come to some conclusions about spirituality and the experiences of old age.

ILLUSTRATIVE BIBLICAL CASES

Caleb

The first narrative pictures one who exemplifies the optimism and courage of spiritual well-being, Caleb, son of Jepunneh. In early adulthood, he explores Canaan to help his people decide whether to conquer it or not (Num. 13:1–6). He represents Judah even though he is a prince from an outsider group (Kenizzites,[2] Josh. 14:6). He calls for his people to conquer Canaanite strongholds and to take the land. Unfortunately, a majority, pessimistic report prevails. Because of his advice, optimistic faith, and loyalty to God, Caleb is promised a blessing (Num. 14:24). In the narrative Caleb gives a stirring speech calling the people to overcome their fears and to "go up at once and possess it [the land]; for we are well able to overcome it" (Num. 13:30).

In later scenes of the story, Caleb continues to exemplify the optimistic leader. In his old age, he says he feels as healthy and vigorous as ever. Caleb reminisces freely in Joshua 14 and suggests a plan for conquering the hills of South Canaan (Josh. 14:6–15;15:13–19). Caleb speaks openly about age forty when he was a spy in Canaan and gave the minority recommendation. He reflects on the events with a great deal of satisfaction. Forty-five years later, he remains positive and confident. His words indicate feelings of spiritual well-being.

Examine me now! I am now eighty-five years old. I am still as strong as I was in the day when Moses sent me; my strength now is as my strength was then, for war or for traveling. So now give me this hill country of which the Lord spoke on that day; for you heard on that day how the Anakim were there, with great fortified cities; it may be that the Lord will be with me, and I shall drive them out as the Lord said. (Josh. 14:10b–12)[3]

On the surface, Caleb would be an excellent model for those who see old age as an extension of middle age. He still believes in his ability to conquer. His health seems good and he remains productive. On the other hand, before the reader concludes that old age is an extension of middle age, one should examine other details in the narrative. The Bible does not explain how Caleb conquers Hebron, but the story mentions how he adapts realistically to conquer Debir. He takes Debir (Kiriath Sepher) by his wits and wealth, not by battlefield strength. Instead of fighting the battle personally, he wisely assesses the situation and offers his daughter Acsah to whoever will conquer the city for him. Othniel, son of Kenaz, Caleb's brother, leads the battle and marries Acsah. These actions and attitudes indicate feelings of personal integration, psychological health, and personal wholeness. Caleb combines optimism with a realistic appraisal of declining strength (Josh. 15:14–17). These traits indicate his sense of well-being.

The narrator goes beyond the words and actions of Caleb to evaluate Caleb's spiritual pilgrimage. First, the narrator attributes Caleb's success to following God fully and completely (Josh. 14:14). Those words explain why Moses spoke a blessing to Caleb (14:9). The narrator concludes that Caleb inherits the blessings of land because throughout his life he does not deviate from loyalty to his God and achieves his dream. Second, Caleb ranks high in the opinion of the narrator because he achieves a position of leadership. That achievement explains why Caleb receives the respect the narrator gives him in the story. Caleb has the respect of the community. Hence, Caleb demonstrates spiritual maturity in his relationships with God, self and others.

The narrative deals separately with the issues of well-being and maturity. Caleb's own words express feelings of spiritual well-being. He feels good about his health, reminisces freely about the past, and has a high degree of satisfaction with his life. His optimism pushes him to attempt the impossible at every phase of his life. Old age does not defeat him, only forces him to seek alternate ways to accomplish the same thing. His optimistic realism keys his successful journey from young adulthood to old age and an ever present sense of well-being. On the other hand, the narrator describes the spiritual maturity of Caleb. In this sense, the narrator explains Caleb's success more in the terms of mature and positive relationships, the signs mentioned by Moberg as characteristics of spiritual maturity.

Barzillai

The second story about an elder focuses on one who helps David, the founder of the united kingdom of Israel. Barzillai the Gileadite from Rogelim (East and North of the Jordan River) represents a subdued but contented form of spiritual well-being. A narrator relates most of the story. The Bible tells nothing about earlier days of his youth. As an older, wealthy man, Barzillai enters history in two scenes.

The first scene relies almost totally on narration. The story describes Barzillai's rescue of David during a revolt. Absalom, David's oldest living son, successfully engineers a coup. David, losing the support of the people, flees to the wilderness. His loyal forces are demoralized and defeated. Barzillai and two others supply the loyal troops with "beds, basins, pottery, wheat, barley, meal, parched corn, beans, lentils, honey, curd, sheep, and cheese." They rescue the thirsty, hungry and weak army of David (2 Sam. 17:27–29). The only discourse recorded in the scene quotes an evaluation of the plight of the army (2 Sam. 17:29). Without those supplies, the people say, the army would not have survived to fight again.

The narrator stresses the generosity of Barzillai. The long list of items donated to David's forces illustrates the wealth of Barzillai and friends. Obviously David would wish to have a wealthy benefactor like Barzillai at his side. The narrator points out later, however, that Barzillai thinks for himself (2 Sam. 19:32–40).

In the second scene, Barzillai the Gileadite reappears after David has defeated Absalom and humiliated his unfaithful friends. The story resumes with Barzillai talking with David as the king prepares to return to Jerusalem. The narrator mentions Barzillai's age for the first time. He is eighty years old. The scene ends with David kissing and blessing Barzillai before both go to their respective homes. The closing dialogue between King David and Barzillai shows the stature of the benefactor and how his age becomes a factor.

The words of Barzillai show him to be a modest man, aware of his declining senses and energies. David asks Barzillai to go with him to Jerusalem. The king promises to take care of him. Barzillai replied to the king:

How many days of the years of my life are left, that I should go up with the king unto Jerusalem? I am this day eighty years old; can I distinguish between good and bad? Can your servant now taste food and drink? Can I hear any more the singing of men and women? Why then should your servant be yet another burden upon my lord the king? Your servant would like to go only beyond the Jordan, why should the king repay me with such a reward? Let your servant, please, turn back, that I might die in my own city which contains the grave of my father and my mother. (2 Sam. 19:35–37)

Barzillai's statement points out the secular or political purpose of the narrative (Glueck 1967; Sakenfeld 1978, 1985). He says nothing that reflects overt religious devotion. Still, the dialogue reflects a sense of well-being.

Barzillai demonstrates an acceptance of his age and its limitations. He knows that he has limited time left. At age eighty he should step aside in favor of another who would have more time left to serve the king and to enjoy the court. His age does not interfere with serving the king, but only from accepting a prestigious position at the court. He does not shy away from responsibility. He does not withdraw from life; rather, he passes on position and power to one who will enjoy it longer and better.

Aware of his limits, Barzillai refuses the prestigious job. As many eighty-year-olds testify, the senses frequently dull. Barzillai knows that he would be a poor food and wine taster. His sense of taste is so bad that he could not protect the king. His hearing losses limit his singing. He would not enjoy the court as much as a younger person. So he recommends his servant (son) Chimham for the position.

His comments on his infirmities reflect the way older people talk. Barzillai does not deny losses he is experiencing as he ages. He does not see old age as an extension of middle age or a time to accumulate wealth or glory. At the same time he remains at peace with his situation. His life satisfaction is high.

Death also does not threaten Barzillai. He is rooted in his home town and wishes to remain there to face death. Jerusalem does not tempt him. He is ready to die. Wholeness is his primary value. He wants to remain near the grave of his ancestors. He expects to be buried soon in that tomb. A sense of rootedness and openness to death indicates a maturity and sense of well-being found in well-adjusted elders.

David, not a narrator, evaluates Barzillai within the narratives of Samuel and Kings. The incident concludes when David accedes to Barzillai's request: "And the King answered, 'Chimham shall go over with me, and I will do for him whatever you wish and what you suggest, I will do for you' " (2 Sam. 19:38). The king then kissed and blessed Barzillai. With this, Barzillai returned to his place.

Later on, facing death in Jerusalem, David does not forget the generosity of his faithful friend. He asks Solomon to be faithful to the family of Barzillai: "But continue to be faithful (*hesed*) to the descendents of Barzillai the Gileadite, and let them eat at your table, for so they treated me (faithfully) when I fled from Absalom your brother" (1 Kings 2:7).

David states that the key to Barzillai's generosity is his faithfulness. His connectedness and compassion merit the same kind of favor for his kin. The king uses the word for faithfulness that the Bible generally reserves for God's covenant faithfulness to the people of God. David thereby elevates the financial support of Barzillai to the level of support that God shows for Israel. On this basis, David praises Barzillai for his loyalty and guarantees his descendents royal support and well-being.

In summary, the narratives about Barzillai show him as a man who exhibits a keen sense of well-being. Those feelings remain despite declining senses and vigor. His feelings of well-being may be reinforced by his wealth, but seem to be powered more by his rootedness and an absence of fear of death. Only later, in another narrative, does anyone judge Barzillai's motives and spiritual maturity. The narrative on the death of David brings in a theological perspective. Faithfulness powers Barzillai's actions. Actions of faithfulness secure Barzillai's relationships and so the future of his family. The motive of faithfulness dominates God's actions and becomes the primary sign of Barzillai's spiritual maturity.

Naomi

After hearing the stories of older, affluent, powerful men, the struggles of Naomi come as a shock (Glueck 1967; Sakenfeld 1985; and Trible 1978). Her climb to spiritual well-being and maturity travels through the isolation of widowhood (Cf. Isa. 54:4; Lam. 1:1, 5:3–4 and Rev. 18:7). When she moves to Moab, she travels with a husband and two sons (Ruth 1). Her sons marry but all three men die, childless. Without male support she becomes vulnerable in her society. Family ties fail. No one comes to rescue her.

A key to interpreting the narrative comes in isolating its dialogues. Narrators set the background for the story and make comments throughout. A commentary places the final scene of the book into the history of the Davidic dynasty. However, dialogues between Naomi and her daughters-in-law and between Naomi and the women of Bethlehem provide turning points for the story and evaluations of God's role in Naomi's pilgrimage. Ruth, Boaz and the kinsman redeemer complete the story within the structure of these turning points.

Several dialogues in the story express the devastation widowhood thrust upon Naomi. Naomi has only daughters-in-law to support her. She tries to convince them to leave her also. Her sense of worth hits a new low. No option remains but to return to her people in Bethlehem. Orpah and Ruth must return to their families. Naomi is an older widow who no longer is desirable for marriage. She can offer them nothing. Her daughters-in-law would be better off in their "mother's house." She expresses her despair to Ruth and Orpah, exaggerating her hopelessness with sarcasm, saying, "Should you on account of them [waiting for marriage to her unlikely, potential sons] deny yourselves the opportunity for marriage? Oh no, my daughters! My situation is far more futile than yours, for the hand of the Eternal [divine name] has struck me" (Ruth 1:13).

Loss of loved ones, status, financial standing and its accompanying grief test the faith of widows. The "curse" of widowhood reminds all how much security and connectedness fuel feelings of well-being. When tragedies strip away hope and relationships, a religious person feels trampled by God.

Unknown to Naomi, her security stands beside her. The narrator mentions that Ruth the Moabitess cements herself to Naomi. She will not leave her mother-in-law in her emptiness. Orpah obeys her and returns home. Ruth shows the surprising side of honoring the older generation. Ruth vows that she will abandon her religion, home country and even her burial place to stay with Naomi. Ruth provides the connectedness to enable Naomi to move from emptiness to fullness. She honors her mother-in-law most by disobeying her.

Naomi illustrates how spiritual maturity may be connected with feelings of spiritual well-being. Life's events sometimes flow through emptiness to wholeness. Under these circumstances, hope for renewal and stabilization depends on at least one faithful relationship. Loss of well-being tests severely a faith stance. Naomi expresses her feelings of abandonment in the following statement: "Do not call me *Naomi* [sweetness], call me *Mara* (bitterness), for *Shaddai* [the mighty one] has made my life bitter. I went away full, but the Eternal has brought me back empty. How can you call me *Naomi,* when the Eternal has leaned on me; when Shaddai has brought a disaster on me?'' (Ruth 1:20–21).

Naomi's movement from emptiness to fullness and a sense of well-being is charted by speeches to and from the women of Bethlehem. The narrative turns on Naomi's speech of despair (Ruth 1:20–21) and the victory song from the women of Bethlehem (Ruth 4). Between these key moments, Ruth and Naomi work together to find a male relative who will help them. Ruth works hard picking up grain behind the harvest workers (gleaning). The Bible requires that some grain be dropped as food for the poor. She follows the counsel of Naomi until she gets Boaz to assume their support and to marry her. Eventually, the birth of a son to Ruth and Boaz restores Naomi's sense of life satisfaction. In the words of her female friends, God is taking away the emptiness of her bitter years. "And the women said to Naomi: 'Blessed be the Eternal one, who has not withheld a redeemer from you today! May his name be perpetuated in Israel! He will renew your life and sustain your old age; for he is born of your daughter-in-law, who loves you and is better to you than seven sons' '' (Ruth 4:14–15).

Naomi's spiritual maturity shows up in a number of ways. Her maturity begins with wholeness in intergenerational relationships. Ruth's friendship and support ignite sparks of strength throughout the book. Naomi, even in her despair, has great pride. Her pride shows when she will not ask her daughters-in-law to remain with her when she has nothing to offer. A second time her pride appears is when Ruth must ask to glean in the fields. Naomi allows Ruth to glean but cautions her about the dangers of gleaning. She does not ask Ruth to glean though it is an accepted way widows feed themselves. Shaken by circumstances, Naomi depends on Ruth to regain her confidence. Respect from Ruth restores Naomi's self-respect.

Second, a restored Naomi regains her boldness. Cultural safeguards do not work for Naomi and Ruth. Naomi's husband's family does not assume its responsibility for their welfare as the culture expected. Naomi's kinsman redeemer disappears instead of taking care of them. When the time and place were correct, Naomi boldly suggests that Ruth request that Boaz cover her with his cloak (coat). In this gesture he would take responsibility for them. She sends Ruth to the fields at night to woo him. Naomi and Ruth risk everything to break the failure of their patriarchal system. Naomi wisely develops a bold plan for Ruth's success. Ruth and Boaz complete the story. Naomi's bold plan (Ruth 3:1–5), Ruth's courage and Boaz's generosity give Naomi's story a happy ending.

Third, though strained by circumstances, Naomi retains her relationship with her God. Her strong language against *Shaddai* and the Eternal One indicates a continuing and open communication with God. During the dark days, Naomi blames God for difficulties. Her friends later express her joy for the way the Eternal granted her security. In the same song, her friends praise Ruth as the source of success. The journey from emptiness to fullness helps Naomi mature spiritually. In the words of the women, the infant belongs to Naomi, his grand-mother. She has earned her well-being and maturity.

CONCLUSION

Of the three examples of spiritual well-being and maturity discussed, several characteristics appear in each one of them. They exhibit courage, confidence, and an attitude of openness. Emotionally they vary because of life's circumstances. Naomi experiences emotional highs and lows because her security is threatened and her losses are greater. Caleb is the perpetual optimist and Barzillai is the modest, realistic elder. Caleb seeks roots and Barzillai appreciates and returns to them. Naomi comes to her roots to seek a measure of hope and spiritual well-being. In every case, the elderly find wholeness in interconnectedness.

Circumstances influence feelings of spiritual well-being. Naomi expresses fear and uncertainty until she finds security with Ruth and Boaz. Life satisfaction increases when circumstances improve for the elderly. Spiritual maturity is less tied to circumstances. Hardship and challenge can produce character and maturity.

The single factor which shows up in all three elders is that of faithfulness. That appears in two senses. One form of faithfulness is that of friendship and loyalty to family, king, and nation or tribe. The other form of loyalty is religious. Faithfulness to God especially appears in the Caleb narrative. Faithfulness to the king and family dominates the Barzillai narrative. Intergenerational faithfulness anchors the Naomi-Ruth story. Faithfulness motivates the elderly characters in all three narratives.

Naomi's experiences are the most relevant of the three personalities for the majority of those in the fourth quarter of life. Women outnumber men in the older age groups. Many of these women never find security in the home of some Boaz. They must find spiritual maturity without a concrete sense of well-being. Developing spiritual maturity under these conditions remains possible, but difficult.

In summary, following the guidelines of human science research and literary criticism helps readers analyze case studies of the elderly found in biblical narratives. No one pattern emerges in three biographical sketches. As with interviews of elders, the merging of methods turns up a variety of characteristics of spirituality. Recognizing well-being depends more on external circumstances than does maturity. Findings generally confirm Moberg's distinction between well-being and maturity and the characteristics which he attributes to both. At the same time, the sketches isolate additional factors that point toward a sense of well-being and that direct the developmental aspect of spiritual maturity.

For example, the narratives point out that rootedness and financial security aid feelings of well-being in old age. Rootedness especially prepares one to face death. On the other hand, faithfulness in relation to God and others motivates and sustains the journey to maturity. These conclusions underline the relational interdependence required for acquiring a sense of well-being and spiritual maturity.

NOTES

1. The *Journal of Religious Gerontology* 7(½) (1990), deals with spirituality and aging in important articles.

2. The Kenizzites were a non-Israelite ethnic group that presumably penetrated the Negeb (southern plains) of Israel from the Southeast. These southern tribes were eventually subsumed under the tribe of Judah. The plural form "Kenizzites" surfaces but once (Gen. 15:19) in a promise the Eternal one makes to Abraham (Kuntz 1992).

3. All Bible translations in the article are those of the author.

REFERENCES

Birren, J. 1990. Spiritual maturity in psychological development. *Journal of Religious Gerontology* 7(1/2), 41–54.

Chenail, R. 1992. A case for clinical qualitative research. *The Qualitative Report* 1(4), 1, 3–6.

Clements, W. M. 1990. Spiritual development in the fourth quarter of life. *Journal of Religious Gerontology* 7(1/2), 55–70.

Clinebell, H. 1992. *Well being*. New York: Harper San Francisco.

Eisner, E. W. 1981. On the differences between scientific and artistic approaches to qualitative research. *Educational Research* 10(4), 5–9.

Glueck, N. 1967. *Hesed in the Bible*. Cincinnati: Hebrew Union College Press.

Harris, J. G. 1987. *Biblical perspectives on aging*. Philadelphia: Fortress.

Hutchinson, F. 1991. *Aging comes of age*. Louisville, Ky.: Westminster/John Knox.

Kuntz, J. K. 1992. Kenaz. *Anchor Bible dictionary* 4, 17.

Missinne, L. E. 1990. Christian perspectives on spiritual needs of a human being. *Journal of Religious Gerontology* 7(1/2), 143–52.

Moberg, D. O. 1990. Spiritual maturity and wholeness in the later years. *Journal of Religious Gerontology* 7(1/2), 5–24.

Payne, B. 1990. Spiritual maturity and meaning-filled relationships. *Journal of Religious Gerontology* 7(1/2), 25–39.

Sakenfeld, K. D. 1978. *The meaning of Hesed in the Hebrew Bible*. Missoula: Scholars Press.

———. 1985. *Faithfulness in action*. Philadelphia: Fortress.

Seeber, J. 1990. Spiritual maturity and wholeness—A concept whose time has come. *Journal of Religious Gerontology* 7(1/2), 1–4.

Thibault, J. M., J. W. Ellor, and F. E. Netting. 1991. A conceptual framework for assessing the spiritual functioning and fulfillment of older adults in long-term care settings. *Journal of Religious Gerontology* 7(4), 19–43.

Trible, P. 1978. *God and the rhetoric of sexuality*. Philadelphia: Fortress.

8 Honor Thy Mother: Aging Women in the Jewish Tradition

Dena Shenk

INTRODUCTION

To what extent does Jewish religious ethnicity provide continuity in the lives of Jewish elders and particularly, Jewish women? Being Jewish is viewed here as a source of identity and continuity for Jewish women as they age. The main avenues for this continuity which will be explored in this chapter are traditional roles as they are defined within the family. We will explore patterns in the Jewish aging experience which are fostered by Jewish tradition. In many ways in fact, children are expected to take over the roles of their parents. In large measure, the next generation takes over the roles and responsibilities within the family and Jewish community. At the same time, there is discontinuity in this experience because of generational differences and historical and cultural changes.

Many religious and cultural traditions stress respect for the aged and honoring one's parents. Perhaps the most notable aspect of the Jewish tradition is the element of limits on the responsibilities of children for their aging parents and the clear priority of caring for one's children, the next generation.

There are several levels of tension and ambivalence in the relationships between Jewish children in the United States and their aging parents. One dilemma relates to the strong values of education and ''success'' versus closeness of the family in the Jewish tradition. In American society, occupational success often necessitates geographic mobility, which complicates the maintenance of close family relationships. A second dilemma relates to the stated ideals for relations with one's mother and father and the reality of these relationships both in traditional times and the present.[1] A third dilemma relates to the differences between today's generations of aging Jewish parents and their children, and the concurrent expectation that the children will likely fill the roles of aging Jewish parents in the future. These tensions provide the background for the following discussion.[2]

My emphasis is on aging Jewish women, first, because of the predominance of women among the elderly Jewish population and, second, because of the paucity of information which focuses on them. The primary roles of women have been within the family and it is within that context that Jewish women have traditionally found continuity as they aged. I will begin by discussing religious ethnic identity as a source of continuity in the Jewish aging experience. Traditional sources will be used to provide the background for this consideration of adaptation to the life cycle issues of old age within the Jewish context in the United States. This is followed by a consideration of family responsibilities and roles, specifically, motherhood, caregiving, grandmotherhood, late-life marriage and widowhood as they are experienced by aging Jewish women in the United States today.

RELIGIOUS ETHNIC IDENTITY AS A SOURCE OF CONTINUITY

My view of the aging experience of Jewish elderly as relatively continuous draws on the concept of ethnicity "as fluid, as a resource rather than a solid countable variable" (Gelfand and Berresi 1987). I am using the concept of religious ethnicity to describe the case of Jewish women in the United States. An anthropological version of ethnicity, as Climo explains

focuses on ethnicity as a resource which is situationally invoked in response to changes in people's lives. The issue of understanding ethnic difference becomes one of understanding when and how aging individuals draw on their ethnic background to make sense of their life experiences. (1990:165–6)

Similarly, Luborsky and Rubinstein (1987) have looked at ethnicity as a resurgent phenomenon in late life, one around which people rework life course "themes," as that concept has been used by Kaufman (1986). Life themes are the topics around which particular individuals organize the stories of their lives. I suggest that ethnicity is also used to cope with specific incidents and changes in people's lives, such as various aspects of the aging experience which require adaptation and adjustment. In these ways, Jewish culture and religion as ethnic heritage informs the aging process and provides a theme of continuity in the lives of Jewish elders.

This continuity is at the same time cause for the recognition that one is "becoming one's mother." As a woman becomes an older Jewish woman, she will be taking over the roles previously filled by her mother and will likely fill those roles in similar ways, following the teachings of Judaism as taught within her family. Basha, of Barbara Myerhoff's *Number Our Days,* described "domestic religion" as it was taught to girls from their grandmothers: "These things were injected into you in childhood and chained together with that beautiful grandmother, so ever since infancy you can't know life without it. . . . When it goes in this way, I describe, Jewish comes up in you from the roots and it stays with you all your life" (1978:235).

As Susan Schneider points out, "when we consider the relationships within the Jewish family, we risk getting caught in a tangled web of myths and damaging stereotypes about Jewish women" (1985:268). She discusses the contradictory myths of the "Yiddushe Mama" and her daughter the "Princess" and points out that "there are many ironies in this juxtaposition, not the least of which is that the Princess is expected to become the Mama as soon as possible after she marries and/or has children of her own."

The recognition comes in its own way for different people that they are aging within their family and Jewish community. For example, I recall a conversation at my grandmother's funeral about twenty years ago. There was a discussion among my father, his brother and sister, acknowledging that they were now the oldest generation within the family. It was a chilling moment for them, to begin to see themselves as fulfilling the role of elders within our family. For myself the recognition of this "cycle" comes when I sit at the Seder table, no longer among the children, but as the parental generation, with my own children taking part in the ritual questioning and storytelling. Or at Chanukah, when I recall for my children my glorious memories of those festive days spent among my cousins in my aunt and uncle's home. "First we would eat mounds and mounds of latkes" (potato pancakes). "Then, with the smell still filling the house, we would each pick a corner," I explain to my own son and daughter. "Tell us about the piles of presents," they urge. And in this way, I pass on the values and traditions of life within our Jewish family.

AGING IN THE JEWISH TRADITION AND LIMITS TO FILIAL RESPONSIBILITY

Our understanding of the Jewish aging experience may be framed in terms of the biblical and talmudic traditions of respecting the aged and honoring one's parents and the primacy of love and care for one's children over one's parents. We must also consider how these traditions are interpreted by Jews in American society and to what extent they affect the reality of their lives. While the biblical and talmudic traditions clearly urged respect for the aged and honoring one's parents, there is both a dearth of references to aging women and evidence of unequal treatment accorded aged men and women. What old women are assumed to have in common with old men is the infirmities that come with old age. Less often in the traditional sources is there clear evidence that older women equally share the honor, respect and wisdom that come to men in old age. Old age for men brought wisdom and honor: "Thou shalt rise up before the hoary head, and honor the face of the old man" (Lev. 19:32).

Respect for the aged is clearly admonished to assure maintenance of the elder within the family and larger Jewish community. The first duty that children have to their parents derives from the Fifth Commandment to "honor thy father and thy mother." This first appears in Exodus 20:12 and in the second version of the Ten Commandments this commandment is amplified: "Honor thy father and thy mother, *as the Lord thy G-d commanded thee, that thy days may be long, and that it may go well with thee,* upon the land which the Lord thy G-d giveth thee" (Deut. 5:16).[3] The relative importance of honoring one's mother is explained in the *Mekhilta of Rabbi Ishmael,* Pisha, chapter 1:

"Honor your father and your mother." I might understand that because the father precedes in the text, he should actually take precedence over the mother. But in another passage, "You shall each revere his mother and his father" (Lev. 19:3), the mother precedes. Scriptures thus declare that both are equal.

The sages taught and used scriptural passages to support their view that the Bible itself equated the fear of father and mother with the fear of G-d (Patai 1977:484).

The Talmud built upon the biblical basis, spelling out the significance of the respect one must show to one's parents and how it should be expressed. Although many of the talmudic examples refer to fathers only, the implication that they refer to treatment of both mother and father is generally assumed. At least three talmudic tracts refer specifically to a son's treatment of his mother.[4]

The primacy of love and care for one's children over one's parents is also part of the Jewish tradition. We find it stated in the Talmud that: "A father's love is for his children; the children's love is for their own children" (Babylonian Talmud, tractate, *Sotate,* p. 49a). Glueckel of Hameln, whose *Memoirs* offers insights into German-Jewish life and thought during the seventeenth century, wrote about a father bird struggling to transport his three fledglings across a windy sea (Klagsbrun 1980:203). He asked each bird in turn if they would do as much for him and provide for his old age. The first two replied that they would and, being liars, were dropped into the sea. The third fledgling replied: "My dear father, it is true you are struggling mightily and risking your life in my behalf, and I shall be wrong not to repay you when you are old, but I cannot bind myself. This, though, I can promise: when I am grown up and have children of my own, I shall do as much for them as you have done for me."

There is considerable discussion of the meaning of the terms "reverence," "respect" and "honor" of one's parents in the talmudic literature. Rashi wrote: "What constitutes 'reverence/yirah?' He [the son] shall not sit in his [the father's] place, nor speak in his place, nor contradict his words. And what constitutes 'honor/kibood?' He gives [him] food, and drink, provides [him] with clothes and shoes, brings him in and takes him out" (*Kiddushin* 31). Thus, respect encompasses psychological and symbolic elements (what the tradition calls "reverence"), as well as physical and caretaking needs (what the tradition calls "honor"). Natalie Joffe (1949) quotes an Eastern European Jew in the United States who expresses how this was interpreted and experienced:

You cannot imagine the respect I felt for my parents. . . . There is a Jewish expression for it which explains it so well, *derekh erets* (lit. "way of the land," but meaning respectful demeanor). . . . It is not fear. If it were fear, then the respect would be asked of the child, and my parents never asked for anything. (241)

The Jewish family unit ideally encompasses expectations of interdependency and mutual responsibility. The Book of Ruth exemplifies the ideal of interdependency and caretaking across the generations. It explores the mutual responsibilities of family members in general and the relationship between the elder and younger generations in particular. The relationship between mother-in-law and daughter-in-law is exemplified in the support, nurture and comfort of Naomi and Ruth for each other.

The dynamics between the members of the family is summarized by Dulin (1982):

Just as the old nurtured and cared for the young, so were the young expected to support and provide a dignified life for the old. . . . The old were an integral part of these dynamics. They assured proper transmission of property to their children, and taught and cared for the young to assure the proper transmission of tradition and law. (83–84)

"Parents . . . had to provide for the children, protect them and teach them (Lev. 19:29; Deut. 6:20–25; 8:5; 11:19–21). The children . . . were required to respect and obey their parents (Exod. 20:121; 21:15,17; Lev. 20:9; Deut. 5:16; 21:18020; Prov. 23:22) as well as to help them in the family work (Gen. 24:15; 29:6; 37:12; 1 Sam. 9:11; 17:15)" (Dulin 1982:72). According to Jewish law, it is the responsibility of older people to transmit Torah and life teachings (*veshinamtam levanecha*—"you shall teach these commandments to your children"), and it is also the responsibility of the younger generation to learn. These various roles and obligations are discussed by Linzer (1986).

At the same time, the limits of children's responsibilities for their parents are also acknowledged by Jewish tradition. In the *Code of Maimonides* we find the following:

If the mind of his father or his mother is affected, the son should make every effort to indulge the vagaries of the stricken parent until G-d will have mercy on the afflicted.

But if the condition of the parent has grown worse, and the son is no longer able to endure the strain, he may leave his father or mother, go elsewhere, and delegate to others to give the parent proper care. ("Laws Concerning Rebels," ch. 6, Halacha 10).

While the adult child was exempt from performing the physical aspects of care, he or she remained responsible for arranging care for the parent by others, and was still required to respect the parent (Gutmann 1990:275).

A good example of the balance between requiring respect and allowing for self-preservation is found in a responsum of Rabbi Meir that deals with material care for a widowed mother. When asked whether a widow could demand support from her three sons, Rabbi Meir de Baruch of Rothenberg answered that "children are obligated to support their widowed mother only out of the possessions they inherited from their father. . . . Therefore, any son who would himself be thrown upon charity were he forced to support his mother cannot be forced to do so." He then goes on to reassert the importance of proper respect, saying, "But those sons who have means should support their mother in proportion to their wealth" (Meir de Baruch of Rothenburg, *Responsa,* "Yoreh De'ah," no. 197). The talmudic sources speak of the expectations for continued care of widows. As summarized by Patai (1977:484–85):

When Rabbi Y'huda the Prince codified the Mishna (c. A.D. 200), he included in it precise instructions as to how children must honor their mother after the death of the *pater familias:* she must be assured the same living conditions which she enjoyed while her husband was alive, and not even the slightest change must be introduced into her circumstances. (M Ket 12:3, quoted in Patai 1977)

There is strong emphasis in the Hebrew Scriptures and Jewish tradition on the wisdom of the elders and the importance of learning from and respecting them on that basis. As the Midrashic dictum goes, "One who takes counsel with the old will not falter" (Midrash Rabbah, Exodus 3). In fact, the Hebrew word for old, *zaken,* is thought to possibly be an acronym for the words *Ze She' kanah Hokhmah*—"he who has acquired wisdom" (Blech 1977:71). The aged command respect "because their conversance with the facts of life and the workings of nature were assumed to have refined their wisdom and their common sense" (Smolar 1985:5). Even when the elders forgot what they knew, they were to be kept secure within the "frame of life" of the family and community. As the Talmud teaches, "We must be careful with an old man who has forgotten his learning because of his incapacity, so as not to shame him, and to treat him with dignity. For were not the broken tablets placed side by side with the whole ones in the Ark [of the Covenant]?" (Sanhedrin 96b; Berakhot 10a).

Despite all this stated positive regard for the aged, the frailty and physical decline of old age were always feared (Gutmann 1990:275). This fear is evident in the plea: "Do not cast me off in old age; when my strength fails, do not forsake me" (Ps. 71:9). The physical deterioration and emotional depression that often accompanied old age were recognized throughout the Bible. One of the most powerful descriptions is from the book of Ecclesiastes (12: 1–7). The author uses metaphors to describe the various parts of the body: "The guards of the house" are the arms; "men of valor," the legs; "maids that grind," the teeth; "ladies that peer through the windows," the eyes; and the "doors to the street," the ears.

> So appreciate your vigor in the days of your youth, before
> those days of sorrow come and those years arrive of
> which you will say, "I have no pleasure in them";
> before sun and light and moon and stars grow dark,
> and the clouds come back again after the rain:
> When the guards of the house become shaky,
> And the men of valor are bent,
> And the maids that grind, grown few, are idle,
> And the ladies that peer through the windows grow dim,
> And the doors to the street are shut
> With the noise of the hand mill growing fainter,
> And the song of the bird growing feebler,
> And all the strains of music dying down;
> When one is afraid of heights
> And there is terror on the road. . . .
> Before the silver cord snaps
> And the golden bowl crashes,
> The jar is shattered at the spring,
> And the jug is smashed at the cistern.
> And the dust returns to the ground
> As it was,
> And the lifebreath returns to G-d
> Who bestowed it. (Ecc. 12:1–7)

Under certain conditions and for some individuals, old age was seen as a "true blessing. It was considered as an ideal age [if] . . . the old person not only lived to old age, but also attained the blessing of a family, wealth, honor and respect" (Dulin 1982:128). It is within the framework of these traditional writings and beliefs that we can understand the aging experience of Jewish women in America today.

FAMILY RESPONSIBILITIES AND ROLES

Leo Simmons in his early examination of the role of the aged in seventy-one nonindustrial societies, observes that "throughout human history the family has been the safest haven for the aged. Its ties have been the most intimate and long-lasting, and on them the aged have relied for greatest security" (1945:176). Growing old as a Jewish woman means aging within the family. "The Jewish people are sustained by the strength of the families, and by the values that are learned within them" (Reuben 1987:122). The aging Jewish woman generally performs a range of roles within the family, including mother, grandmother, spouse and widow. The way these roles are enacted by a particular aging Jewish woman within her family and community will be affected by her stage of life and health, as well as the dynamics of her particular family system. For example, the extent of assistance and support that she is able to give and receive will vary based on her health and economic status.

Motherhood in Old Age

A central role of the Jewish woman is generally that of mother. What "counted" for the elderly Jews that Barbara Myerhoff (1978) studied as they reviewed their accomplishments was

above all the rearing of children who were well-educated, well-married, good citizens, good parents in their own right, children who considered themselves Jews and raised their children as Jews, and who respected their elderly parents. . . . The old women had the deck stacked in their favor. Nearly always they had maintained closer ties with their children than the men, and fairly or not, it was they who were considered most responsible for "how the children turned out." (266)

Much of what has been written about Jewish mothers has been the creation of American Jewish writing. We can begin by looking at the classic Jewish mother joke: How many Jewish mothers does it take to change a lightbulb? Answer: None. "That's okay, I'll just sit here in the dark." This is analyzed by Susan Schneider (1985) in terms of the realities on which the stereotypes were based: "the self-sacrifice of the mother who did without in order to feed her children, . . . or the mother's concerns for her children's safety during sieges, pogroms, and famines" (269). Expression of the same behavior in different circumstances in the United States is no longer as appropriate. Suppression of her own needs and desires in "less-straitened circumstances" gives us the lightbulb joke. The novelist E. M. Broner describes a generation of Jewish mothers living "a life of nurturing, of feeding others and starving one's self" (Davidson & Broner 1980:191).

The situation should be viewed in light of the adaptations required by changing expectations after immigration to America. Jewish women in Eastern Europe had shared responsibilities with their husbands in family and community life. They had helped support the family and make decisions. Women now relegated to the home in America "put the same energies into the raising of children that previously had gone into paid labor *plus* home responsibilities" (Schneider 1985:270).

There are important differences between mother-son and mother-daughter relationships. The old Jewish proverb, "A son's a son till he takes him a wife. A daughter's a daughter the rest of her life," suggests different expectations for the relationship with daughters and sons. The relationship with sons is based on nurturing and "mothering." The emphasis is humorously portrayed by Jewish poet Heinrich Heine in his *Germany: A Winter's Tale* (1944) describing how his mother received him when he visited after an absence of thirteen years. She questioned whether he was fatter or thinner and exclaimed that after thirteen years he must be hungry: "Now, what would you like for dinner?"[5]

The Middle Eastern Jewish women who were interviewed by Susan Starr Sered (1989) reported "that it is better to have daughters because daughters have more mercy and compassion than do sons, and daughters care if their elderly mothers are sick or unhappy" (317). Stated in another way, women—both as daughters and as mothers—are seen as the keepers of the family, the caregivers and transmitters of tradition. Closer relationships are thus more likely to be maintained with the mother's family. This is documented by Doris Francis (1984) from her comparative study of Jewish elderly in Cleveland, Ohio, and Leeds, England. The families of the American Jews had stronger ties while in Europe with maternal family, and this continued in America. The relationships of women and their mothers is clearly complicated by the fact that the daughters will be expected to fulfill the same roles as their mothers.

"Mutuality, interdependence and positive connection" are reported to characterize the Jewish mother-daughter relationship in later life (Bromberg 1983). This emotional closeness was also found in the family structures of the Slavic and Italian women in a comparative study (Krause 1978). But the Jewish women tended to seek geographic separation, not living in the same household or neighborhood as their mothers. They expressed both feelings of closeness and a striving for independence. An important theme that flows through the literature on American Jews in general and on the Jewish elderly in particular is "the constant tension between obligation and independence. . . . The conflict between the desire for individuality and the obligation to family is not easily resolved" (Sanua 1981; Weintraub 1985, cited in Glicksman 1991). That tension is certainly played out among mothers and daughters. In addition, significant lifestyle differences between adult Jewish daughters of the 1980s and 1990s and their mothers have created a veritable "tradition of change" over the past three generations. In particular, as Jewish women postpone childbearing or don't have children at all, the pattern of the daughters' lives differs radically from that of their mothers and grandmothers, and the reconciliation between the generations that typically occurs with the birth of the first grandchild now occurs much later, if at all (Schneider 1985:276–277).

Caregiving

What does this mean for the relationship of adult Jewish daughters and their mothers in illness and when they require care? It is a common fear of elders in our society "not to be a burden." Bart discusses the phenomenon of older Jewish parents who live frugally in order to save money to use if they should become ill or disabled. She comments that these parents are reluctant to be in need of help from their children for fear of putting the relationship "to the test which it may not survive" (1967). It is commonly recognized that in our society, women have typically been the ones responsible for care of their aging parents as daughters or daughters-in-law. We noted above that the Jewish tradition both enjoins children to care for their parents and sets limits on these obligations. It is the clear limits of these obligations which appear to be uniquely Jewish.

Adult daughters, often caught between the pressures of caring for their children and their aging parents, have been called "the sandwich generation." Bart and other researchers on the Jewish family suggest that Jewish women are more devoted to their children than to their parents (Bart 1967). As we have seen above, while the adult child was exempt from performing the physical aspects of care, he or she remained responsible for arranging care for the parent by others, and was still required to respect the parent (Gutmann 1990:275). There has in fact been a long history of nursing homes and formal social services for the Jewish aged in America. Jewish communities generally developed formal services to meet the basic needs of older members of the community because it was recognized that these needs could not be met by the family without support. This approach is notably different from the pattern for the dominant American society, and the limits for expectations of care for the elderly are not as clearly defined in the dominant American society.

Grandmotherhood

The strength of the extended family within the ideal Jewish tradition carries over to the recognition of grandchildren as a blessing in old age. This is demonstrated in the following proverbs: "To be old and to live to see children and grandchildren was indeed a gift from G-d" (Prov. 17:6) and "Grandchildren are the crown of their elders" (Prov. 17:6). Grandchildren in fact, inherited the responsibilities of their parents to care for their grandparents in their old age.

Although grandparents are "peripheral to the day-to-day business of living" (Monk 1987:158), the relationship is often an important one to Jewish grandmothers and their grandchildren. The role of Jewish grandmother is an important one in a tradition where "roots" and a link to the future are sought within the family. "In addition to radiating and receiving unconditional love, grandparents often provide a 'safety net' during times of family transition or stress" (Isaacs 1987:87). The collection of poetry written by "Shayneh Maidelehs" (beautiful children) for their Jewish grandmothers focuses on several themes: storytelling (that is, recounting family history and roots), food, love, trust and warm relationships (Newman 1989). Another example is the recent collection of Jewish folk tales entitled *My Grandmother's Stories*. This collection uses the context of a young girl visiting her grandmother as the format for the telling of stories rooted in the grandmother's Russian Jewish heritage (Geras 1990).

How has this traditional relationship of grandmother and grandchild been adapted by American Jewish families? Abraham Monk characterized the Jewish grandparental functions in American society within five styles. The functions include (1) head of the family and (2) transmitter of family history and values:

There are several others which are increasing in frequency. The funseeker relaxes strict parental codes of behavior and indulges the grandchild. The surrogate parent takes over in situations where the mother works, is divorced or incapacitated. The distant grandparent visits infrequently, bringing presents and often maintaining a relationship over the telephone. (1985:5)

While we have been viewing Jewish identity as a source of continuity in the lives of the Jewish elderly, as Glicksman points out: "A strong Jewish identity . . . is not always a buttress against the problems of old age. If children and grandchildren are highly assimilated or intermarried, a strong sense of Jewish identity can cause pain and rifts among the three generations. This again is part of the struggle to balance both Jewish and American values" (Glicksman 1991:23).

Late-Life Marriages and Widowhood

The marital relationship of most Jewish couples is purported to be more equal than the American norm and based on a "partnership model." In a study of Jewish wives based on anecdotal interviews (Schwartz and Wyden 1969), one of the recurring themes was that husbands and wives used each other as sounding boards, often discussed business or professional problems with each other, and appeared to be more supportive of each other in many ways than non-Jewish couples. By contrast, "while Jewish women expect that their husbands will be their best friends, in 'ethnic,' non-Jewish working-class families women expect to have a network of women friends and most often do not expect friendship from their husbands" (Schneider 1985:329).

What is the nature of these marital relationships in old age? "Studies on the marital quality of such (long-lived) marriages tend to fall into groups; those that find a trend toward progressive devitalization with age and those that point to alternating cycles of marital satisfaction" (Monk 1987:154).

A Jewish woman whose spouse dies must face the same changes and adjustments that all widows face. But the experience of becoming a widow must be viewed within the cultural context and value system we have been discussing. Robin Siegel, a social worker who has studied Jewish widows suggests that "the very values which foster and promote Jewish family life are the same values which cause the widow's transition period to be that much more difficult" (quoted in Schneider 1985). One of the women Siegel interviewed describes her feelings in the following way:

I would like to remarry, but I'm skeptical. I would like to because I'm used to being a pair and sharing. To me life is nothing if you don't share it with someone. . . . I'm not afraid of living *by* myself, I'm afraid of living *for* myself. I have never lived just thinking of me; I'm always used to thinking of someone else. Buying something that someone else likes, and cooking something that someone else likes. In the widow's group they taught us to do things FOR ME, but I'm not that kind of person. (Quoted in Schneider 1985:408–9.)

The experience of widowhood is clearly different for Jewish women and men. "Unlike a man whose spouse dies, a woman faces loss of caste status, loss of financial or class status, and a regrouping of friendships or a change in friendship patterns as she ends up spending time with other widows" (Schneider 1985:41). In contrast, on a recent visit to a retirement community in Florida, the author was told about the "casserole brigade" who come out in force when an older man is left alone.

While religious beliefs are often reported by widows to provide strength and support through this difficult transition, "bereaved Jewish women are much less likely than men in the same position to seek solace from (formal) religious observance. . . . Since in Judaism both ritual leadership and ritual participation have been male activities, Jewish widows often feel that they have no meaningful connection to religious life without men" (Schneider 1985:410). Therefore, the formal religious structure to which widows often turn for support through the grieving process does not provide the same support for Jewish widows. The formal stages of grieving and the ritual prayers cannot provide support for widows who do not feel "at home" in the synagogue or temple.

Thus, the experience of widowhood for older Jewish women must be understood within the context of Jewish tradition and values as they are experienced in the United States. The adjustment to widowhood for the Jewish woman is commonly experienced within the context of the family, rather than the larger formal religious community.

CONCLUSIONS

The ideal Jewish traditions as presented in biblical and talmudic teachings provide the backdrop for adjustment to old age within the Jewish family and community. These religious traditions can provide a thread of continuity in the life of the older Jewish woman. These traditional values can also lead to issues and conflicts due to the diversity within the Jewish community and changes that are occurring from one generation to the next.

While many American Jews do not seriously study religious traditions, religious knowledge is commonly passed on informally by parents and grandparents within the context of the Jewish family. These shared religious traditions include respect for the wisdom of the aged, and the expectations and limits of responsibilities to one's children and parents. It is most notably the limits financially and physically that differentiate the Jewish traditional expectations of care for one's aging parents. While Jewish children and grandchildren are expected to provide care and support for their aging parents and grandparents, their obligations to their own children are primary. These limits of responsibility towards one's aging parents are perhaps the most important and unique aspect of the traditional framework and expectations.

Let us look again at the three dilemmas identified in the introduction. The strong value placed on education and "success" leads to minimal tensions in regard to closeness of family for Jewish older women. The value of "success" is primary. While adult children are not typically available to provide daily care, elderly Jewish parents do not expect their children to forgo career opportunities in order to remain geographically close to their parents. The parents' pride in their children's success is their reward and the family remains close within the framework of limited responsibilities. Second, the ideal relationship between a Jewish daughter and her aging mother is discussed throughout this chapter. The ideals and reality are also addressed although they need to be more fully explored through empirical research. Finally, the differences between Jewish parents and their children and the simultaneous expectation of continuity of roles should also be studied through further empirical research. While there is of course continuous change, there is also apparently continuity of Jewish traditions and values passed on from grandmother and mother to daughter.

It is within the context of these values and expectations, in conjunction with general American values, that the process of aging is experienced by aging Jewish women in the United States today. Perhaps most importantly, a perspective informed by traditional Jewish views on old age helps us to see this time as the final stage of the life cycle, rather than a deterioration toward death.

NOTES

1. See Blidstein (1975, Introduction:xiii–iv) for a discussion of two possible misapprehensions that address this relationship between "the unique quality of each relationship and . . . generalized rules." The two warnings are first, while there is apparently a wealth of guidelines and norms presented, there is actually a paucity of materials on the topic in the traditional literature. Second, "it should be obvious that a survey of normative materials on an aspect of the family does not presume to capture the family as a lived experience."

2. See Gutmann 1990 for a comprehensive discussion of the diversity within the older Jewish population.

3. See also Lev. 19:3, where the Children of Israel are commanded to fear their mothers and fathers. The Hebrew word for "fear" refers to a commandment requiring respect, rather than truly "fear" as in the English usage, which means to be afraid.

4. These are about Rabbi Tarfon (Jerusalem Talmud, *Kiddushin,* chapter 1, paragraph 7), Rabbi Ben Natinah (Jerusalem Talmud, Peah 81) and Rabbi Joseph who: "When [he] heard his mother's footsteps . . . would say, 'I will rise before the approaching *Shekinah'* (Divine Presence)" (Babylonian Talmud, *Kiddushin,* p. 31b).

5. Quoted by Theodor Reik, 1962. *Jewish Wit.* New York: Gamut Press, p. 83, as quoted by Patai (1977). English translation of Heine by Herman Salinger, New York.

REFERENCES

Bart, Pauline. 1967. Depression in aged women: Some sociocultural factors. Ph.D. diss., UCLA.

Blech, Benjamin. 1977. Judaism and gerontology. *Tradition* 16(4), 62–78.

Blidstein, Gerald. 1975. *Honor thy father and mother—Filial responsibility in Jewish law and ethics*. New York: KTAV Publishing House.

Bromberg, Eleanor Mallach. 1983. Mother-daughter relationships in later life: The effect of quality of relationship upon mutual aid. *Journal of Gerontological Social Work* 6(1), 75–92.

Climo, Jacob. 1990. Transmitting ethnic identity through oral narratives. *Ethnic Groups* 8, 163–79.

Davidson, Cathy N., and E. M. Broner, eds. 1980. *The lost tradition: Mothers and daughters in literature*. New York: Frederick Ungar.

Dulin, Rachel Zohar. 1982. *Old age in the Hebrew scriptures: A phenomenological study*. Ann Arbor: University Microfilms.

Francis, Doris. 1984. *Will you still need me, will you still feed me, when I'm 84?* Bloomington: Indiana University Press.

Gelfand, Donald E., and Charles M. Berresi, eds. 1987. *Ethnic dimensions of aging*. New York: Springer.

Geras, Adele. 1990. *My grandmother's stories—A collection of Jewish folk tales*. New York: Alfred A. Knopf.

Glicksman, Allen. 1991. *The new Jewish elderly—A literature review*. New York: The American Jewish Committee.

Gutmann, David. 1990. Caring for the frail Jewish aged—Myth and reality. *The Journal of Aging and Judaism* 4(4), 271–87.

Isaacs, Leora. 1987. Intergenerational families. *Journal of Aging and Judaism* 2(2), 84–93.

Joffe, Natalie F. 1949. The dynamics of beneficence among Eastern European Jews. *Social Forces* 29, 238–47.

Kaufman, Sharon. 1986. *The ageless self, sources of meaning in late life*. Madison: University of Wisconsin Press.

Klagsbrun, Francine. 1980. *Voices of wisdom*. New York: Jonathan David Publishers.

Krause, Corinne Azen. 1978. *Grandmothers, mothers and daughters: An oral history study of ethnicity, mental health, and continuity of three generations of Jewish, Italian, and Slavic-American women*. New York: American Jewish Committee.

Linzer, Norman. 1986. The obligations of adult children to aged parents: A view from Jewish tradition. *Journal of Aging and Judaism* 1(1), 34–48.

Luborsky, Mark, and Robert Rubinstein. 1987. Ethnicity and lifetimes: Self concepts and situation contexts of ethnic identity in late life. In Gelfand, Donald, and Charles M. Beresi, eds., *Ethnic dimensions of aging*. New York: Springer.

Monk, Abraham. 1985. Response. In *Jewish grandparenting and the intergenerational connection: summary of proceedings*, 5–6. New York: American Jewish Committee.

———. 1987. The "new" and the "young" aged. *Journal of Aging and Judaism* 1(2), 146–65.

Moskowitz, Faye. 1991. *And the bridge is love*. Boston: Beacon Press.

Myerhoff, Barbara. 1978. *Number our days.* New York: E. P. Dutton.

Myerhoff, Barbara, and Andrei Simic, eds. 1977. *Life's career-aging: Cultural variations in growing old.* Beverly Hills: Sage Publications.

Newman, Leslea, ed. 1989. *Bubbe Meisehs by Shayneh Maidelehs—An anthology of poetry by Jewish granddaughters about our grandmothers.* Santa Cruz, CA: HerBooks.

Patai, Raphael. 1977. *The Jewish mind.* New York: Charles Scribner's Sons.

Reuben, Steven C. 1987. Old age: Appearance and reality. *Journal of Aging and Judaism* 2(2), 117–22.

Rich, Adrienne. 1977. *Of woman born: Motherhood as experience and institution.* New York: Bantam.

Sanua, V. D. 1981. Psychopathology and social deviance among Jews. *Journal of Jewish Communal Service* 58(1), 12–23.

Schneider, Susan Weidman. 1985. *Jewish and female—Choices and changes in our lives today.* New York: Simon and Schuster.

Schwartz, Gwen Gibson, and Barbara Wyden. 1969. *The Jewish wife.* New York: P. H. Wyden.

Sered, Susan Starr. 1989. The religion of relating: Kinship and spirituality among Middle Eastern Jewish women in Jerusalem. *Journal of Social and Personal Relationships* 6, 309–25.

Simmons, Leo. 1945. *The role of the aged in primitive society.* New Haven: Yale University Press.

Smolar, Leivy. 1985. Context and text: Realities and Jewish perspectives on the aged. Paper presented at annual meeting of the Conference of Jewish Communal Service, Baltimore, June 3.

Weintraub, Robin. 1985. Two systems of values among elderly Jewish Americans: Their manifestations in holidays, rituals, and everyday activity. Paper presented at the annual meeting of the American Anthropological Association, Washington, D.C.

IV Participant Observation

9 A Social Milieu for Spirituality in the Lives of Older Adults

Susan A. Eisenhandler

Literature is a repository of cultural imagery and meaning. Reading and discussing literature necessarily involves the evocation of self in relationship to others as the individual reader moves through the imaginative social world created by an author. Some of the others who create the social relations and context for reading include the fictional characters themselves, the people who read and discuss the work, and literary critics whose popular or scholarly commentary shows just how varied one's understanding of an imaginary world can be. Although research on creativity (Wilson 1986: 8) indicates that "The reading of literature is a type of experience to which social scientists have paid very little attention," reading is best understood, I would argue, as a wonderful example of a solitary, meaningful activity that draws heavily upon the individual's social ties to others and to her or his socialization within a culture in order for the activity to be completed. As the individual initiates and engages in the process of reading, the reader draws upon the collective imagery, meaning, and social history stored within the symbol system of language. Thus reading is an intrinsically social form of interaction; it is an active social encounter with others and with the encompassing culture.

This paper describes some of the spiritual themes which emerged in two classes that were part of a series of weekly reading and discussion groups designed for older adults. The spiritual content of the group's discussions suggests that some secular literary sources contained sufficient thematic content and dramatic tension to provide the imaginative and real social experiences that led to deliberate reflection. For instance, two short stories read and discussed by these older adults provided insight into what was valuable and meaningful to them and what they hoped they were leaving as a social and ethical legacy to their friends and to younger generations. The activity of reading gave older adults a chance to take some steps on a spiritual journey that moved them beyond the daily concerns of living to a place where questions about the enduring values of life as well as questions about justice and fairness could be raised. Secular sources were the basis of our reading, but the activity of reading was treated by these older adults as a special kind of experience, a much anticipated activity that brought them out of themselves, closer to others and to spiritual concerns.

THE SOCIAL SIGNIFICANCE OF LITERACY AND SPIRITUALITY

Although there is evidence that television has as strong a following among the elderly as it does among younger age groups (Moss and Lawton 1982), it is also true that reading is a highly valued activity for many older adults. As some research has suggested (Myerhoff 1978), the printed word may be honored differentially among groups of the elderly. That is to say, the cultural, historical and religious development of some groups has instilled a deeply felt appreciation for the written word even among those group members who may have had little formal training or education in reading and writing. Myerhoff's research suggests that oral and written language allow the elderly to sustain the symbolism that is central to individual and collective narratives concerning the meaning of life. Indeed, it is this fluency in language, and in some sense, faith in language, that enabled many of the elderly Jews of Venice, California, to achieve an equilibrium, to "manage ideological complexity" and to integrate real contradictions in living confronted in late adulthood (Myerhoff 1978: 218–219). This capacity to think, reflect and to give expression to one's present and past permitted these elderly to age well despite their poverty, attenuated family relationships and increasingly confined social world.

For Myerhoff the crucial process involved in successful aging is one of acculturation to a group that offers what she called "dynamic" opportunities for integration and continuity of self. One might say that the elders she observed were able to make myths—to continue to impart substance and meaning to their lives. The continuous construction of meaning and the debate about the nature of what made life meaningful provided social cohesion for the group and ego integrity for the individual. As one elderly woman in Myerhoff's study put it, "We fight to keep warm." Debate and dialogue brought the elders together, and as Myerhoff noted, it made people invisible to the larger social world visible to each other.

The kind of social solidarity and support that emanated in part from the value and respect placed upon literacy by the elderly Jews, is in stark contrast to the social settings of British public libraries described many years ago by Richard

Hoggart in *The Uses of Literacy* (1958). Hoggart's evocative and exhaustive analysis of the impact of mass literacy on working class life offers a different portrait of elderly readers. Hoggart observed that "old men who fill the reading rooms of the branch public libraries," are lonely and isolated, yet they seek "a sense of home and neighborhood" in the reading rooms. "This is the special refuge of the misfits and left-overs, of the hollow-cheeked, watery-eyed, shabby, and furtively sad. . . . A few make for one of the items of sect-journalism and resume their endless cult-reading . . . some turn leaves aimlessly or stare blankly for ten minutes at one page"(69).

Hoggart points out that the group ties and oral traditions characteristic of working-class literacy cannot be sustained among the elderly men who take refuge in these reading rooms. "After a while the atmosphere is so depressing that you begin to think that NO AUDIBLE CONVERSATIONS ALLOWED is an instance of warm-heartedness in the midst of officialdom, a sensible allowance for the fact that so many regulars talk to themselves" (Hoggart 1958: 69-70). In this case, a setting expressly intent on fostering intellectual, social and spiritual growth does not readily achieve those ends because bureaucratic constraints dominate interaction and stifle the possibility of growth.

The full expression and value of literacy is found in settings and social relations which engage both individual and group in purposive and longstanding discussion of ideas and meaning. This kind of social interaction may also be conducive to the discovery of "symbolic immortality." Symbolic immortality is defined by Lifton and Olson (1974:59–60) as the "psychological process of creating meaningful images." They add that engagement in this process of creating meaning establishes a sense of connection to time and to others. These connections move the person beyond the realm of individual concerns.

Participation in this process evokes transcendent meaning and the possibility of further transformation and development of self and identity. Lifton and Olson suggest that the transcendent quality of human life finds expression in a quintet of ways: the individual may come to understand his or her biological, creative, theological, natural or experiential immortality. The social-psychological significance of these forms of symbolic immortality is that "feeling moments of experiential transcendence or a strong sense of relation to one of the other modes of symbolic immortality enables one to affirm the continuity of life without denying death" (1974:71).

Such an affirmation of life is part of what Erikson (1963) alludes to in his discussion of ego integrity in late life. Understanding the integrated meaning of one's life is the only effective foil against the fragmentation of meaning, the despair, that one faces when confronted with the death of self, which is a part of each person's life. Indeed, Coles (1990) has written that working up such an integrated moral vision is a regular feature in some children's lives. "The task for those boys and girls is to weave together a particular version of a morality both personal and yet tied to a religious tradition, and then (the essence of the spiritual life) ponder their moral successes and failures and, consequently, their prospects as human beings who will someday die" (Coles 1990: 109). Among older adults, the search for settings and methods that foster ego integrity and symbolic immortality has renewed interest in the process of life review first elaborated by Butler (1963). Various offshoots of life review such as poetry groups (Lyman and Edwards 1989) and guided autobiography (Birren and Deutchman 1991) are the kinds of group experiences that make the discovery of meaning their focal point.

At the most general theoretical level, spirituality is often associated with the idea of transcendence; a spiritual experience or set of experiences is understood to transform the individual's relationship to God or to a divine force and to intensify the person's engagement with life by deepening an appreciation for its struggles and joys. Implicit in this conception is the notion that heightened spirituality and explorations in spirtuality, as well as spiritual encounters themselves, change the person's awareness and understanding of self and of others. As the illustrative quotations below suggest, even among those most fully immersed in particular religious traditions, spirituality is often acknowledged to be something that cannot be completely captured in intellectual terms or by the discipline of contemplative life. For example, Thomas Merton defines spirituality as a way of living that goes far beyond the realm of thought.

Spiritual life is not mental life. It is not thought alone. . . . It is not just a life concentrated at the "high point" of the soul, a life from which the mind and the imagination and the body are excluded. If it were so few people could lead it. And again, if that were the spiritual life, it would not be a life at all. If man is to live, he must be all alive, body, soul, mind, heart, spirit. Everything must be elevated and transformed by the action of God, in love and faith. (Merton 1958: 27)

The spiritual life is first of all a *life*. (Merton 1958: 46; emphasis Merton's)

This understanding of spirituality is echoed and expanded in recent works on feminist spirituality. As FitzGerald (1986: 287) points out, "Today our spirituality is rooted in experience and in story: the experience and story of women . . . the experience of the poor and the oppressed of the world; the experience of aging." The social wrapping that surrounds spirituality is also recognized by Carr (1986).

Spirituality is deeply informed by family, teachers, friends, community, class, race, culture, sex, and by our time in history. . . . As a style of response, spirituality is individually patterned yet culturally shaped. Implicit metaphors, images, or stories drawn from our culture are embodied in a particular spiritual style. (50)

Other works on feminist spirituality such as Gray (1988) and Anderson and Hopkins (1991) emphasize that "Women's renaming of the sacred is . . . life-affirming rather than life-separating or life-distancing. Our naming of what is sacred finds meaning in things that have never before been found important, much less sacred.'' (Gray 1988:2) This emphasis on the transcendent in real life is a central theme for the women interviewed by Anderson and Hopkins (1991:120–121). ''Underneath the question of whether spiritual life is easy or difficult, far deeper than that question is the truth of how a woman actually lives her life. The important issue, one woman told us, is not how to develop spiritually but how to live authentically.'' Putting aside the presumptive factor of gender for another time, it is clear that each of the definitions above features a spirituality that is embodied in daily human concerns. This may not have been what William Sloan Coffin originally had in mind when he spoke about faith as ''passion for the possible,'' but his phrase neatly captures a common thread in the meaning of spirituality.

In the Judeo-Christian tradition, spirituality may be discovered and practiced within the context of everyday life. For example, as Kegan (1980:438) notes in an acknowledgment of Buber's work ''The Hasidic vision testifies to a sacredness in the everyday, a spirituality to be found in the concrete world.'' It is this concrete aspect of spirituality which emerges in group discussions of literature when questions are raised about justice, love and the meaning and purpose of living.

In the present analysis, spirituality is best understood as an experience with meaning, an active engagement with ''symbolic immortality,'' that takes the individual beyond a narrow band of self-interested concerns. Incipient spiritual experiences can be found in social contexts that promote the value of literacy and in social contexts that create, however ephemerally, the group cohesion and living culture that enables individuals to probe meaning. These ''social attachments'' are a requisite condition of moral education (Durkheim 1961) for the old as well as the young. Reading groups for older adults bring people together and out of themselves. In this way, reading groups encourage reflection and deliberation of spiritual concerns.

This social milieu conducive to spiritual exploration and development exists within a larger macro-organizational framework whose central features, modernization and urbanization, have had a dramatic impact on the lives of the aged and the social value placed upon their lives. For example, Gutmann (1987) sounds a warning about the effects of ''deculturation'' and ''demythification.'' Part of the process of ''deculturation'' is that ''as the aged lose their cosmic connection, they also lose the power to control the cultural imagery in their favor'' (Gutmann 1987: 240).

In sum, deculturation and the weakening of the extended family have major effects that particularly disadvantage the aged. They lose their special developmental milieus, they lose their special bases for self-esteem, and—as a secularized culture loses its power to ensure civil behavior and to control the grosser manifestations of narcissism and rage— the aged lose their traditional character as hero, and take on their modern character, as victim. The weak face of aging appears. (Gutmann 1987: 251)

Like other low status groups (such as women or particular religio-ethnic mi-
norities) in our society, the elderly may only be able to rise to higher, nonstig-
matized status among those who are similar to them. The marginalization of
some groups and individuals by dominant groups insures that marginalized voices
are heard in small contexts rather than in larger, mainstream ones. In addition,
as Gutmann suggests, "special developmental milieus" are lost as the transformation from gemeinschaft to gesellschaft and the shift from personal to bureau-
cratized social relationships becomes the organizational framework for day to
day life. The simultaneous movement away from religiously informed epistemology to secular or scientifically informed epistemology further weakens the
moral authority that was the traditional basis for values and norms that endorsed
longevity and eldership (Fischer 1978).

Yet it is possible that remnants of "developmental milieus" exist (Myerhoff's
community is one example) and are thriving in the various "urban villages"
(Gans 1962) which shape the social basis of life within metropolitan areas. It is
also possible that functionally similar milieus may emerge in the niches of large-
scale social service and human service programs. In other words, innovative
"developmental milieus" may be unintentionally created in response to the social
forces that impel and sustain the marginalization of some groups like the elderly.
Such humanistic milieus personalize rather than depersonalize life and contribute
to human and social development by giving people the time and place to work
through the kinds of issues that open identity to change, transformation and
growth.

THE READING GROUP AS A SOCIAL MILIEU FOR
SPIRITUALITY

An example of a "developmental milieu" which makes it possible to raise
such issues was an education program offered through a grant from the Connecticut Humanities Council. The six-week series of classes entitled, "Images
of Aging," was open to older adults in the greater Waterbury, Connecticut,
area. A core group of ten older adults, eight women and two men, was joined
from time to time by two "floaters." In this short time the ten older adults who
continuously shared the reading and group discussion created a social setting
conducive to open dialogue and to certain kinds of intellectual experiences and
growth. Two of the most lively group discussions were ones where spiritual
concerns—questions about the meaning of life and the meaning and value of
old age—dominated.

Before delineating some aspects of spirituality that arose in response to reading,
a few characteristics of the group and its social setting need to be described. As
the teacher of the course on images of aging, I was able to observe and record
the questions and discussions that followed each reading the group completed.
The text used in the course was *Images of Aging in Literature,* published in
1977 by the National Council on Aging. This reader includes six short stories

as well as an extract from a play and a selection of poems. The class met for ninety minutes on Monday mornings in late winter to early spring of 1991.

It was surprising to me that the poetry selections did not stimulate spiritual discussion. However, two short stories educed spiritual concerns and themes. The stories were "A Worn Path" by Eudora Welty and "The Sudden Sixties" by Edna Ferber. Both stories are quiet and slow-paced. Both feature female protagonists who are familiar rather than exotic. One woman, Phoenix Jackson, is described by Welty as "an old Negro woman." The other, Hannah Winter, is introduced by Ferber with this epigram. "The old sob song used to say, 'She's somebody's mother.' Hannah Winter is anybody's mother."

The narrative of each story is built upon a challenge (one concrete, the other more intangible—involving social-psychological adaptation) that each woman faces in her old age. Each story poses dilemmas for which there are no "happy" endings. Hence, these fictional worlds with fictional problems seemed quite real. As one might find in the works of O. Henry and Saki, a bittersweet quality permeates the women's stories. This flavor as well as the realism of the issues does not permit much in the way of sentimental response from the reader.

The group of ten older adults who formed the core of this reading group ranged in age from sixty-seven to eighty-nine. The average age was seventy-three and the median age was seventy. All eight women and two men had completed high school. Four of the women had some college education. Only one, who had worked all of her life as a high school English teacher, had completed the baccalaureate.

Compared to a national sample of their contemporaries, this group was better educated (this makes sense because the course was purely voluntary and the group was formed as a consequence of self-selection). Nine had also participated in other educational programs (an average of ten such courses over the past five years, a median of five courses in five years) offered through the same organization (Older Adult Service and Information System—OASIS). Only one woman had never attended a course offered through OASIS. Clearly the group was well acquainted with the OASIS variation of classroom culture.

The only other important social characteristic that distinguished this group from its contemporaries was marital status. Given the average age of the group and its gender composition, one might expect that most members would share the status of widow. However, six of the ten (five women, one man) were married (two of these were second marriages). The other four (three women, one man) were single (three widowed, one divorced).

SPIRITUAL THEMES AND ISSUES THAT EMERGED IN DISCUSSION

The Necessary and the Joyful—Their Value and Difference in Life

To create Phoenix Jackson's tale Welty draws upon then extant patterns of racial and socioeconomic inequity in the rural South. The aged Phoenix embarks on a daylong journey from her home to the city to obtain a much needed medicine for her grandson. In the course of what would be a simple task for a younger woman, Phoenix's body betrays her and stymies her efforts to walk to the city. Because she falls and has to be set to rights by a young hunter, she has an opportunity to steal a nickel that falls from the hunter's pocket. She does not steal the nickel as revenge for his insult, " 'I know you old colored people! Wouldn't miss going to town to see Santa Claus.' " Nor does she do so without understanding what she has done, " 'God watching me the whole time. I come to stealing.' "

There is a higher principle involved in this theft as readers learn by the tale's end and after Welty paints a trenchant vignette of how demeaning Christian charity can be. After obtaining her grandson's medicine, completing her duty, Phoenix has ten pennies left in hand. She considers the sum and, " 'This is what come to me to do. . . . I going to the store and buy my child a little windmill they sells, made out of paper. He going to find it hard to believe there such a thing in the world.' "

The discussion that followed this reading was characteristic of what Kohlberg (1973) terms "postconventional thinking." Statements featured extensive commentary on the rightness of Phoenix's actions even though she violated several moral principles. The context of "embedded relations" (Gilligan 1982) also figured in talk about why Phoenix was right to steal and was right to use the stolen pennies and the donated pennies to buy a present. The group's initial emphasis on "moral reasoning" and the problems of old age and social injustice faced by Phoenix, gave way to observations, anecdotes and remarks, with everyone participating, about the value and meaning of money, health and of paper windmills—the toys that give children pleasure, but the toys which are by their very nature insubstantial.

This last idea generated a couple of issues that were seriously considered: (1) What should the older generation, grandparents in particular, pass on to younger generations and grandchildren regarding the things that give life meaning and purpose? and (2) What obligation and responsibility do older people have to other older people and to other younger people, to make their lives better (less of a hardship and happier)? I call these two queries spiritual because in order to answer them older adults considered and weighed events and experiences from their own lives. They were transported via the short story to an arena where "symbolic immortality" was a focus. The elderly group delineated the values they lived by and some of the values they hoped they had passed on to their children and grandchildren. Much of the discussion centered on the nature and meaning of a good life—a life where people do not have to steal as God watches them.

Phoenix's predicament was addressed in three ways by the group. The first theme, one which engendered reminiscence and several anecdotes, was the value of a nickel. As one woman observed, everyone in the group understood the times "when a nickel meant a lot." Everyone had shared the historical experience of knowing that "five pennies is a nickel" and knew why "the nickel meant so much to her [Phoenix]." The group's unanimous assessment went beyond understanding the theft: a second theme revolved around their feeling that Phoenix had been justified in taking the nickel from the hunter. "She lived for the little boy and that's what kept her going" was an initial response from one woman. Other group members added to this thought. Taking the nickel was acceptable "well, because that's what keeps her spirit going," "by that time [in the story] her body was weakened," "it was an uplifting thing for her," "she got more pleasure out of that [buying a toy] than using it for something she wanted herself."

The group gradually settled on the idea that the stolen nickel combined with a nickel of charity from another woman allowed Phoenix to "bring happiness [the toy] . . . more than bitterness" [the medicine] to her grandson. "She balanced it [her responsibilities to the child] well," one member concluded, and another added that Phoenix displayed "a sense of justice." "She was enjoying herself by buying something for a child—she was buying an impractical gift."

This discussion led into the third theme, the rightness of this decision despite Phoenix's admission that "God watching me all the time I come to this." The windmill, "the impractical gift," was good because it came from love and justice and created joy for the boy and the elderly grandmother. This spiritual insight was, ironically, the cause of much collective complaining about the lack of joy that modern toys brought to grandchildren, which is, of course, yet another kind of spiritual pondering.

Conflict between Family Needs and Individual Needs

The biographical details Ferber created for sixty-year-old Hannah Winter focus on Hannah's family relationships and the fact that at sixty she no longer recognizes who she is.

In her hurry and nervous apprehension she looked, as she scuttled down the narrow passage, very much like the Rabbit who was late for the Duchess's dinner. Her rubber-heeled oxfords were pounding down hard on the white marble pavement. Suddenly she saw coming swiftly toward her a woman who seemed strangely familiar—a well-dressed woman, harassed-looking—Hannah had just time to note, in a flash, that the woman's smart hat was slightly askew and that, though she walked very fast, her trim ankles showed the inflexibility of age, when she saw that the woman was not going to get out of her way. . . . Next instant Hannah Winter brought up with a crash against her own image.

Hannah's startling discovery of "this murderess who had just slain, ruthlessly and forever, a sallow, lively, high-spirited girl of twenty," prompts reverie and deliberation of what her life has meant and what will unfold in her future. Like Phoenix, Hannah has found meaning and self within familial relationships. Yet in contrast to Phoenix's experience, "life had tricked Hannah Winter." After running into the mirror Hannah attempts to rebel, to put her own interests and desires, dormant so long, ahead of her daughter's.

In reading and responding to this story, older adults were intensely empathetic (their responses were very personal, whereas the responses to Phoenix were also sympathetic but more distant) to Hannah's plight and her search for a way to treat herself and her family fairly. The spiritual concern here was for weighing and deliberating the older generation's need for opportunity, change and development against the need of the younger generation for care and services of what Hannah called a "second assistant nursemaid."

The group concluded that whereas Phoenix was compelled to care for her grandson, "it was not necessary for Hannah to do that." With one vocal exception, the group was infuriated and disappointed when Hannah "gave in" to her daughter's request that Hannah care for her grandson and granddaughter. As one woman said with the group's assent, although Hannah "decides to take care of the grandchildren to let her children enjoy themselves," she is not "making her own plans," but instead abdicates "her time" to a daughter whose attitude is "you have nothing to do; you can come care for your grandchildren." The selfishness of the daughter's request and Hannah's "giving in" was not "uplifting" to Hannah or inspiring to the group. Nine members of the group agreed that Hannah would "pay the price for it." The lone dissenter thought that it was fair for Hannah to recognize that her babysitting offered the daughter and son-in-law some chance to have a "good time." Group members were very disturbed about the outcome and several agreed with one woman who said, "I just would not put up with it." Three people took my suggestion to rewrite the ending to the story before our next class. The new endings all featured an assertive Hannah who said that her time was her own, that she wanted her independence and that Marcia could pay someone to babysit.

The story hit close to home on the issue of intergenerational equity. The unfairness of expecting older people to put their lives on hold or to sacrifice their needs to accommodate their children was a central, spiritual theme. It provided a stark dilemma that is not easily dismissed. What is the proper balance between an older person's need for growth and development and the need to respond to family responsibilities in a generative manner?

A question raised by one woman, "Did Hannah ever recognize the meaning of her life?" gets to the heart of what troubled the group about Hannah's old age. Ferber implies strongly that Hannah had the chance to uncover the meaning of her life in old age, but missed her opportunity to do so because she acceded to her daughter's needs. It was left to our dissident to point out that the grandchildren could have benefited from Hannah's self-sacrifice even though taking care of her grandchildren closed Hannah off from personal and spiritual development.

CONCLUSION

Both stories served as vehicles for the emergence of transcendent, and therefore, spiritual concerns. Discussions centered on the meaning and value of life, and the reason for living and for growing old in circumstances, personal and social, which do not enhance life and are often unremittingly harsh and unfair. Conspicuously absent from the discussions were overt references to institutionalized religions or programmatic theological interpretations. These two particular readings stimulated the kinds of responses that did not arise with respect to other readings. Perhaps this was an unlikely "developmental milieu," and one that only functioned to move older adults beyond sociability and bonhomie in two classes (one-third) out of six. Nevertheless, it represents the kind of bureaucratic milieu that is a routine feature of outreach programming for older adults and shows that there is much to be learned about what people take away from these experiences. It also hints at the problems "aging enterprises" perpetuate by underestimating the intellectual abilities and spiritual concerns of older adults, all of whom are deserving of being offered the kinds of activities which provide food for thought as well as food for the body.

Despite serious gaps in our knowledge about reading and our misreading of some lives and literature (Heilbrun 1988), the individual engaged in the interrelated process of reading, thinking and speaking about a written text uses a social milieu as well as biographical experience to interpret and make sense of a text and to understand his or her relationship to that material. Insights based upon reading and discussion open the individual to the possibility of intellectual, personal and social development. The dialogue that is engendered as a response to reading may also create a climate which is conducive to spiritual growth or at the very least to the consideration of spiritual issues. Indeed, it was the anonymous author of the fourteenth-century book devoted to spirituality and contemplation, *The Cloud of Unknowing,* who made the point that reading, thinking and praying are necessary for spiritual development. They are "helps" advisable for all.

Engagement by older adults in the kinds of reading groups described here does not guarantee that spiritual issues will emerge or prevail in discussion. The reading group does, however, establish a regular milieu for the consideration of spirituality and symbolic immortality—the meaning of an individual's life (here, particular fictional lives and upon reflection the member's own life) is probed from a larger perspective. Thus a few of the cosmic connections that suffuse individual lives are delineated and considered. In these small groups some of the powerful imagery and the special qualities of old age are reclaimed symbolically. As important as these groups may be for their members, reclaiming the cultural power of the elderly (Gutmann 1987) will succeed only if it is part of a larger societal effort that reiterates and actively promotes the intrinsic value of life at any age.

Societal support and concern for the value and meaning of life needs to be consolidated and articulated in institutional settings and public arenas. However, many observers have cautioned us about an opposite trend. For example, Moody has noted (1986: 12) that the search for meaning in late life has shifted ground from the search for whole meaning in a public sphere to the privatized search for "the meaning of my life." In addition, Bellah et al. (1991: 285) have

commented that "The impulse toward larger meaning, thankfulness, and celebration has to have an institutional form, like all the other central organizing
tendencies in our lives, so that we do not dissipate it in purely private sentiment."
The older adults described in this qualitative study were interested in moving
questions about meaning back to a public sphere where they could listen to other
perspectives and share their own ideas. Their attempt to locate themselves and
others as members of that public sphere through a class involving reading and
responding to literature is a shard of evidence that the quest for meaning is real.
Whether this kind of commitment is an epiphenomenon or is long-lived remains
to be seen.

As far as this group was concerned, each person was ready and willing to
take another class, as one woman put it, "just for the chance to think big and
talk strong again." These discussions invigorated and stimulated older people.
Similar programs may assist older adults in their continuing intellectual, social
and spiritual development by providing a regular setting for group interaction
and readings that require thought and reflection. I hope that educational programs
for the elderly will more consistently offer what the poet William Meredith
(1987: 107) has described as "hand-clapping lessons for the soul." The good
news is that we need only tax our imaginations as much as we tax our material
resources in order to encourage and nurture a social milieu for spirituality.

REFERENCES

Alvarez, R. A. F., and S. C. Kline, eds. 1978. *Images of aging in literature*. Washington,
    D.C.: National Council on the Aging.
Anderson, S. R., and P. Hopkins, 1991. *The feminine face of God: The unfolding of the
    sacred in women*. New York: Bantam Books.
Bellah, R. N., R. Madsen, W. M. Sullivan, A. Swidler, and S. Tipton. 1991. *The good
    society*. New York: Knopf.
Birren, J. E., and D. E. Deutchman. 1991. *Guiding autobiography groups for older
    adults*. Baltimore: Johns Hopkins University Press.
Butler, R. N. 1963. The life review: An interpretation of reminiscence in old age.
    Psychiatry 26, 65–76.
Carr, A. 1986. On feminist spirituality. In J. W. Conn, ed., *Women's spirituality:
    Resources for Christian development*, 49–58. New York: Paulist Press.
Coles, R. 1990. *The spiritual life of children*. Boston: Houghton Mifflin.
Durkheim, E. [1925] 1961. *Moral education*. New York: The Free Press.
Erikson, E. H. 1963. *Childhood and society*. 2d ed. New York: W. W. Norton.
Ferber, E. 1978. The sudden sixties. In R.A.F. Alvarez and S. C. Kline, eds., *Images
    of aging in literature*, 48–73. Washington, D.C.: The National Council on Aging.
Fischer, D. H. 1978. *Growing old in America*. New York: Oxford University Press.
FitzGerald, C. 1986. Impasse and dark night. In J. W. Conn, ed., *Women's spirituality:
    Resources for Christian development*, 287–311. New York: Paulist Press.
Gans, H. J. 1962. *The urban villagers: Group and class in the life of Italian-Americans*.
    New York: The Free Press.

Gilligan, C. 1982. *In a different voice: Psychological theory and women's development.* Cambridge: Harvard University Press.

Gray, E. D. 1988. Introduction. In E. D. Gray, ed., *Sacred dimensions of women's experience,* 2–5. Wellesley, Mass.: Roundtable Press.

Gutmann, D. 1987. *Reclaimed powers: Toward a new psychology of men and women in later life.* New York: Basic.

Heilbrun, C. G. 1988. *Writing a woman's life.* New York: W. W. Norton.

Hoggart, R. 1958. *The uses of literacy.* Middlesex, Eng.: Penguin.

Kegan, R. 1980. There the dance is: Religious dimensions of a developmental framework. In C. Brusselmans and J. A. O'Donohue, eds., *Toward moral and religious maturity,* 404–440. Morristown, N.J.: Silver Burdett.

Kohlberg, L. 1973. Stages and aging in moral development—Some speculations. *Gerontologist* 13, 497–502.

Lifton, R. J., and E. Olson. 1974. *Living and dying.* New York: Bantam.

Lyman, A. J., and M. E. Edwards. 1989. Poetry: Life review for frail American Indian elderly. *Journal of Gerontological Social Work* 14, 75–91.

Meredith, W. 1987. His plans for old age. In *Partial accounts: New and selected poems,* 107. New York: Knopf.

Merton, T. 1958. *Thoughts in solitude.* New York: Farrar, Straus and Giroux.

Moody, H. 1986. The meaning of life and old age. In T. R. Cole and S. A. Gadow, eds., *What does it mean to grow old?,* 11–40. Durham: Duke University Press.

Moss, M., and M. P. Lawton. 1982. Time budgets of older people: A window on four lifestyles. *Journal of Gerontology* 37, 115–23.

Myerhoff, B. 1978. *Number our days.* New York: Simon and Schuster.

Welty, E. 1978. A worn path. In R.A.F. Alvarez and S. C. Kline, eds., *Images of aging in literature,* 31–44. Washington, D.C.: The National Council on Aging.

Wilson, R. N. 1986. *Experiencing creativity: On the social psychology of art.* New Brunswick, N.J.: Transaction.

10 Life Narrative and Spiritual Journey of Elderly Male Religious

Edward J. Quinnan

Within a variety of religious traditions the elders of the community have frequently been accorded a position of preeminence. What accounts for the respect in which these individuals are held? To gain some insights into the relational and spiritual development of such elders, I undertook to study a group of elderly, celibate men who were members of a Roman Catholic religious community. A communal lifestyle offers an ideal setting in which to do participant observations. By conducting interviews I was able to explore participants' constructions of their lives and their use of religious themes to explain aspects of life and aging.

As a younger member of the same community I am an "insider." Yet, as someone three decades or more their junior, I am outside of the formative experiences of these men. They entered the community and became full, functioning members prior to the reforms of Vatican II. The men of this sample were socialized into a religious structure distinctly different from the rest of their cultures.

At the period in which these men entered (1924–1951) the monastic influence predominated, in distinction to the lifestyle of a parish priest. Therefore a rigid boundary existed between those entering religious life and the rest of society. All letters had to pass through the hands of the novice master, the religious superior in charge of the novitiate, or through a delegated censor. The novice master functioned as a gatekeeper, even deciding which members of the religious order would have access to the novices. The structure of the early years of religious formation effectively built a wall between these individuals and the outside. Within the walls of the novitiate the novices spoke Latin (an idiosyncratic form of Latin, at that). Even today these men make use of Latin phrases and references, even telling jokes in Latin, thus maintaining a camaraderie but also excluding those who did not share their history.

After Vatican II the boundaries within the order became more permeable. Individuals were to take responsibility for their own activities. Latin gradually fell out of use. Members engaged in diverse activities which frequently immersed them in work outside of community structures. The difference in training, in expectations of conduct, even in language, separate the generations.

For some members of the older generation the reforms which have occurred are interpreted as criticism (the previous model was flawed). Others see the changes as a return to the roots of the community (the original community formed in reaction to the restrictions of the monastery, not in conformity to them). Thus as an interviewer I could be viewed through a number of lenses: as one of the newfangled members finding fault with the old, as someone completely outside a given individual's experience, or as the future of the community. While I may be viewed as a generational outsider, from a structural perspective I am a member of the same community and so have full access to the public events of a community house.

The position of being an insider and an outsider well suits a participant observation study. As an insider I have access to individuals and a general familiarity with community life. As a perceived outsider I have a position from which to ask questions. The outsider cannot be expected to know the experience of other participants and so can request to be educated, triggering a familiar role for teachers (a role played by most of the participants at one time or another).

A question frequently put to human science researchers involves the external validity of a study. Elderly, celibate men committed to a communal lifestyle form a select subpopulation. To what extent can one generalize to other populations? In keeping with the human science tradition of exploring the breadth of experience (Strauss & Corbin 1990), the use of this sample can help to establish the sweep of religious and spiritual factors employed in the aging process. Further, these men have lived their lives as public figures, as teachers, administrators, preachers, retreat directors and representatives of a variety of professions. They have influenced, and continue to influence, thousands of people. This small population has communication nets which cross denomination, social class, national boundaries, and educational levels. They have utilized their experience in providing pastoral care and academic discourse. A small population may have a disproportionate voice. In addition, the experience of these men may help to illuminate the lives of other elderly, who are faced with finding meaning and coherence in the later years of their lives.

DESCRIPTION OF STUDY

The religious order to which the participants and myself belong has a variety of houses or local communities. One of these, in metropolitan New York, has

Table 10.1
Interviewees' Ages and Years in the Religious Order

Name	Age	Years in community
Fr. Aherne	73	52
Fr. Boyle	80	62
Fr. Caldwell	69	51
Fr. Donnelly	79	62
Fr. Eagen	78	62
Br. Feeney	86	41
Fr. Gallagher	89	67
Fr. Herrlich	84	62
Br. Keck	84	62
Superior	64	42
Director	63	44

a partial retirement wing and an infirmary wing, with a number of fully employed individuals also residing in the building. This local community houses fifty-six individuals. The house has a superior who sees to the needs of the residents and that the norms of the religious order are observed. The infirmary has its own administrator, charged with the physical care of the infirm, including coordinating nursing and medical attention.

The infirmary occupies the bulk of the building, and has graduated levels of care. The superior, the director of the infirmary, and I identified eighteen mentally alert members of the house over sixty-five years of age. Absence from the house, medical conditions, and disorientation eliminated many members. I wrote to the eighteen members and explained that I wished to interview them on their life histories, particularly in the areas of friendship and spirituality. The superior then followed my letter with one of his own asking if the individual wished to participate. Nine members agreed to be interviewed.

The names in Table 10.1 are pseudonyms. The names attempt to reflect the ethnic background of the participants. Seven were born in the United States and two in Europe. Two of the interviewees worked in Asia for years, and one spent

Table 10.2
The Interview Format

	Intimacy	Friendship	Spirituality
Childhood			
Formation			
Ministry			
Present			

considerable time in the Caribbean, South America, and Europe. The superior of the community and the director of the infirmary are also listed for comparison purposes.

In the first interview I spent approximately two hours with each participant. After this initial phase I produced a preliminary summary of the themes raised by community members. I mailed a copy to each interviewee and requested a follow-up interview. Seven agreed. During the follow-up interviews I lived in the house for a week and took the opportunity to interview the superior, director of the infirmary, two nurses, and four nurses' aides. In this way I contextualized the interviews by including the perceptions of caregivers and by observing these men as they interacted with one another.

The initial interviews were structured around the subjects' experiences of intimacy, friendship, and spirituality over four different time periods, rather than by specific questions. Each individual was encouraged at the beginning of the interview to describe his family and to describe interactions, rather than present abstractions. The subjects quickly moved into telling their stories, with rich biographical detail, and were prompted by the interviewer to cover each of the twelve cells in Table 10.2. The interviews were each audiotaped and subsequently transcribed.

The interviews were examined by means of a metaphorical analysis (Thomas, Kraus, and Chambers 1990). This approach attempts to interpret the experience of an individual as a text (Ricoeur 1979), which can be analyzed much as a work of literature. The analysis moves from individual metaphors into themes which run through a given interview, and between interviews. The end result of the analysis was the identification of themes which connected the metaphors.

Initially I focused on the relationships experienced by these individuals. In the course of my analysis, however, I recognized a congruence between the types of relationship these men established and their experience of spirituality. For the purpose of this paper I have returned to the initial interviews in order to focus more strongly on the religious themes and metaphors employed by the participants. The interviews with the administrators and nursing staff, as well as my observations, supplement the interviews with the nine elderly participants.

The interpretive technique of metaphorical analysis has much in common with the therapeutic interview, which looks to construct a life story from the patterns which emerge in an individual's life. The analysis, however, departs from the therapeutic in examining trends seen across individuals. The particular question addressed in the analysis will be: how do the participants make use of religious and spiritual themes in order to explain their experience?

FINDINGS

As the participants in the study related their life experiences they shared at least four ways in which they made use of religious and spiritual metaphors. Religion could be used as a boundary by which one identifies oneself through membership in a group. Secondly, religion and spirituality provided an inter-generational connection. Spirituality was also used to interpret life events, putting one's life in the context of a spiritual journey. The nine men varied, however, in the format they used in speaking of their journey, including how they looked at the future. Lastly, these men displayed a cohesiveness in their accounts which connected the domains of spirituality, intimacy, and friendship.

In the course of the analysis I began to draw a distinction between religious and spiritual themes. Religious themes, as I define them, address norms, de-nominational expectations, dogma, and formal ritual. Spiritual themes deal more with the relationship between individuals and their God. The two are connected, but differ in their selective emphases.

Religion as a Boundary

Many of the participants used religious belief systems to establish a boundary of affinity and difference which was used for the purpose of constructing identity. Inclusion within a religious community, parish, or denomination provided a sense of inclusion. In many ways the religious beliefs and rituals were extensions of family boundaries, of family identity. Most of the interviewees spoke of family prayers in the evenings, of attending liturgies as a group, of engaging in a number of religious activities. Being part of the family meant being part of a faith community.

Fr. Herrlich most strongly presented a boundary based on religious identifi-cation, which he associated with home. Herrlich, who comes from another culture, looks back on his family and finds it inconceivable that a family member would cross the religious boundary. "I think there was never such a mentality as sometimes here [the United States]. Parents that are complaining that 'What should I do, Father? My daughter, she is with a Jewish fellow. She gave up the faith, she is not going.' That never came. It was impossible [chuckling] in my family."

Early in his religious training Herrlich left his homeland for Asia. His missionary experience occupies a central place in his life narrative. One event which he strongly stressed was the conversion of the head of a Buddhist monastery. Convincing another of the value of one's way of life to the extent that the other wishes to join provides a sense of validation. The monk redrew his personal boundary to exclude himself from one group (Buddhist) and include himself in another (Herrlich's).

Not all families experienced such a clean division between "us" and "them." Both Br. Feeney and Fr. Caldwell mentioned the conversion of one parent to Catholicism for the purpose of marriage. Caldwell sees religion as dividing his family: "There was, I come from a steel town, iron and steel, and there were a lot of Presbyterians around there who oppressed the Irish, and the Irish were all down and out." His parents straddled this division. The continued contact with non-Catholic relatives blurred the religious boundary.

Br. Feeney and Fr. Gallagher offered few comments on denominational differences and instead highlighted differences in their experience of God. Feeney finds most Catholics lacking in their appreciation of the Eucharist: "They say yeah, that's right, but they don't know what the hell they're talking about half the time, they really don't." Denominational differences have less impact on Feeney than do differences in the understanding of religious belief. Gallagher sees religious training as setting people apart: "but their value [value in established prayer times] became more and more clearly manifest to me as the years grew on, and I saw religious and non-religious [people] as they grew up in life, and saw the difference, that I had a special advantage that they did not have."

For Feeney and Gallagher identification with Catholicism provided an insubstantial boundary. Of greater importance were the traditions of prayer and belief. These two men espouse a more vigorous living out of faith.

Br. Keck recognized denominational boundaries in his youth and recalled having many Protestant friends when growing up, and of his being tempted to baptize the younger ones when no adults were watching. Keck wanted to be assured of the safety (salvation) of the youngsters, and of placing Keck and his friends on the same side of the religious boundary. Later, one of his sisters converted and married a Protestant man. Keck's family recognized this as a break between the family and the newlyweds. When Keck next visited his mother, she told him that she would not visit her daughter. Keck picked up the phone and told his sister that he and his mother were coming for the weekend. He summed up this story with the comment: "All that stuff must be forgotten."

While observing religious boundaries early in life, Keck minimized them in later years. Caldwell, too, while acknowledging religious differences, found them essentially without foundation. He instead prefers the concept of universal salvation, a belief in life after death without distinguishing between denominations. The positions of Keck and Caldwell may reveal religious norms giving way to spiritual convictions.

Fr. Donnelly, a recovering alcoholic, relates differences in religious upbringing, race, and class among those in his Alcoholics Anonymous meetings. Yet all of these melt in the light of the shared experience of recovery and the Twelve Steps. The coming together for mutual support, for prayer, and to see one another through difficult times has provided Donnelly with a sense of inclusion which he did not find in decades of life within the religious community. The shared spirituality of the Twelve Steps now provides Donnelly with a sense of identity.

These men, though trained in a period which drew rigid boundaries around the Catholic community, have allowed this boundary to become more permeable. Inclusion has less to do with taking the label Catholic, than with a shared experience of prayer, of relationship with God. When questioned about their spirituality or prayer, the participants did not respond with dogma or formulas, but struggled to express their encounters in prayer and the beliefs generated by their prayer. Though many began religious life having a strong identification with traditional belief and formal ritual, they have expanded the sense of affiliation to include those who share a similar posture before God.

Intergenerational Ties

Religious themes linked the participants to their parents. As the interviewees followed the thread of their religious beliefs, they acknowledged them as rooted in their parents' actions. These men also connect themselves with younger generations through religious activities. They spoke of performing baptisms, weddings, and funerals for nieces and nephews. They maintained ties with students over the years, and found themselves connected with the children of their students. The participants provide a continuity between past generations and new generations, within the community as well as outside of it.

Most frequently the interviewees saw their religious observance as connected with their mothers. Fr. Donnelly stated, "The whole question of vocation and nearness to God I attribute mainly to my mother." Fr. Eagen related how his mother blessed each of her children with her wedding band, a gesture she learned in Ireland. When he announced his intention to become a priest, she responded that she had been praying for five years that he would. Fr. Boyle considered his mother to be a holy woman, and he held that "I certainly entered the religious order because of her prayers." Fr. Gallagher said of his mother, "And in one sense she is responsible for my vocation in many ways, cause of her own, shall I say, holiness."

Less frequently individuals associated their fathers with religious observance. Br. Feeney and Fr. Eagen both spoke of their mothers and fathers as mutually engaged in prayer with the family. Fr. Aherne, on the other hand, remembered his surprise as a boy when he went to his cousins' house and saw their father lead prayer. Frs. Aherne and Gallagher had fathers who were frequently absent, and thus had no sense of a religious connection with them. Fr. Donnelly experienced his father's religious devotion as meant for others outside the family. Fr. Caldwell's father converted to Catholicism in order to marry. "He [Caldwell's father] hadn't been raised a Catholic, he was a convert, and she [Caldwell's mother] was very careful not to push things at him." In Br. Feeney's family it was his mother who was the convert, yet she was the most devout member of the family.

While Fr. Eagen viewed his mother as particularly influential religiously, he also recalled the impact his father had on his beliefs. Fr. Eagen had been cautioned by his father, "You're too bright and you ask too many questions, you are going to lose your faith." Especially after his father's death this became a driving concern, that he remain faithful. In becoming a priest Eagen fulfilled his mother's hopes and observed his father's warning.

Fr. Herrlich similarly found his father to be influential and followed in his father's footsteps. Herrlich's father was a school teacher and cantor in the church, who left his family to fight abroad in World War II and never returned. Herrlich trained to be a teacher, entered the religious order, and then volunteered to go to the missions in Asia, never returning to his homeland. Br. Keck, too, recalled the influence of his father in his religious upbringing. Father and son had an agreement about playing soccer on Sundays. Keck as a child could play only after attending mass twice on a Sunday. Keck carefully fulfills his religious obligations.

It was in their families that participants became grounded in their religious beliefs and ritual. In carrying these beliefs and activities into the present they safeguard a heritage and tradition. In passing on their spirituality they engage in a form of generativity. Whereas for the parents religious belief was a component of family life, for the interviewees religious and spiritual beliefs have become the focus through which they connect with family.

Fr. Aherne made frequent references to his "kids." Many of these individuals came into contact with him as he taught undergraduates and lived with them in the dormitories. He read from a letter he had recently received: "I will never forget the September Sunday 25 years ago when we first met in the dorm. You touched me in a way that you never realized." Aherne peppered his conversation with remembrances of students and younger friends. He offered a family photograph sent him by one of the students from the dorm. "By jolly, just to look at those kids, he must have been a pretty proud man; they looked like awfully nice kids." Fr. Aherne has become involved with the children of his students, performing baptisms and weddings. His influence and presence extends across the generations, into the lives of students' children and the children of nieces, nephews, and cousins.

Within the community Fr. Aherne also nurtures relationships with younger members. Three of the community members with whom he feels particularly close were all in their twenties, whereas he was in his sixties, when their friendships first began. Ten years later he still maintains close contact with these three men. Fr. Eagen also maintains a warm rapport with younger members of the order. At lunch on one occasion a number of candidates considering application to the religious community were in the dining room. Fr. Eagen waved for them to join him. He engaged the group in conversation and anecdotes, drawing them out in the course of half an hour. He and Aherne specifically mentioned the desirable qualities the young bring to the order.

Frs. Aherne and Eagen represent one group within the order and Fr. Donnelly another. Since the time of their religious formation the order has undergone numerous changes. Donnelly has a difficult time dealing with the young. For him the tradition carries greater weight, and the changes are painful. "I find that being with my own, the old, the other grey beards has been a big help to me. I've grown progressively less tolerant of new ideas, you know, of the younger religious, the way they dress, the way they act, and anything they do that's not something I did, is bad." Donnelly invests himself in his AA community: "But the spirituality they develop through the program is really working, it's devotion and practice, you know, that these people are really taking their lives and turning them right around." So while Donnelly does not experience generativity with regard to younger members of the order, he does enjoy contributing to the growth of the members of his AA group.

Fr. Eagen sees a number of individuals for spiritual direction and refers to them as his "spiritual children." Fr. Herrlich likewise acts as a spiritual director and retreat director for numerous individuals who come to him. Even I, who was with him a relatively short time, found myself entrusted with Herrlich's message. He did not merely relate his experience to me as an interviewer, but delivered his story in the manner of an impassioned sermon given to a prospective disciple. The conversion story of the Buddhist monk occupied a central place in Herrlich's narration. The passing on of belief is something Herrlich both described and demonstrated.

The ministries in which these men have engaged reflect traditional aspects of fathering. Br. Keck spoke of moderating soccer teams, acting as a scout master, and coordinating altar boys, which also doubled as an early form of after-school care, in which he sponsored basketball games and other sporting events. Fr. Aherne, besides teaching, also gave of his time in the dormitory with students, listening to their hopes and struggles. At one point in the interview, Aherne began to muse aloud about one of his students who was in his second marriage, wondering if the man had "regularized" the marriage (obtained an annulment for the first marriage). Aherne functioned as a father would, worrying over the state of a son's marriage. Fr. Eagen, though infirmed, still engages in education, having a small number of students come to him in the infirmary. These three men as well as the other interviewees still continue to be present in the lives of relatives, former students, current students, younger members of the order, in many ways acting as father figures, bearing the title "Father" or "Brother."

Spiritual Journey

The theme of spiritual journey is more inclusive than those of religious boundaries and intergenerational ties, and may in fact encompass these two previous themes. The journey can incorporate one's inclusion or exclusion from a denomination or congregation. Br. Keck addressed his own development in telling of his wish to baptize Protestant friends but then later in life forcing his mother to accept her daughter who converted. The journey also includes the formation of relationships over time, and the place of religion in these relationships. The participants traced their faith journeys from parents and important individuals in their life journeys.

The interview format lent itself to the formulation of a life progression which included spiritual themes. Yet several individuals disregarded the interview format and spoke spontaneously of their spiritual journey. This is a familiar vehicle seen in scripture, hagiographies, and religious autobiographies. While each individual related events which constitute a religious or spiritual journey, they varied in the format. The participants fall into three categories of journey: those interpreted in light of climactic events, those which showed slow, steady growth, and those consisting of a series of significant events.

Climactic Events

Fr. Herrlich well exemplifies the use of religious journey to structure a life narrative. He left his family and homeland to go to Asia as a missionary. His story climaxes in the details of his imprisonment and solitary confinement: "And it was so wonderful in this prison. Ah! How wonderful You are. And over and over, many times. Said how sweet can be a chain with you. [sucks in breath] That I kiss the chain. And still I have to do something, otherwise I thought my heart will burst. So on my knees, in the darkness—we had no light—I went to the wall and kissed the wall." His imprisonment led him to a spiritual insight or conversion, which he continues to experience in the present.

Herrlich reserves the language of intimacy for God alone, speaking of "being conjoined purely in love with God." He intertwines his fingers and changes the cadence of his voice as he speaks of being joined with God. The prison became a transformative opportunity in which Herrlich discovered that God had come to him.

Herrlich has extended the theme of allowing God to come and be heard into the past and into the future. In the story of being instrumental in the conversion of a Buddhist monk to Catholicism, Herrlich urged the monk to pray: "Oh God, if you exist, please help me to know you that I may love you." The experience with the monk happened prior to the imprisonment, yet Herrlich used the same metaphor of prayer as a waiting for God. Herrlich interprets the earlier encounter with the monk in light of his later prison encounter. Since his imprisonment Herrlich has traveled and preached extensively, using his prison experience to entreat others to wait for God. Even in the interview itself, Herrlich moved from simple dialogue to a dramatic presentation of his experience. Through gesture, tone of voice, and narrative he preached and appealed to me to wait for God.

Fr. Donnelly, by contrast, spoke of a life of superficial prayer. The first few years in the order were terrible, which he compared to a prison camp. "We were never taught really how to meditate with any ease.'' He had the impression that they knelt for show. It wasn't till he was about sixty, when he began a Twelve Step program, that Fr. Donnelly had a sense of spirituality. In Alcoholics Anonymous Donnelly found a way to come in contact with God, and with God in other people. ''I pray in the morning, I pray in the afternoon, I pray at meetings, I pray. You know, it's a wonderful life.'' ''I'm a grateful alcoholic.'' The recognition of his addiction became the central theme through which Donnelly translates his early family experience (tracing the line of alcoholism), his decline in his middle years, and his metamorphosis in later life.

For Frs. Herrlich and Donnelly a transformative spiritual event has become the central metaphor of their lives. While they will relate stories from childhood to the present, the organizing principal is the climactic event. The life narrative is organized to lead up to this central incident and to lead away from it. Fr. Donnelly explicitly talks of ''before AA'' and ''after AA.'' Rather than simple linear sequencing these men use a bidirectional sequence centered on what they consider their life's revelatory milestone.

Slow, Steady Growth

The other participants did not cite a given event as climactic. Two of the interviewees described their experience as a gentle growing in a sense of themselves and their place in the world. Fr. Boyle described himself as someone intellectually stimulated by theology and related subjects. He began in a more speculative vein, and then came to appreciate ''the difference between thought about God, and the presence of God.'' His prayer has evolved, though at first he questioned what he was doing: ''Is it the thought of God or it is the presence of God? I was helped a great deal more, I think, in my practice, by the Jesus prayer than by ejaculatory prayer. It's more or less habitually in my mind and my heart.'' Boyle found his prayer simplifying to an uncomplicated repetition of the name ''Jesus'' over the course of the day, rather than using words to provide content for his prayer.

Fr. Boyle knows a great deal of theology, even for a priest. I mentioned a newly published article and he was immediately able to derive the sources of its argument and its place in a historical context. Boyle, however, has shifted from an appreciation of speculative ideas to the language of theology used to express a spiritual reality. He searches for words to describe his experience. Similarly, in his work he began by producing some sermons on the relationship between the members of the Trinity. Boyle found himself leaving behind the thought process and becoming caught up in the phenomenon of love within the Trinity, and between God and himself. The thought process, the sermon writing, the training in prayer, all moved to a relationship of love best expressed in the name of Jesus.

Even in those areas where Boyle faults himself he reveals the focusing of his experience. He finds fault with himself in lacking a spontaneous wish to be with others. ''I sometimes feel guilty that I do feel drawn and attracted toward the

Father and toward Jesus, but not, not—it doesn't overflow, it doesn't set me on fire to go out and give it to somebody else.'' Everyone in the community who mentioned Fr. Boyle, however, praised him for his generosity, his ability to spend time with the seriously ill and delusional. Boyle judges himself by a stricter standard than do his companions. What standard does Boyle use? He places himself in the context of Christ. Those behaviors and motivations which deviate from the norm of Christ become the focus of Boyle's attention and his desire to change.

Like Fr. Boyle, Fr. Aherne speaks in terms of a growing simplicity of prayer. Prayer as hard work has gradually shifted to prayer as spending of time with God. This approach to prayer is consistent with Aherne's sense of intimate relationships. The degree to which a person is present to another defines intimacy. The quality of being present to God defines prayer. On a retreat Aherne told his director ''the presence of God was intruding on the meditation. . . . '' The experience of prayer seemed to be at odds with the technique or form of prayer. His director exclaimed, ''You couldn't ask for more could you!''

Aherne related a childhood with a distant father and many older siblings, who formed a buffer between him and his mother. In contrast to all the other participants, Aherne referred more frequently to his siblings than to his mother or his father. It is as though he grew up in the company of peers, who provided parenting. Rather than a vertical relationship, with the implication of power dynamics, Aherne speaks most frequently using horizontal images, with a sense of solidarity. Whereas most of the other participants had little contact with younger members of the order, Aherne has maintained close friendships with individuals in my generation. In the eucharistic liturgy, rather than bowing to altar or tabernacle, Aherne turns and bows to the congregation, exemplifying his preference for horizontal connections.

For Aherne the boundaries between prayer and encounters with other people, the boundaries between congregation and presider, have gradually eroded. He has experienced a slow process of integration. The challenge for him now rests in training others to trust the dynamics of prayer. As a retreat director Aherne encourages others to worry less about the form of prayer and invest more in establishing a simple relationship with God.

Series of Significant Events

The remaining five individuals spoke of their journey as a number of small events, which they used to interpret their experience. Fr. Caldwell and Br. Feeney both experienced health crises in their youth, which had an impact on their life experiences. Frs. Caldwell and Eagen both found their parents' illnesses and death to have had profound impacts. Brs. Feeney and Keck spoke of their work prior to entering the order, and Fr. Gallagher of his extended high school experience prior to entrance. All spoke of their time in the novitiate. Eagen and Keck spent a great deal of time relating their experiences overseas. Each of the five also spoke of being moved to the infirmary community. Frs. Caldwell and

Eagen have had years of physical infirmity in which to a degree they came to terms with their illness. They find it more difficult to adjust to decreased contact with more active community members. Feeney and Gallagher see themselves as having left the ranks of the useful and have a hard time adjusting to increasing infirmity.

While the previous two subcategories of spiritual journey had a positive valence, the five men in this last category have no such commonality. The variety of events have both negative and positive qualities attached to them. Eagen and Keck relate more positive than negative events. Caldwell and Feeney seem to have a balance of positive and negative events. Gallagher presents himself as falling below the mean in most endeavors, and has ended in the infirmary where he feels himself with no useful function.

Comparison of Journeys

The journey narratives of the first two categories (climactic events and slow, steady growth) have a cohesiveness not found in the last category (series of significant events). The four individuals cited in the early categories had already interpreted their life experience in light of a few important themes or metaphors. The narratives were already characterized by organizing principals, or a plot.

The individuals whose journeys were characterized by a series of significant events presented less of a coherent whole. Have these individuals yet to complete a life narrative? This seems more likely than an explanation that these men had a higher level of dissatisfaction. Keck voiced very little dissatisfaction and Eagen only slightly more. By contrast, Donnelly (in the climactic category) had many more negative events. Yet, by using a conversion theme (AA), Donnelly gave the life narrative a positive trajectory. For the majority of the men in the third category there existed a conflict between their expectation and their experience.

The men in the first two categories were able to relate clear growth and development. Life events occurred in a sequence, around a significant event, or in a growing integration of themes across the various domains of life. The five men in the last category voiced a number of metaphors which resist being unified into a set of cohesive themes.

Fr. Caldwell, whose journey was a series of events, frequently returns to a sense of isolation. He has an unmet hope of being connected with others. "I think like most human persons, I have both a great need and capacity for love, and that's a very serious problem in the community." While he speaks of his sense of isolation, according to the administrator, he visits everyone on his floor daily. Caldwell's religious beliefs revolve around a sense of inclusion, yet his experience is of alienation.

The men in the last category share with Caldwell a sense of having reached an impasse. Caldwell finds himself blocked by his sense of alienation. Eagen, who has always relied on his charm and wit, has fewer and fewer opportunities to exercise these qualities. Feeney, Gallagher, and Keck defined themselves in terms of their work, and they now find themselves physically unable to continue as they had. They await whatever task God has for them. The men in the two earlier categories continue to have a sense of movement forward, not found among those in the last category.

The Future

A theme related to the three types of spiritual journey is the view of the future expressed by the participants. The two men who experienced the journey as climactic events and the two who experienced journey as slow, steady growth offered little comment on the future. Donnelly and Herrlich intend to continue living out their transformative experiences. Aherne and Boyle viewed themselves as simply continuing on the paths which they find unfolding before them. Boyle offered the statement: ''But I don't want to yield to the idea that because you're any older therefore you should do less or you should fade, fade away.'' These four men did recognize changes in themselves with age, as in Donnelly finding himself less tolerant of new ideas. They each, however, have an optimism about their aging. The events and developments which gave meaning to their past continue to give meaning to the present.

The five participants in the category of journey as a series of events have less optimism about their aging. Br. Feeney refers to himself as a ''dead pigeon.'' With the loss of his health, he no longer has the ability to work, the thing which gave life much of its meaning. His continued life he attributes to something God wants accomplished. ''But there's something He wants done, and it hasn't been finished yet and maybe you think I'm crazy, but I can't help it, that's the way I feel about it.'' Fr. Gallagher similarly speaks in terms of God's plan as it has unfolded. Gallagher feels that his continued presence in religious life is a testament to God as Gallagher has had little to offer. He, like Feeney, awaits God's call: ''Well if God wants to take me, He certainly knows, He put me on here, can take me off. [Laughing] He let me hang on here a long time!'' Both these men have a sense of waiting for death.

Br. Keck speaks in more pragmatic terms, of wanting to train someone to take over his responsibilities. Keck has recognized that he is slowing down. In the anticipation of death he wishes to pass his knowledge on to another, lest his experience be wasted.

Frs. Caldwell and Eagen offered no comments on their own deaths. Instead they reflected on the deaths of loved ones. For themselves they spoke in terms of their infirmities, of ways in which their actions are impeded. The struggle for the two of them is to find ways to continue to function in light of physical handicaps. Ultimately they view their situation in terms of decline.

Cohesiveness of Themes

Rather than finding distinct religious themes, which were separate from friendship, relationships, work, and so on, the participants provided narratives in which overarching themes united the various aspects of life. Frequently these themes were overtly religious, as in the spiritual journey. The journey tied together experiences across the domains of life.

Fr. Aherne provides an example. He made use of numerous metaphors to convey the importance he places on the quality of presence found in a relationship. He identifies intimacy as this quality of presence between people. When speaking of his brother he states, "But, for me he was always kind of a special person. But I didn't kiss [with emphasis] him, I didn't put my arms [with emphasis] around him." Aherne knew that he and his brother had an intimate relationship because of the time they spent with one another, because of the way in which they were present to one another.

Aherne, in defining prayer, offered the image of: "a very old married couple sitting in their rocking chairs on the porch. It's very important that they be with one another, but they don't really have to say anything." As Fr. Aherne found himself responding to loved ones, so he expected to respond to God in prayer. The content of prayer became much less important than the act of settling into an attitude of attention to God. In Aherne's journey he has learned to value the growing simplicity of prayer.

As these men related a life narrative, they revealed remarkable consistency both across domains and over time. Fr. Aherne valued the quality of presence, across intimacy, spirituality, and friendship. Fr. Caldwell maintained a continuity of themes over his lifetime. He returned frequently to his sense of distance or separation from other people, which he can trace to childhood. He told one story which graphically conveyed this theme:

You never kissed people in our family, you just shook hands. When I was a little tyke I once crawled up in her [paternal grandmother's] lap. She used to wear beautiful, lovely silk dresses, and smelled of lovely perfumes. And, I did the same thing with my other grandmother. Anyway, she took her right hand and knocked me across the room. "We don't do this kind of slopping in our family."

Fr. Caldwell brought his struggle with personal distance into the order as well. (It may be that he remained in the order because of his childhood training.) He lived the rules but feels that he relinquished some of his humanity because he was never able to come close to another. "You've never been a completely human person; you can't be in every respect once you take on our type of life, once you decide that you're not going to get married."

Caldwell found his early training in prayer to be superficial, without depth. Caldwell bemoans the fact that he has never shared his deepest beliefs, never connected with another in prayer. "The most important thing in one's total existence is, you never share at all, the other person's fundamental beliefs, where they stand with regard to their love of Jesus." The distance exists even between those dedicated to prayer. In contrast to Aherne, Caldwell related no experience of a communal sense of prayer.

While Caldwell feels alienated from others, the people around him comment on his openness. On one occasion I observed a group of students in the dining room. As they left, Caldwell introduced himself to several, and learned something about each one. He acts as an impromptu chaplain for two groups outside the house. The sense of isolation, rather than paralyzing Caldwell, prompts him to act. Yet he is also comfortable with the isolation and will derail any attempt by another to move too close. Caldwell related several stories in which he rebuffed a companion who attempted to broach the gap between them. Caldwell experiences conflicting desires and actions.

Aherne and Caldwell provide examples of a phenomenon common to each of the participants. Each man portrayed himself in a particular way, producing a set of life themes. The communication pattern of Aherne's family or the distance in Caldwell's became part of their style of relating, which extended itself into prayer and liturgy. Even the discrepancies between the self-presentation of participants and others' perceptions of them are reflected in their life accounts. Fr. Eagen, for instance, uses pious language and maintains the traditional role of priestly behavior. Some of the nursing staff, however, dislike him because they find him both pious and critical of them, which strikes them as contradictory. In fact, during the interview, a nurse's aide entered the room to see if Eagen had rung for assistance. He responded, "Does it show on your machine there, dear? Check your glasses." After she left he turned and asked if he were wrong to have said this.

Individuals did reveal more than one face which they presented to the world. Some faces were complementary and therefore produced a more unified narrative. Others, however, stood in tension with one another. Eagen has two distinct ways of presenting himself: wisecracking and pious. These two components seem at odds, yet he related stories of himself which show both present in him as a child. In conversation Eagen displays a quick wit and an ability to banter. He moves easily from this mode into one in which he makes use of pious gestures and words. The other members of the house, who volunteered information about Eagen, typically chose one face and interpreted his behavior in light of it. Eagen, for his part, has utilized these sides of his personality in establishing relationships. He has the largest network of friends and acquaintances of any of the participants. He was one of the more difficult men to schedule for an interview because of his numerous social and pastoral commitments. His friends praise his wit, and his detractors comment on his condescension. Does Fr. Eagen lack integration, or is he a more complex and sophisticated individual?

The cohesiveness of the themes intersect with the participant's account of his spiritual journey. Cohesion stresses connections. Journey, on the other hand, adds a trajectory, places the pieces in the context of a plot. Eagen has been consistent in his wisecracking and his piousness. Yet the one quality does not inform the other. The pieces do not fall into a sequence. By contrast, Fr. Boyle spoke of his distress at not being filled with enthusiasm for others. Other members of the house, however, reported Boyle's commitment to even the most difficult bedbound individuals. Boyle's narrative includes a growing identification with

Christ, and Christ's devotion to others. It is in light of this exemplar that Boyle judges himself wanting, and so redoubles his efforts. Even in his failings, Boyle displays a consistency and a movement toward his ideal, integrating his intellectual life, his spiritual beliefs, and his behavior within the community.

Conclusion

It is in the construction of a spiritual journey that these nine men have added meaning to their lives. Not all have been equally successful in producing a unified whole in the journey narrative. Those who have arranged their experience in a coherent plot with a clear trajectory differed from the other participants in having an interpretive theme or event. Donnelly is a "grateful alcoholic." Herrlich came through the trauma of prison with a firm sense of God's action even in the midst of helplessness. Aherne has found less need to do and more need to be with God and others, simplifying his relationships. Boyle has undergone a change in intellectual appreciation of relationship with the Divine, to an experience of this relationship, to a thirst to have this relationship flow into his connections with others.

The four men who characterize their lives as part of a unified journey have many details in common with the other five participants: loss of parents, premature deaths in family, childhood traumas, difficulties in establishing friendships, and so on. It is in the ordering of the details that the groups differ. Those men who lack a plot for their narrative have experienced a conflict between expectations and experience, or a conflict between the themes they espouse. The conflict blocks the construction of a coherent narrative.

DISCUSSION

The analysis of the above life histories is consistent with the work of Erikson and the developmentalists who follow his approach. Erikson (1959) posits the last two tasks of life as generativity versus stagnation and as ego integrity versus despair. Part of generativity is the begetting of children. Yet Erikson looks beyond the producing of another generation to include that which is entrusted to those who follow. Generativity includes the passing on of a legacy, which may include art, forms of government, philosophy, and spiritual values. Erikson defines ego integrity as an acceptance of one's life as lived, as a recognition that one's life is one's own responsibility, and as a realization of the significance in the flow of people and events which have contributed to this life. In the passing on of the life narrative the elder can accomplish both of these life tasks.

Generativity reaches a peak of intensity during the middle years (Ryff 1986), though the consequences of this period will extend forward in time. The men in my sample each demonstrated a form of generativity, mostly through their investment in the lives of students, retreatants, younger relatives, and younger members of the order. They continue to reap the benefits of these relationships, by being welcomed into the lives of the next generation, through the performing of weddings and baptisms, in being invited to ordinations and vow ceremonies.

Integrity marks later life. According to Erikson (1959), this process includes a life review in which the individual finds significance in the events which have made up his or her life. Ryff (1986) perceives elderly individuals as engaging in the construction of self-narratives. In the light of the present, an individual pulls together the details of the past in a way consistent with current experience. The novelty of the present stimulates the older person to reevaluate previously constructed patterns. From this period of self-examination the person in later life assembles a new life structure. The updated narrative also has implications for the future, establishing a valence on the direction in which the individual travels. Am I declining? Am I growing, maturing?

The participants in this study use a spiritual journey motif as the template on which to construct a life narrative. I have drawn a distinction between those who have produced a cohesive set of themes and those who have constructed a journey. The difference between the two lies in the degree of integration evident. Those marked by cohesion have parallel sets of themes which are carefully distinct. The overarching themes do not mutually support and interpenetrate one another. By contrast, those who have constructed life journeys have pulled together the themes of life and climactic events into a coherent whole. I find that the four individuals who were able to arrange their life experience in a meaningful plot demonstrated integration.

The social process of communicating the life narrative seems crucial to the process. Marshall (1986) found that those who identified themselves as privately reminiscing about life events had not yet completed the process. Those who reported that they had engaged in social reminiscence, had talked about their past with others, were more likely to have demonstrated success in the process. Generativity and integrity remain linked. Part of the construction of a life story involves passing it on to another.

Scripture can, in part, be seen as the product of this self-reflective process. The life histories of the few who reached old age served to link the community with its past, and to provide a backdrop by which present experience could be interpreted. The Jewish and Christian scriptures explicitly make use of individual lives in order to convey meaning across time. Abraham and Sarah, Isaac and Rebekah, Jacob and Rachel, and Joseph and his brothers form the bulk of the book of Genesis. This family history provides a model for finding meaning in the events of life. So too, the life of Jesus of Nazareth is a narrative that ties together the experiences of life in a provocative way. Religious and spiritual traditions have preserved life narratives and offer themselves as templates for the construction of contemporary life structures.

The elderly men interviewed in this study have the time and the need to make sense of their lives in light of present events. Struggling to arrive at a new integration includes communicating the process to others, particularly younger generations. They place current experience in the context of a lifetime, while providing a service to younger contemporaries. Their religious themes also take the long view, examining significance over historical time. These men are in a position to appreciate religious insights and to be able to interpret them in light of a lifetime. Those who have achieved a level of integrity provide an interpretive function for the rest of the community. Not only do they look for meaning in their own lifetime, they also enter into dialogue with the experiences of those who have gone before them. These elders, and perhaps untold others in widely varying situations, build tradition, preserving significance over lifetimes.

REFERENCES

Baruch, G. K. 1984. The psychological well-being of women in the middle years. In G. K. Baruch and J. Brooks-Gunn, eds., *Women in midlife,* 161–80. New York: Plenum Press.

Bee, H. L. 1987. *The journey of adulthood.* New York: Macmillan.

Connidis, I. A., and L. Davies. 1990. Confidants and companions in later life: The place of family and friends. *Journal of Gerontology: Social Sciences* 45(4), S141–49.

Cumming, E., and W. E. Henry. 1961. *Growing old.* New York: Basic Books.

Erikson, E. H. 1959. *Identity and the life cycle.* New York: International University Press. (Reissued by Norton, 1980).

Field, D., and R. E. Millsap. 1991. Personality in advanced old age: Continuity or change? *Journal of Gerontology: Psychological Sciences* 46(6), 299–308.

Levinson, D. J. 1978. *The seasons of a man's life.* New York: Knopf.

Litwak, E. 1989. Forms of friendships among older people in an industrial society. In R. G. Adams and R. Blieszner, eds., *Friendship: Structure and process.* Newbury Park, CA: Sage Publications.

Marshall, V. W. 1986. A sociological perspective on aging and dying. In V. W. Marshall, ed., *Late life: The social psychology of aging.* Beverly Hills: Sage Publications.

Rabinow, P., and W. M. Sullivan. 1979. The interpretive turn: Emergence of an approach. In P. Rabinow and W. M. Sullivan, eds., *Interpretive social science: A reader,* 73–101. Berkeley: University of California Press.

Ricoeur, P. 1979. The model of the text: Meaningful action considered as a text. In P. Rabinow and W. M. Sullivan, eds., *Interpretive social science: A reader,* 73–101. Berkeley: University of California Press.

Ryff, C. 1986. The subjective construction of self and society: An agenda for life-span research. In V. W. Marshall, ed., *Late life: The social psychology of aging.* Beverly Hills: Sage Publications.

Steinbach, U. 1992. Social networks, institutionalization, and mortality among elderly people in the United States. *Journal of Gerontology: Social Sciences* 47(8), S183–S190.

Strauss, A., and J. Corbin. 1990. *Basics of qualitative research: Grounded theory procedures and techniques.* Newbury Park, CA: Sage Publications.

Thomas, L. E., P. A. Kraus, and K. O. Chambers. 1990. Metaphorical analysis of meaning in the lives of elderly men: A cross-cultural investigation. *Journal of Aging Studies* 4(1), 1–15.

V Interview and Survey Research

11 Generativity as Pragmatic Spirituality

Robert L. Rubinstein

> In our age the I-It relation, gigantically swollen, has usurped, practically uncontested, the mastery and the rule. The I of this relation, an I that possesses all, makes all, succeeds with all, this I that is unable to say Thou, unable to meet a being essentially, is the lord of the hour. This selfhood that has become omnipotent, with all the It around it, can naturally acknowledge neither God nor any genuine absolute which manifests itself to men as of non-human origin. It steps in between and shuts off from us the light of heaven.
>
> —Buber 1966:56

Traditional views of religion have stressed a distinction between the domains of the sacred and the secular; an elaboration of the domain of the sacred; and an accounting of the duties within everyday life owed to the sacred or the divine. This is, no doubt, a Western folk model of the cultural architecture of religion, although its extension to other societies is questionable.

However, within our own society, the distinction between the sacred and the secular in fact maps only poorly onto the cultural notion of the person or the American folk model of the person. Now, it is true that Protestantism has been seen as the cause or catalyst of the capitalist, as well as the American, character. Nevertheless, religious behavior is increasingly seen as distal to the person and as "voluntary," and less a function of bounded communities of similar people, language, customs, and denomination. Further, American religions, and their ways of viewing persons spiritually, are widely diverse. All formal religions have sectors that range from the secular to the deeply mystical, from the local to the universal. And, while specific religions suggest or dictate the nature of what should be believed, in fact what doctrinal components persons actually believe or accept vary widely and individually. The extent to which religious ideas are inherent to the basic notion of identity that each person has also vary widely.

Many analysts of American culture have stressed characteristics of a culturally defined sense of personhood that appears largely devoid of spiritual content. For example, the American self has been viewed as autonomous, commercial, goal-oriented, independent, proactive, self-reliant, in consonance with the American character (Hsu 1972; Clark and Anderson 1968). Again, while some may argue that these are characteristics that have been stressed in Protestantism and through rationalism, there is little about these adjectives that, for example, speaks of a personal or community-based relationship with God. They are primarily characteristic of the person in the secular realm. They are ways of getting on in the world that "is." They can be things of the I-It relationship. They say little specifically about the unseen. They are about the here and now.

In this chapter I want to address the voluntary or extraneous nature of spirituality in our cultural definition of the person. In a certain way, recent work on "the constitution of the self in cultural context" has not treated the spiritual dimension of the person in American society. Perhaps it is the case that the culturally defined self is not innately "spiritual." However, I believe that it is possible to make more modest claims about the nature of spirituality in everyday life, given the cultural definition of the person. If we redefine the spiritual component of the culturally constituted self purely in terms of the temporal and developmental aspect of the folk model of the person—the self through time—this component of the self is the subject of a refocusing. I argue that this is especially true on the latter portion of the life span.

However, once we begin to consider "the self" through time we are no longer necessarily within the context of the sacred, but rather with the practical business of everyday life, the realm of the secular. The spiritual concerns within the domain of the secular may be seen as pragmatic "self-work" within the cultural architecture of the person.

As each person ages, she is faced with the facts of finitude, with the tying up of loose ends, and the need to maintain connections that provide for care when one is old and "on the way out." Thus, regardless of religion each individual, as a cultural entity, is left with a very great deal of pragmatic self-work, facing issues of self-care needs, the perpetuation of deeds, the support of loved ones, futurity, continuation of the self, life review and the like. These issues have often been subsumed by the term generativity. Thus I would define the self-work around issues of generativity as a form of pragmatic spirituality, because this work deals with the transition from late life to death and takes account of some of the culturally defined ways in which the self can continue on after death.

DEFINING GENERATIVITY

Generativity has several definitions, all of which involve connections of the self with a future that will continue on after one is gone. This notion was initially defined by Erik Erikson (1963) as "an interest in establishing and guiding the next generation." The potential developmental conflict between generativity and stagnation was for him one epigenetic adult developmental stage and was primarily concerned with generative activities around issues of biological reproduction and parenting. More recently, Erikson and others have extended the notion of generativity to different activities that may not specifically be seen as parenting and may include other modes of transgenerational connection that are symbolic, technical, cultural, or knowledge-oriented. For example, Kotre (1984) reconfigured Erikson's notions into four generative types: biological generativity (fertility and the begetting of children); parental generativity (child raising and the initiation of children into family traditions); technical generativity (that which is accomplished by teachers of all sorts); and cultural generativity (creating, renewing or conserving a system of symbols or meanings). One aspect of this list that is significant is that these are tasks that can exist over the entirety of the adult life span. Thus, for example, cultural generativity (as well as other forms) may be enacted by those of extreme old age.

THE SPIRITUAL NATURE OF GENERATIVITY

I want to argue here that generativity has a spiritual component. While generativity is a notion that has been developed in the context of humanistic psychology, we can as well identify a spiritual nature to it. In essence, this aspect may be found in several components of generativity, including the following: a caring, nurturing or loving attitude; concern for the self through others; a concern with the nature of personal finitude; concerns about the post-death condition of the self; the possible equation of godliness with otherness; and (possibly) care of the self through a diffuse concern with the condition of the world (leaving the world a better place than one found it). Religious-based ethics generally teach behaviors that are generative.

Now, we must be sure to note that, in actuality, most generativity is enacted within family contexts and does concern activities that may be circumspectly seen as nurturing the next family generation, as in Erikson's original formulation. Some of the larger extensions of generativity, for example a concern with the world or the condition of the planet and its people, may be seen as alternatively deriving disparately from traditions of political involvement, social activism from a spiritual basis, or even class-based notions of social responsibility. Nevertheless, they share common ground in that they feature a concern with human well-being and a concern for the health of the self through the condition of others. These are quintessentially activities that link, rather than divide, people.

Lifton and Markusen (1990) provide another example of some of the components of generativity. They document two forms of modern genocidal thinking in a matrix of sociopolitical systems that have dominated much of our thinking in the twentieth century. Thus, they equate the genocidal mentality and social structure of Nazi Germany with the mentality and social structure of nuclearism. This is a mentality that is based on schismogenic thinking (Bateson 1972), the establishment of a nuclear elite that is permitted to develop and manage a nuclear culture; and a failure by them to grapple, on personal terms, with the very real effects of nuclear war. One solution to the problem of genocidal mentality, Lifton and Markusen feel, is a psychological shift in the content of symbolic immortality (what lives on after us; or in terms of this chapter, generativity), to include a focus on "the species self" or the entire species itself as an object of generative action. They note, "In addition to the feeling that, 'I live on in my children and their children, in my people, in my nation,' one now has the sense that 'I live on in humankind' " (1990:260). They note the following:

Consider the striking phenomenon of very old people joining actively in the antinuclear movement. One might wonder at their doing so, since they appear to have so little time left in their lives to be concerned about. But in actuality, as they approach death, older people can be deeply concerned about what will remain of their fundamental human connections: Will their family, people, tribe, nation—and now species—continue to thrive? Older people raise these questions about modes of symbolic immortality, at whatever level of consciousness, because they feel the meaning of their entire lives to be at issue. They may therefore have more at stake psychologically than anyone else in keeping the species going." (1990:261)

GENERATIVITY VERSUS NARCISSISM?

Lifton and Markusen refer to the possible development of a species self as a phenomenon occurring in modern historical context, that is, at a certain time in response to certain conditions. The construct narcissism has also been viewed in relation to generativity. Narcissism has also been seen in such a historical context, as a personality development especially attuned to the events of modern times (Lasch 1979).

Narcissism and generativity have an ambiguous relationship with one another. Narcissism, a psychological construct, refers to an unhealthy or overestablished focus on the self and one's own perspective and an inability to maturely focus on the needs of others without regard to one's own primal needs. Nemiroff and Colarusso (1985) interpret, from a psychoanalytic perspective, aging itself as a narcissistic injury to self.

However, it is possible to see how aspects of generativity, or a focus on the self through others—might be compatible with narcissism. We may view generativity as a mature or, in a psychoanalytic sense, a socialized manner of dealing with personal finitude, with death. There are some with personalities well within the norm who may view generativity—toward family, people, species—as an appropriate and mature enactment of developmental strivings in later life. However, there are also those with narcissistic personalities who are able to appropriately recognize finitude and transfer their narcissistic concerns from the self via the self to the self via others. Narcissists may seek eternal monuments to the self in the glory of that that they have left behind. Narcissism may thus in part find an outlet in nurturing others. In a sense narcissists subscribe to a theory of the kingly self elaborated by Kantorowicz (1957) in his discussion of medieval political thought. There, the king is viewed as having two bodies. The first body is his natural body, subject to human declivities; the second body is the political body, which survives despite the frailties of the natural body. Narcissism's only recourse is to an eternity of self; other options are hard to contemplate.

SPIRITUALITY IN A CULTURE THAT FOCUSES ON INDIVIDUALS

To the extent that religion is a negotiation of Self and Other, I and Thou (Buber 1970), and a world of relations, such negotiations can be difficult in a society that increasingly focuses narcissistically on the self. Indeed, the epistemology of spirit in a culture of individualism is often unclear. Socially, from Tocqueville to Bellah (Bellah et al. 1985; Greenhouse 1992), America has often been analyzed as a society with a distinctive tension between person and community, self and other. Historically, there has been and continues to be change in focus on the individual or the community. And the observation by Lasch (1979) and others that narcissism is a historically situated product and is on the rise has developmental aspects as well. The increased interest on youthfulness and bodily beauty in popular culture has been part of an historic change in which "midlife" is now extended into what recently had been the domain of old age (Turner 1984; Hepworth and Featherstone 1982). There is an increased commoditization of self-care, youth, beauty, health, sexuality, and athleticism. Further, the locus of responsibility for bodily maintenance is the individual. Communities are on the decline as the units of care. Politically, the enactment of narcissistic greed and behavior has been subject to few political controls, particularly since the early 1980s. Narcissism can be one aspect of individualism, can be a denial of community and can act to promote interpersonal avoidance (Greenhouse 1992).

Narcissism also has an important role in generativity. However, the situation regarding self and other in generativity is ambiguous. We will turn to this next. While Erikson defined generativity as an interest in nurturing and guiding the next generation and exemplified this by parenthood, he also acknowledges (as does Kotre) other forms of generative behavior that include the passing on of knowledge, values and symbol systems. Kotre refers to generativity as "outliving the self." What is outliving the self in spiritual terms? Outliving the self refers to the mature recognition of personal finitude and the enactment of symbolic continuation. The self can only exist, through time, through others. The actual burden of self will dissipate at death; the products and essence of self will continue on.

Debate about the nature of these products has a long history in Western culture. For example, in Plato's *The Symposium,* there is a lengthy debate between Socrates and Diotima on just this topic. Diotima notes:

Mortal nature seeks, as far as may be, to perpetuate itself and become immortal. The only way it can achieve this is by procreation, which secures the perpetual replacement of an old member of the race by a new. . . . If you will only reflect you will see that the ambition of men provides an example of the same truth. . . . the love of fame and the desire to win a glory that shall never die have the strongest effects upon people. . . . Those whose creative instinct is physical . . . believ[e] . . . that by begetting children they can secure for themselves an immortal and blessed memory . . . ; but there are those whose creative desire is of the soul, and who conceive spiritually, not physically, the progeny which it is the nature of the soul to conceive and bring forth. If you ask what that progeny is, it is wisdom and virtue in general; of this all poets and such craftsmen as have found out some new thing may be said to be begetters; but far the greatest and fairest branch of wisdom is that which is concerned with the due ordering of states and families, whose name is moderation and justice. (Plato 1951: 88–90)

GENERATIVITY LOCALIZED IN INDIVIDUALS

While generativity has most frequently been seen as a psychological or developmental construct, it also has a cultural component (Alexander et al. 1991). The way in which the self is culturally constituted shapes how that culture's members view death and generativity. A key variable here is the manner in which continuity—substantive or symbolic—is built into the system. For example, American culture provides for the cross-generational transmission of family names—through men; this continuity of symbol and substance is built into the system.

Becker (1973) discusses the perception of death in Western culture, in a book that can be viewed as a somewhat unconscious ethnography of Western attitudes to death. He suggests that individuals are caught in an inescapable paradox of the limitless imagination encased in bodily finitude, based on the Western distinction between the domains of body and self. Ultimately this duality collapses into material nullity. Heroism and monumentalism are some responses to this existential void, a development from "the ache for cosmic specialness" that people may have.

In American culture, where an increasingly individualized notion of the self dominates, death clearly signifies an end. Unlike in many other societies, there are few collective social, ritual, spiritual or interpersonal mechanisms to ensure continuity. Generativity is, in part, a cultural response to finitude and termination of the culturally constructed self in a society governed by individualism. Again, behaviors undertaken to foster generativity are largely autonomous of specific religious systems concerning an afterlife. Rather, these generative actions are the practical spirituality of everyday life.

GENERATIVE PERSPECTIVES

In the remainder of this chapter, I wish to present and discuss some case material from a qualitative research project that concerned the generativity of older women. Case material was elicited through interviews with 161 women, aged 61–93 (mean age of 75) in a study entitled "Lifestyles and Generativity of Childless Older Women." The main purpose of this research was to explore manifestations of generativity among senior adult women with and without children, that is to say, all forms of generativity from parenthood through cultural transmission. The focus of this research project on childless women, who make up some 20 percent of older American women, was in response to an interest in understanding the generative energies and outlets of older women who do not have children. There were six study cells in the research: never-married and childless women; widowed and childless women; currently married and childless women; women who had survived at least half of their adult children; women with one child only; and women with four or more children. A complementary study of older men is currently in the field. Interviews were generally held over three sessions, held once a week for three weeks, lasting a total of six to ten hours. They were tape-recorded and transcribed.

Case 1.   Mrs. Friel, a heavyset yet active seventy-year-old, had been married for forty-eight years. Her husband suffered from emphysema and had curtailed his activities. A practicing Catholic, Mrs. Friel had six adult children, ages forty-eight to thirty. She lived with her husband in suburban Philadelphia. Her eldest children were twins, and all but the youngest lived independently and had their own households and families. Her youngest was born with Down's syndrome, and spent weekdays in a residential facility, but was often home with his parents on the weekends. She was faced with her husband's illness as well as her responsibilities for an ailing, never-married elderly sister who lived nearby. She also had concerns about the long-term care of her youngest son. Yet she felt satisfied that she had instilled enough family feeling in her children that the others would care for him after her own death.

She saw her own generative urges largely in terms of mothering and motherhood. For example, she was asked to list what in her own view were her accomplishments in life. She named "being a mother," taking special care of three of her babies who were born premature. In the nonmaternal areas, she listed her work as a lab technician prior to her marriage and, uniquely, the one time she acted as a best man in a wedding, in place of her husband, whose ship set sail unexpectedly during World War II. Nevertheless, she conceived of her life accomplishments largely in terms of motherhood and the spiritual nature of this role. This theme was often returned to in the interviews.

Interviewer: What activities have you enjoyed during your life?

Mrs. Friel: Well, being a mother . . . That's what I always wanted to be and I enjoyed it very much.

Interviewer: What's the best part about it?

Mrs. Friel: I don't know, just the whole thing. Having a baby and looking at this new baby, this new life and then seeing the child grow and develop. You know, I started out with twins and you see them developing differently, and it's just fascinating to watch this difference in them.

And again:

Interviewer: What do you consider to be the main purpose or task in life?

Mrs. Friel: I would say . . . the main thing in life [is] to be the best mother I could be.

Interestingly, she did not appear to view her role as a mother as including an idea that she would live on through her children. She was more modest and more vague about what, she felt, would live on after her.

Interviewer: All in all, what important things that you've done in your life do you think will outlive you or continue on after you are gone?

Mrs. Friel: Probably a messy basement (laughs). And my craft projects. They'll be around for a long while. . . . No, I don't know if there's anything in particular. Memories of me, I would say, certainly will outlive me, but whether they're good, bad, or indifferent, I don't know.

And,

Interviewer: In the past few years, have you ever felt that there was no one who would remember you when you are gone?

Mrs. Friel: No. I think that there will be some that remember me [but if they don't] it doesn't bother me too much. I know now that at my church they will remember me, and in my Down's syndrome volunteer group, they'll remember me, too.

But in her view the family does assure some sort of continuity. For example, at the end of a very long discussion of family members and their recent doings, she noted: "There's a lot to be said for big families. . . . It gives continuity to and a meaning to your life. You're just a dot on the face of the earth, but I guess you're a part of a family."

Her generative urges were primarily channeled through her role as a mother. She did not appear to be overinvolved in her children's lives, but she was able to continue her role as an active mother because of the continuing needs of her Down's syndrome son. Her relationship with her children and to the future appeared to be touched by a sense of satisfaction and accomplishment. She could see, in her children, what would survive her.

Case 2. Mrs. Cook, vital and active at age seventy, had been widowed for eighteen years. She had one living son and one who had died about five years prior to the interviews, accidentally burned to death in a house fire in a Western state. Her remaining son had been troubled as a youth, and was until recently an active substance abuser, but was now "in recovery." At age forty, he seemed to have finally found a degree of stability and maturity in his life and was in a stable relationship; this pleased his mother.

Her husband had had his own business; she had worked in adult teaching and child care. Her children provided little in the way of generative outlet during her adult years. One had died before ever marrying; and it was unclear if the other, troubled and developmentally late, would find stability and himself have children. Rather, her generative action had been invested in personal relationships and teaching. She noted, "[These relationships] enhance me. So they're not just altruistic. . . . They're what I would call self-actualizing. But I mean I know enough of my past to know there were times I did a lot of things out of duty." And in the following interchange:

Interviewer: Do you see anything of yourself in family or friends.

Mrs. Cook: Well, I see it more particularly in terms of really young people: a great-niece, a friend's daughter . . . and I see it in terms of their ideals and values. They like to be open, to be ready to risk closeness or self-disclosure or to be ready to express it about the positive. . . . It's [a] kind of freedom or expression of warmth.

To be sure, her son's death had had the potential to block or terminate her interest in living and her generative strivings. Indeed, she suffered still from his absence. But she had been able to put some perspective on her loss, and viewed it both as a terrible closing of a door, and an opening as well.

Interviewer: Was there ever a time you felt you were having a second chance to make up for things you may have done badly before or things that had gone wrong?

Mrs. Cook: Well, you're talking in terms of my own mistakes rather than in terms of things like losses. Because I can answer that in terms of loss. I already said that after my son's death, it was a godsend that I was teaching . . . that I had many, many, many adult students in whom I could invest.

And, after his death:

It is hard. It is hard. God knows I was up against all this, these things about not being sure I wanted to continue living. Yet feeling committed to a lot of people who'd given me a lot of support and who loved me and who at this point looked to me somehow . . . to keep on living and live through this thing. So that kept me going. That was a kind of commitment to the people who cared about me and the people who cared about my son. Even the people out there, that I was very close to when I was there. I remember someone telling me just how lost and at sea they all were until I came and then somehow, it was, they could go on. And the night after I got to my son's house, after he died, one of my son's best friends who was housesitting in this big wonderful house, everybody brought food and everybody gathered. And I moved around and met people. And the next night we gathered again, maybe forty or sixty people. Many of them I never met before. . . . So, I felt committed to go on and live and live and eventually have again a rich, full life. And sometimes people get into, I got into, I got into a feeling I couldn't let him down or his memory or what he stood for.

Mrs. Cook started her adulthood with a rather normative generative outlet in her two sons. One died and the other had a troubled life. She found that she could no longer invest in them generatively in the manner in which she had anticipated. However, she had somehow managed to turn from these closed doors to other openings, to find a way. This consisted of friendships, peer-relations, fictive parenthood of friends' children, teaching and mentoring, across many domains. These nurtured her and would, in a small way, outlive her.

Case 3.   Mrs. Grey, 92-year-old woman who never had any children, had been widowed for three years after a forty-year marriage. She had few relatives—her closest were distant cousins who lived in rural Canada—and few living connections. She approached the end of her life with determined planning and with the idea to make as little trouble for anyone as possible. For example, she had labeled all the furniture and possessions in her home with the name of the person who was to get them when she was gone. She had all her worldly affairs settled up and in the hands of her lawyer. She anticipated and in a certain sense was waiting around for her end.

She was keen to cleanly terminate her existence in the world. She had made careful plans for the total disposition of her personal property, effects and savings. She destroyed photos of her husband and his family after his death. She got rid of many books and possessions. She had planned for her own cremation and the scattering of her ashes. She had taken total responsibility for her earthly existence. I asked her if this was deliberate, if when she was gone ''the book would close,'' and she replied that that was her goal, to close the book and be completely gone.

Her sense of generativity was largely in the past and was perceived as a function of her work role as a teacher and student counselor in the United States and abroad.

Interviewer: Thinking of your life as a whole, what have been some of your accomplishments?

Mrs. Grey: Well, the most important to me would be the opportunity to become a teacher and to move from that into personnel work in the public school and college and university. And I guess I could call it leadership of a kind that put me in key positions in certain professional organizations. Which meant a great deal to me. And I would say that, although I had no special dreams about what marriage might do from the standpoint of continuing professional growth, but it did and that made it very nice. . . . And the opportunity to spend twenty years abroad learning about other people. And the kinds of experience which we had were very outstanding to us. Other people do greater things but these were important to us.

Her spiritual focus was clearly of this world and she recognized that her living was primarily a thing of the past. She noted, "Well, as society is today and the changes that I have seen and the changes that there are going to be, I think I would say I lived a fuller life, maybe the fullest part of my life up to age eighty-five. And felt a part of everything. I mean, I wasn't conscious of my age or of people doing something or not doing something because they had an old lady in their midst." Having children would not necessarily, in her view, have made her present any different or affected her sense of generative action. She stated, "If I had children and these children were located professionally in different parts of the United States, whereby I might see them once or twice a year, I don't think my feelings would be any different than they are today, living without children or contacts." She thus faced the future both satisfied and alone:

Interviewer: Who would you say is the most important person in your life right now?
Mrs. Grey: No one.

Mrs. Grey waited for her end, seemingly without fear and with full knowledge that her effects on the world and its people were of the past, were ephemeral and incorporeal, not tangible. They were affected through influence, example, advice, professional concern and knowledge transmission. There was for her a great satisfaction in leaving little materially and no loose ends and in the very act of being present to supervise her own end.

DISCUSSION

Most American religions do articulate beliefs about where the soul goes after death. Yet, after interviewing hundreds of American elders over the last decade or so, I have failed to encounter many people who subscribe uncritically to such beliefs about the afterlife or subscribe to such beliefs without significant doubts or through deeply colored rationalistic glasses. Mostly people say they don't know, aren't sure, or doubt the existence of an afterlife. They are more concerned with the practical matters of earthly endings.

Thus, in our culture, the onus is placed on the individual to construct components of selfhood that will outlive the corporeal self. To the extent that forms of generative outlets are built into the system or are at least normative, these consist of primary and lineal relations. However, the reality is that not all individuals have children, and that some children die prematurely. Thus many normative outlets are blocked.

Because it deals with issues of connections, human continuity, and transcendence, I have argued that there is a spiritual component to the selfwork undertaken at the end of a life. The above cases illustrate rather different dimensions of this self work. Mrs. Friel established her generative outlet through her children. Her children had established themselves in life, but as a senior adult she was still involved in the care of an impaired son, and in arranging for his care after her own death, for the rest of his life. Mrs. Cook saw the generative outlets of her children as "stopped up" and sought the expression of her influence and an outlet for her wisdom in nonkin, mentoring relations. Mrs. Grey, without children and beyond a life of teaching and mentoring, had completed her self work, made arrangements, and decided to go out with as little fuss as possible. These arrangements are not "spiritual" in the traditional sense. They lack reference to the divine or the sacred; they are not "selfless"; rather, they contain components of narcissism and self-centeredness, as does all generative action. Yet they are distinctively spiritual and generative in that they refer to the self through time, transcendence of the self, express support and love, and unity of people through action.

The need to connect through generative action is tied to the cultural architecture of the self in the United States and solves an organizational problem in individualism in how the matrix of the self is constructed. This issue is quite different from, although may be considered complementary to, a religious ethos that promises an afterlife for the soul in return for good deeds.

Generativity is enacted through small components that express love, warmth, nurturance, and support. Yet this work is pragmatic, of daily life as it moves through time, and not grandly religious or spiritual. We may view these acts as small, pragmatic components of spirituality.

NOTE

The data presented in the chapter were collected as part of a research project entitled "Lifestyles and Generativity of Childless Older Women," conducted by R. Rubinstein and supported by the National Institute of Aging. Support of the Institute for this research is gratefully acknowledged. Project interviews were undertaken by the author and colleagues that included Marcene Goodman, Baine B. Alexander, Mark Luborsky and Helen Black. We also wish to thank informants in this study who openly shared their lives and thoughts with us. All names used in this chapter are pseudonymous and some details have been changed to preserve anonymity.

REFERENCES

Alexander, B. B., R. Rubinstein, M. Goodman, and M. Luborsky. 1991. Generativity in cultural context: The self, death and immortality as experienced by older American women. *Ageing and Society* 11, 417–42.

Bateson, G. 1972. Culture contact and schismogenesis. In G. Bateson, ed., *Steps to an ecology of mind*. New York: Ballantine Books.

Becker, E. 1973. *The denial of death*. New York: The Free Press.

Bellah, R. N., R. Madsen, W. Sullivan, A. Swidler, and S. M. Tipton. 1985. *Habits of the heart: Individualism and commitment in American life*. New York: Harper and Row.

Buber, M. 1966. *The way of response*. New York: Schocken Books.

———.1970. *I and thou*. Translated by Walter Kaufman. New York: Scribners.

Clark, M., and B. Anderson. 1968. *Culture and aging.* Springfield, IL: C. C. Thomas.

Erikson, E. H. 1963. *Childhood and society.* New York: Norton.

Greenhouse, C. J. 1992. Signs of quality: Individualism and hierarchy in American culture. *American Ethnologist* 19, 233–54.

Hepworth, M., and M. Featherstone. 1982. *Surviving middle age.* Oxford: Basil Blackwell.

Hsu, F.L.K. 1972. American core value and national character. In F.L.K. Hsu, ed. *Psychological anthropology.* Cambridge, MA: Schenkman.

Kantorowicz, E. H. 1957. *The king's two bodies: A study in medieval political theology.* Princeton: Princeton University Press.

Kotre, J. N. 1984. *Outliving the self: Generativity and the interpretation of lives.* Baltimore: Johns Hopkins University Press.

Lasch, C. 1979. *The culture of narcissism: American life in an age of diminishing expectations.* New York: Warner Books.

Lifton, R. J., and E. Markusen. 1990. *The genocidal mentality: Nazi holocaust and nuclear threat.* New York: Basic Books.

Nemiroff, R. A., and C. A. Colarusso. 1985. *The race against time: Psychological theory and psychoanalysis in the second half of life.* New York: Plenum.

Plato. 1951. *The symposium.* Translated by W. Hamilton. Harmondsworth: Penguin.

Turner, B. S. 1984. *The body in society: Explorations in social theory.* Oxford: Basil Blackwell.

12 Religiosity and Fear of Death in Non-Normative Aging

Sheldon S. Tobin, Elise M. Fullmer, and Gregory C. Smith

Fears of death decline in normative aging, in part because of religious beliefs. These beliefs, however, cannot be evoked or death accepted when non-normative aging occurs as a result of not having yet completed life's tasks—that is, when still having "unfinished business" in the oldest years (Tobin 1991). The non-normative aging group to be discussed consists of elderly mothers caring at home for offspring with mental retardation, and thus whose unfinished business is to continue care until they no longer are able to do so and also to make permanent residential plans for after their deaths.

The chapter begins with a discussion of how religious beliefs relate to acceptance of death and maintenance of subjective well-being in normative aging. Then, the prototypic Mrs. Smith is used to illustrate non-normative aging in the group of mothers studied: Although her religiosity has enriched a lifetime of caregiving, she cannot use her religious beliefs for acceptance of death. Next, we consider manifest and latent meaning of death for these mothers, including the increasing fears of death with age, afterward discussing with illustrations their religiosity and acceptance of death for feelings of well-being. The chapter continues by introducing the four mothers over ninety years of age who, although their religiosity could make death welcomed, refuse to give in to death because of unfinished business. Their pattern may become more normative with the persistence of religious beliefs in future elderly cohorts who will have greater percentages of people with unfinished business from caregiving and from better educations that cause the continued seeking of secular goals at the end of the life course. The final section is a brief synthesis of uses and meanings of religiosity for the non-normative aging mothers.

RELIGIOUS BELIEFS

Three religious beliefs, inculcated at a young age, become salient to the acceptance of old age and of death. A first belief is that a long life is one of God's blessings (Ps. 91:16; and also Prov. 9:11), that longevity is a reward for prior service (Deut. 4:40). Often quoted is "A heavy head is a crown of glory; it is gained in a righteous life" (Prov. 16:31). A second belief, also one of God's blessings, is that a hereafter will contain reunions with departed loved ones. Contrary to the portrayal of heaven as a place where one sits on a billowing cloud strumming a harp, the hereafter is perceived by the very old who hold this belief as a time of rejoining those who are deceased. In turn, these two beliefs are often accompanied by a third belief among religious people who are suffering: It would be God's blessing to die rather than to remain in unendurable pain. Even among those who are not religious, however, aging in the later years is associated with an increasing acceptance of nonbeing as concerns shift to the process of dying, with wishes to not die in pain, immobile, alone and irreversibly confused.

It would be anticipated that in a religious society such as ours, where about three or four persons believe they have a personal relationship with God and also believe in a hereafter (Gallup and Castelli 1989), the strength of these beliefs would, for example, enhance feelings of subjective well-being. Klenow and Bolin (1989) have reported that nearly 70 percent of Americans believe in a hereafter. Yet, as discussed by Levin and Tobin (in press), these beliefs have been insufficiently assessed in studies. Rather, the focus has tended to be on formal religious activities, informal religious practices, and personal assessments of extent of religiosity. A rare exception is Bearon and Koenig's (1990) descriptive study of the religious beliefs among older people, in which they included the item "Heaven is a blessing or a gift from God," with which over three-quarters of respondents were in agreement.

ACCEPTANCE OF DEATH

Death becomes acceptable at the end of life when the perception is that a life course has been lived and that there is no unfinished business. Yet, is it possible, as Kierkegaard (1844) has noted, that we cannot escape the dread of death? Kierkegaard introduced the existential paradox of "individuality within finitude." Whereas each of us has an identity that transcends the natural order of species survival, never can we transcend our personal demise. This dualism of the human condition is the price we must pay for being human. According to Kierkegaard, in becoming human, our consciousness creates the dread, the anxiety regarding our nonbeing. It is only human beings that have this peculiar and greatest anxiety.

I was cognizant of this most human of all anxieties when I began my studies of aging. Then, in my early thirties, I avoided asking elderly persons about death. Reinforcing the decision with Morton A. Lieberman (Lieberman and Tobin 1982; Tobin and Lieberman 1976) not to ask elderly persons about their deaths when relocating to long-term care facilities was also the reluctance of interviewers to query older respondents about their impending death. Typical comments made by the interviewers in the relocation studies, all professional women in their forties who were selected, in part, because of good relationships with their own parents, were, "They will clam up and tell us nothing afterwards," and, "If I have some questions on death at the end of an interview session, they will be so upset that they will never talk to me again." For the interviewers, as well as for me, to uncover attitudes toward this dreaded and suppressed topic would be disastrous for the respondents and for the study.

But then we discovered that our elderly respondents invariably introduced the topic of death. Indeed it was the rare respondent who did not mention that he or she was near death, and also that nonbeing was less feared than the process of dying.

Although I was familiar with Munnichs's (1966) then recent work in which he had reported an acceptance of death among elderly persons in the Netherlands, I was disbelieving of his results. Munnichs had written:

It was extremely surprising to us at the time that there was a great preponderance of confidence and lack of apprehension, though more than half of the number of persons interrogated admitted that they did think about the matter. We realized this unexpected result was that if death was awesome in character for only few exceptions, the field of experience during old age must be of a different nature from what is generally supposed. (p.12)

Of course, Munnichs's finding should not have been so surprising. Nearly a century ago, Scott (1896) reported on a survey in which he found little anxiety regarding death among the elderly, noting the looking forward to a heavenly life. Less fear of death with aging has been a consistent finding since then and has been reported by, among others, Keller, Sherry and Piotrowski (1984) and most recently by Thorson (1991).

How, I then asked myself, could a person of any age accept his or her death? However, because our findings confirmed Munnichs's findings, I had to confront the inescapable truth. Whereas I can do so intellectually, deep down I still harbor disbelief. It probably cannot be otherwise among those of us in our middle years. But at least we can make the attempt to understand why it is that toward the end of life the very old can accept their nonbeing.

Although death in our culture is perceived as loss, perceptions of what is lost varies. Diggory and Rothman (1961) surveyed people and found that seven kinds of losses were associated with the contemplation of death: loss of ability to have experiences, of ability to predict subsequent events (e.g., life after death), of body and fear of what will happen to the body, of ability to care for dependents, loss suffered by friends and family (e.g., causing grief for others), of opportunity to continue plans and projects, and of being in a relatively stable state. It was found that the greatest concern for men was their inability to care for dependents, whereas the greatest concern for women was causing grief to family and friends. Persons between fifteen and thirty-nine selected causing grief to friends as their major anticipated loss through death, whereas those over forty chose the inability to care for dependents. In a later study, when Kalish and Reynolds (1976) included more people over fifty-five, they found that caring for dependents was less important for this age group. What concerned elderly people was not future plans, and not death itself, but rather having no control over how they will die, dying alone, and dying with pain. Thornson and Powell (1988) confirmed that loss of control is a greater concern to the elderly and also found concerns with "whether there is an afterlife or what the next world would be like" (p. 698).

But obviously there is individual variability in how each person conceptualizes the meaning of a long life and also how each person perceives his or her death. The person who feels that death is to be raged against and does so with his or her last gasp is actually dying in the way he or she wishes. Another individual may become more resigned and passive, approaching death in a peaceful manner, as noted by Cato in Cicero's (44 B.C.) essay, "De Senecture," (On old age): "There had to be a time of withering, of readiness to fall, like the ripeness which comes to the fruits of the trees and of the earth. But a wise man will face this prospect with resignation, for resistance against nature is as pointless as the battles of the giants against the gods" (pp. 214–215).

So too do groups of persons differ from other groups regarding the acceptibility of death in old age. Those who share the view that time is too short to achieve self-assigned ambitions cannot accept death. Visual artists, for example, even in very advanced old age, may still be seeking to express the essence of their work. Analysis of interviews with artists in their later years (Tobin 1991) echoed Hokusai, the greatest of Japanese woodcutters, who said on his deathbed at ninety-four that he is just now beginning to learn his craft. Here, however, the focus is on a group of mothers that have unfinished business not because of self-assigned ambitions, but because of uncompleted life tasks: the perpetual parenting at home of mentally retarded offspring and the assuring of viable care after their deaths.

THE NORMATIVE PROCESS IN BRIEF

The adaptive task in normative aging is to preserve the self. Although preserving the continuity of the self is a motive throughout life (see, for example, Lecky 1945), it becomes the central motive later in life because of age-associated losses that corrode the integrity of the self. Essential to accomplishing this task is the ability to perceive control over some everyday things, even if this is inflated belief in control rather than actual control. Concurrently, with the awareness that external events are beyond personal control, and because of the uncertainty over events and their timing, there is less worrying about the future (Kulys and Tobin 1980–81; Powers, Wisoki, and Whitbourne 1992). In turn, blending the past and present, and making the past vivid, provides validation and continuity to the self. Together, beliefs in continuity and control give a sense of wholeness; and most sustaining of feelings of well-being is the conviction of congruence between expected and achieved life goals.

Feelings of well-being are enhanced by the perception of oneself as special in surviving to an advanced old age; these feelings become augmented if accompanied by the religious sense of being personally blessed by God by a long life. In turn, acceptance of death is facilitated by religious beliefs in a hereafter of reunions with deceased loved ones as the concern shifts from preoccupations and fears of death itself, of nonbeing, to fear of the process of dying.

A hereafter with reunions is rarely introduced in interviews with older people unless specifically queried. For ten years now I have asked students in my graduate course "The Latter Half of Life" to ask about religious beliefs in their assignment to interview community-dwelling elderly persons eighty or over. About half their elderly respondents discuss a hereafter with reunions. An example:

Mr. Poulin, an 87-year-old retired autobody welder of French Canadian descent, lost his wife, Suzanne, four years ago. Because they married when he was 17 and Suzanne 16, they had been married 66 years at the time of her death. He maintains a close relationship with his two daughters, who both live nearby and visit on weekends. During the week he socializes with cronies in his public housing complex and volunteers with the Little Sisters of the Poor three days a week. Still, he feels very lonely when he thinks about Suzanne and "the good time we had together." He then added, "But I have friends here, so I don't get very depressed." Now somewhat choked up, he continued by commenting that he especially enjoys his occasional trips to churches and shrines in Canada. A few minutes later when asked what death means to him, he lighted up, smiled and answered, "I am ready whenever the good Lord calls me. It will be good to get back with Suzanne and the rest of the family."

Sometimes the reunion is of a surprising nature:

A lonely 83-year-old woman who has been widowed for 22 years has a shrine in her living room for her dog Rufus who she raised from a puppy and who died eight months ago. A leash hangs from the shrine and as she talks of Rufus she glances over to the shrine and says, "Whenever I get too lonely, I stroke the leash. I'm looking forward to seeing Rufus again." Although she talked about her religious beliefs throughout the interview and frequently her belief in life hereafter, she only mentioned the reunion with Rufus, never with her deceased parents nor with her deceased husband. Her lone companion for eight years, Rufus, is at the center of her thoughts.

Reunions permit feelings of continuity, of immortality, that attenuate the dread of nonbeing. But what is the nature of this immortality? It apparently is different from what Lifton and Olson (1974) have discussed under the rubric of symbolic immortality:

We can see the *sense of symbolic immortality* as reflecting man's relatedness to all that comes before him and all that follows him. This relatedness is expressed in the many kinds of symbolization that enable one to participate in ongoing life without denying the reality of death. Without this unending sense of attachment to aims and principles beyond the self, the everyday formative process we have been discussing—as well as the capacity to feel at home in the world—cannot be sustained. When people believe in such cultural projects and expressions, they feel a sense of attachment to human flow, to both their biology and their history. They feel a *sense of immortality* which enables active, vital life to go on. (pp. 75–76)

They continue by focusing on the five modes in which this sense of immortality is expressed: biological, creative, theological, natural and experiential. The biological mode embodied in historical continuity with offspring and cultural groups recedes in importance in advanced aging. In turn, the creative mode, in which symbolic immortality is achieved through products, is unusual. The theological immortality, specifically the concept of spiritual attainment through rebirth, is not in evidence when very old people discuss reunions with specific others. Nor do reunions embody symbolic continuity with nature. The temporary suspension of time in experiential transcendence, through moments of time that "have an ecstatic quality" similarly does not capture what respondents tell us when they are very old and perceive themselves to be nearing the end of their life span.

The reason that none of these modes fits the symbolic immortality of the very old is that reunions are self-centered. That is, reunions with specific, meaningful deceased persons or pet companions are too concrete and self-focused to suggest Lifton and Olson's "unending sense of attachment to aims and principles beyond the self."

Instructive, and congruent with this perspective, is Erikson's reformulation of the last stage of life in *The Life Cycle Completed* (1982), a book that he wrote when he was in his eighties. Whereas in *Childhood and Society,* written in 1950, he included "investing in the continuity of generations" for achieving ego integrity, this kind of continuity becomes rather irrelevant in his later focus on maintaining "integrality, a tendency to keep things together" as biological deficits corrode an integrated, coherent self. Essential according to Erikson in 1982 is "a timeless love for those few 'others' who have become the main counterplayers in life's most significant contexts" (p. 65). Yet, it is apparent that "timeless love" is secondary to vivid memories of the counterplayers that make one vivid to oneself and give meaning to oneself. Apparently, however, the counterplayers are not only captured in memories of the past because they also become the focus of reunions in the future. To be sure, reminiscence and reunions typically focus on loved ones, particularly parents, spouse and children if deceased, but not always. A woman in her mid-eighties told of looking forward to a reunion with her older brother who cast her out of the family for marrying a man beneath her. Her greatest wish is to confront this brother with how he has wronged her, to chastise him and to tell him that she had a wonderfully successful marriage.

WHEN BUSINESS IS UNFINISHED

The sample consisted of 235 mothers fifty-eight to ninety-six years of age caring at home for an adult offspring with mental retardation (MR). Elderly mothers who continue to care at home for their offspring with MR are becoming more prevalent as the average life span of persons with developmental disabilities increases. Like other elderly mothers, they can achieve a congruence between expected and achieved life goals from the successful launching of their other nondependent children, but unlike other elderly mothers, they are still immersed in child caring, or what Jennings (1987) has called "perpetual parenthood." Their commitment to this life goal, and their gratifications in caring and beliefs that no one can provide the care that they can, makes it difficult for them to relinquish care to others and also to accept their own death. Content on death and religion in the two-hour face-to-face interviews with mothers by clinicians with masters degrees were minimal. Although this was not the main thrust of the research, the data still permit some interesting findings.

An example of how elderly mothers who have mentally retarded offspring at home differ from the portrait of normative aging is Mrs. Molly Jones.

Mrs. Jones at eighty-six feels "old" because of her waning physical energies, and, also, from caring for her quite ill 87-year-old husband. She is poignantly aware of not being her former self. She says, "I'm not like I was. I don't have the energy anymore. I just don't have the patience." She, however, can preserve her sense of self because she continues to care at home for her eldest son Jim who, at fifty-nine, is moderately retarded.

Her other son, 58-year-old Tom, resides less than a block away; and Tom, his wife and their children, Mrs. Jones's grandchildren, form a close-knit family. She is proud of them, particularly of their closeness and attentiveness to Jim. Thus like other elderly people, Mrs. Jones feels she has successfully mothered and launched the next generation. Yet with Jim at home and necessitating daily care, a lifelong task remains. Having cared for Jim for more than half a century, she feels that placing him in a group home would be to abandon him. Although she would prefer that Tom makes a home for Jim, she wishes not to burden him and his wife. She says, "It would be too much of a burden. They should live their own lives and enjoy their children and then their grandchildren."

Noticeably absent is use of the past for preservation of the self. She never mentions anyone from her family of origin. She can only think about the past as it pertains to Jim, that caring for Jim has been meaningful to her since his birth and that the successful rearing of her other child is best reflected in his and his children's closeness to Jim. Never does she describe any attributes or successes of Tom or her grandchildren other than closeness in the family. She communicates that Tom's wife is special too because she also is fond of Jim. Although the interview focused on the mother's relationship with her retarded offspring, there apparently were sufficient open-ended queries to elicit comments on children's and grandchildren's accomplishments.

Caring for Jim, however, is not without its rewards. She says, "He is still my baby. I don't know what I would do without him. Caring for him . . . I just don't have the energy and my husband is so sick. . . . It is so hard but it's what I do." Indeed, she does it well.

As noted by Seltzer, Kraus and Heller (1991) regarding Mrs. Jones and other aging parents of developmentally disabled offspring, "It is now widely recognized that most parents cope effectively and positively with the additional demands experienced in parenting a child with mental retardation" (p. 7). Others too have discussed the benefits retarded offspring can accrue for their families. Baroff (1986) wrote: "Unquestionably the retarded child can stir deep tenderness, enhance patience, and teach us that a person of value is not limited to individuals who are mirror images of ourselves" (p. 333).

So Mrs. Jones obtains gratification from caring for her retarded son Jim as do mothers of young children but, in common with mothers now "old" when she thinks about her other son Tom and his family, she reaps the rewards from lifelong goals. Yet, although she has agreed with the case manager at the day program that a group home is sensible for Jim, she knows that it can never be like the home she has made for him. She worries about the future, is unable to foster inflated beliefs in control, and dreading the eventuality of Jim's uncertain future, she cannot face death with equanimity. She not only says that she cannot let herself think about dying but, as she ponders dying, almost inaudibly adds, "I can't die." Unlike other elderly mothers, she has "unfinished business" that preoccupies her thoughts.

Religion sustains Mrs. Jones in her caregiving. Jim is God's special gift to her, not as a cross to bear but as a special child to care for and to mother. Like other mothers who live to advanced old age, she has a feeling of specialness. But although she shares with others beliefs in being personally blessed by God by a long life and hereafter with reunions, she cannot use these beliefs to her advantage as mothers can who exhibit normative aging when very old. If she was certain that she would outlive Jim, she could feel blessed for her long life. Also, she cannot consider reunions with lost loved ones, particularly her parents, while immersed in caregiving. Because of unfinished business, she cannot sleep peacefully and accept her approaching death.

Mrs. Jones reveals the paradoxical aging that is characteristic of our mothers. Like younger mothers nurturing young children, she accrues gratification in caregiving. In turn, if the adaptive task in aging is to preserve the continuity of the self, this task is assured because of perpetual motherhood. Enhancement of the self and well-being is further bolstered by perceptions of having successfully launched other children. Yet, these foundations are undermined by awareness of unfinished business which will remain unfinished following her death.

MANIFEST AND LATENT MEANINGS OF DEATH

Respondents were asked to complete the Sentence Completion Test (SCT) *Death is . . .* stem. Responses were scored on a five-point scale from most negative to most positive. A score of 1 was given for fear or denial of fear as reflected in responses such as "I am afraid to go just now" or "I would not be afraid if she was taken care of." A score of 2 was given for themes of loss, where responses encompassed "nothing," "could not take care of him," and "to lose everything." A score of 3 was given when themes were neutral in tone, with responses such as "natural" or "inevitable." Scored 4 were themes of relief from pain or suffering such as "he will let me die in peace" and "ease my pain." And a score of 5 was given when there was a trancendental quality as reflected, for example, by sentence completions of "going to heaven" and "meeting my maker."

The modal response (146, or 62.1 percent) was a score of 3 (death as "natural" or "inevitable"). About one-third (forty-six, or 34.1 percent) gave completions receiving scores of 1 or 2 (indicating fears or loss) and, in turn, less than one in five (forty-three, or 18.3 percent) scores of 4 or 5 (indicating that death is either a blessing because it brings relief from worldly pain or contains welcomed reunions). The modal response, the naturalness or inevitability of death, captures only the most manifest level of the meaning of death. Although responses to the SCT *Death is . . .* stem do not suggest a great fear of dying, responses to the query that followed, in which the focus on death is in the context of caring for offspring, do indeed reflect great fear. The question that was asked was: *Has being a parent and caregiver of a mentally retarded son/daughter affected your feelings about your own death?* Because many had communicated an answer to this question when completing the SCT *Death is . . .* stem and others chose to avoid this topic, only about one-half (115 of the 235, or 48.9 percent) of the mothers answered this question.

Of the 115 mothers who answered the question, 10 were selected at random to develop a typology, but as will be readily apparent, there was little, if any, variability. Of the ten, six completed the stem with responses of "natural" or "inevitable." In the order of my analysis of these six cases, the first woman, who had completed the stem with "a matter of fact," responded to the open-ended query by saying, "I don't want her to go before me." The second, whose completion was "the end of life," said "I hate the thought of leaving her, I wish I could live forever." The third, fourth and fifth respondents completed the stem with "inevitable," the third answering the query with "I would like to be with him when he dies," the fourth with "I hate to think about not being around for him. I don't know how my death will affect him," and the fifth with "I worry about him. He'll miss me." The sixth, who completed the stem with "the end, no more," answered the query with "I worry leaving him to fend for himself. His sister has her own health problems so she can't care." Mrs. Jones is like these six in having completed the stem by saying "natural," but then she answered the query by adding that she tries not to think about her death and ended with the comment, as noted earlier, "I can't die."

The two who gave stem completions reflecting acceptance of death revealed similar concerns in their responses to the query. A woman whose completion was "relief" answered the query with "I want to be here forever to give care." The other woman, whose completion was "the end of my worries," answered the query with "To the extent that she is not settled yet." The responses of this woman reflect an ambivalence shared by our respondents: "It is good for me when I do not have to worry any more but it could be terrible for my child."

The two of the ten who introduced fear or loss revealed the same concerns. One woman whose completion was "I know I should not be afraid" (implying her fear), answered, "I wish I could live forever to take care of her." The other woman, whose completion was "a terrible loss," answered, "Everyday I ask God to stay on earth so I can help him."

The combination of less than one-half of responses to the *Death is* . . . stem revealing great fears and fears expressed in response to the query reveals the internal conflict regarding death of these mothers: If they were not perpetual parents, death would be acceptable. At the most manifest level, the modal response to the *Death is* . . . stem indicates the suppressing of fears by these mothers. However, as soon as the focus shifts to death in the context of their offspring, content in the less manifest level, which is unable to be suppressed, is revealed. Death is greatly to be feared. The fear is so ubiquitous among these mothers that there is almost no variability in their responses to the open-ended query. Put another way, whether death is natural, feared or acceptable at the most manifest level, it is a fear that cannot be suppressed because of its severing of their lifetime of caring and its condemnation of their offspring to an unknown future.

The containment of the underlying, less manifest fear, however, is weakened with age. As death draws closer, suppression of fears becomes less possible. Responses to the *Death is* . . . stem show both a decrease in acceptance of death with age and an increase in fears and losses in the sample. Themes of fear and loss are indeed greater with each older age group: 15.5 percent of 58- to 69-year-olds gave themes of fear or loss, whereas 20 percent of 70- to 79-year-olds, but a much higher 38.5 percent of 80- to 96-year-olds and, in turn, 21.7 percent of 58- to 69-year-olds gave transcendental themes of relief of suffering or a welcomed hereafter, compared to 15 percent of 70- to 79-year-olds and 11.5 percent of 80- to 96-year-olds. Although the distribution is not statistically different from chance, the inverse association between age and acceptance of death is counter to normative aging. Corresponding to this inverse association, responses to the Likert-scaled interview item "Life is too short" increased from 70.6 percent agreement for the 58- to 69-year-olds to 71.3 percent for those 70 to 79, and then to 80.8 percent for those 80 to 96. Additionally, interviewers' assessments of respondents who have great difficulty dying in peace increased in the three respective age groups, from 10.1 percent to 16.3 percent and then to 19.2 percent, while their assessments of great fears of death rose from 10.1 percent to 13.8 percent and then to 23.1 percent. Although, therefore, only a minority of the elderly mothers at any age revealed great fears of death, fears increased with each sequential age group.

Corresponding to the lessening acceptance of death with age is a movement away from humanism. Mothers in the sample often discussed how rearing a retarded child made them more understanding of, and sensitive to, other people. With advancing age, however, the meaningfulness of rearing a retarded child was more narrowly focused on how devoted they have been to their offspring, and on how proud they are of providing a lifetime of home care. Humanism thus becomes the devotion of their lives to another human being, actually to an extension of themselves.

A secular definition of spirituality, however, suggests stability with age and, paradoxically, spirituality possibly more easily achieved than for normative mothers. That is, if spirituality is defined as interpretations of one's personal life and of the world, the devotion to perpetual parenthood readily affords a secular spiritualism. In aging, interpretation of one's personal life is generally reflected in the sense of continuity when confronted with age-associated assaults that corrode the self, and interpretation of the world usually involves connectedness, which can be to one's God, to meaningful groups of others and to family. Perpetual parenthood provides for both continuity and connectedness, narrowly focused though they may be. At the same time, the presence of a kind of humanism and a secular spirituality, spirituality in the form of attachment to religious beliefs, is less evidenced as death becomes increasingly unacceptable.

RELIGIOSITY AND ACCEPTANCE OF DEATH

Religiosity was measured rather superficially. Mothers were simply asked whether they were "not religious," "somewhat religious" or "very religious." Clearly, this simple single-item query does not capture intrinsic religiosity, the kind of religiosity G. Stanley Hall (1896; 1915) may have believed holds the promise of attenuating the existential dread of nonbeing. Evidence to support Hall has been forthcoming. Klenow and Bolin (1989) found that "strong religious intensity" was associated with belief in a hereafter. Yet, evidence as to whether extrinsic or intrinsic religiosity matters more for lessening death fears is mixed. Kahoe and Dunn (1975), for example, found an association with intrinsic but not extrinsic religiosity, whereas Bolt (1977) with extrinsic but not intrinsic religiosity. Thorson and Powell (1988), in summarizing the disparate results from the many studies, observed that inconsistency is related to conceptual and methodological differences, as well as to sampling. Homogeneous samples cannot be expected to reveal associations. When Thorson and Powell (1988; 1990) used a heterogeneous sample, they found a relationship. They also concluded from their study and other studies that death anxiety is lower and intrinsic religiosity higher in later life.

In our study, of the 235 mothers, only 14 (2.6 percent) responded to the query *Are you religious?* by choosing the alternative "not religious," whereas "somewhat religious" was selected by 105 (44.7 percent) and "very religious" by 116 (49.4 percent). It is apparent, however, that the "somewhats" often reflected nonparticipation in formal religious activities rather than intrinsic religiosity. Because of stigma attached to the mentally retarded when these mothers had their child, many neither attended church services nor had their son or daughter attend Sunday School. Yet, our subsample of fifty-nine respondents who were difficult to recruit to the study because they do not use day programs for their mentally retarded offspring were often referred to us by clergy. Apparently, many mothers become known to clergy through the religious activities of their family members. It seems that some clergy seldom see these mothers except at occasions such as funerals and weddings. It obviously would have been preferable to use a measure of intrinsic religiosity uncontaminated by practices. Given the religiosity of the sample, if their aging was normative, it would be expected that religious beliefs inculcated earlier in life that are salient to the older years would be in evidence. But salient religious beliefs were not very evident. Nor was the expected association between religiosity and these beliefs. Mrs. Smith exemplifies the difficulty these non-normative mothers have in using their religiosity for accepting death.

At eighty-seven and twice widowed, Mrs. Smith lives an isolated rural life caring for her 62-year-old retarded daughter Janey. Her other daughter, aged seventy, lives two miles away and is expected to make a home for Janey when she dies. Mrs. Smith said that she is very religious and the interviewer wrote, "She is very religious and feels that God gave her the responsibility of caring for her mentally retarded daughter and she will live up to that responsibility until the day she dies. I believe she will do this." She will do so because "God gave me this cross and I have to carry the cross." This comment reflects her ambivalence at this time in her life. Janey has always been "my honey, my heart" and now "she is still my baby" at sixty-two years of age. But at eighty-seven Mrs. Smith also says, "I have lived a secluded life due to caring for my daughters. I brought up the girls myself. I got remarried again. He was an alcoholic but a good person. It has not been a gratifying life." The inroads on her feelings of well-being are magnified because of her increasing inability to provide care. An operation for cervical cancer several years ago has led to incontinence, she has a broken shoulder and painful arthritis of the hip. Physically weakened and isolated, she completed the SCT *Death is . . .* stem ready to go: "Prepared to die." She also answered the question that followed with, "Her sister will take good care of her."

Missing in her response to the SCT *Death is . . .* stem is reference to any of God's blessings either in the form of relief of pain or a hereafter. Very religious persons can be expected to introduce these themes in advanced old age, especially those who, like Mrs. Smith, consider themselves no longer to just be "older" or "elderly" but now "old." To perceive oneself at eighty-seven as "old" is certainly to recognize the nearness of death. For Mrs. Smith, an acceptance of death must relate to the continuity of care for Janey rather than in her personal relationship to God.

Mrs. Smith contrasts with the three mothers over eighty who gave transcendental completions to the SCT *Death is . . .* stem. Two of the three were able to perceive their business as finished; and because both have high life satisfaction, they also reflect the association between transcendence in SCT *Death is . . .* stem completions and subjective well-being.

SUBJECTIVE WELL-BEING

Despite the fear of the future, these elderly mothers feel gratified in the present in their caregiving and also from their successes as they reflect on how they have carried out their self-assigned life task of caring for their retarded offspring and how their other children have made out. Their subjective well-being was assessed by the Life Satisfaction Rating (LSR) of interviewers (Neugarten, Havighurst and Tobin 1961). Subjective well-being, like religiosity, has not been sufficiently and accurately conceptualized for older persons. In addition to current affects, their subjective well-being should encompass satisfaction with present and past life. Thus, we (Neugarten, Havighurst and Tobin 1961) added the congruence between expected and achieved life goals in the life satisfaction assessment of subjective well-being.

The importance in the specification of well-being was evidenced by Thomas and Chambers (1989) in their study of elderly men in New Delhi and London. The groups differed markedly on what they regarded as central to well-being. The dominant theme among the Englishmen was dread of incapacity of becoming useless and dependent. For the Indian men there were three interrelated themes: importance of family, salience of religious beliefs, and satisfaction with the present life situation. Given their divergence and the substantive content of the well-being for the Indian men, it is understandable that the association between religiosity and well-being was found to be greater among the Indians than among the Englishman.

If in the assessment of psychological well-being greater attention can be paid to developing age- and culture-specific instruments more relevant to the groups under study, then associations of this construct with religiosity may be more likely to emerge and be more meaningful than those associations that have hereto been identified.

As expected, the LSR assessment of subjective well-being is associated with health status (correlations above 25), socioeconomic status (r = .15) and social supports (also about .15). Higher LSR was also associated with religiosity (r = .16) and with completions of the SCT stem (r = .19) that reflected an acceptance of death, a sense that it would relieve their suffering and bring a welcomed hereafter. Stated another way, those mothers who say they are very religious or who can accept death are more likely to have greater subjective well-being.

A statistical regression analysis showed that both religiosity and responses to the SCT *Death is . . .* stem reflecting acceptance of death equally added to the explained variance in LSR; that is, they were additive because the two measures were not associated with each other, which was unanticipated. Indeed, similar percentages of the very religious, as well as the somewhat religious, were accepting and nonaccepting of death. Of the 116 very religious, 22.4 percent were accepting of death and 23.3 unaccepting; and of the 105 somewhat religious, an equal 16.2 percent were accepting and unaccepting of death. Although the two dimensions of extent of self-reported religiosity and of acceptance of death have generally been associated (for example, in my students' assignment of interviewing normative aging persons eighty and over), an association was not evidenced in this non-normative sample. Given the apparent association between religiosity and acceptance of death, why the lack of association of self-reported religiosity and of acceptance of death for these mothers?

The interview data show the sample to be predominantly Christian (126 Catholics of 235, or 53.69 percent; 97 Protestants, or 41.3 percent; and 7, or 3 percent of Seventh Day Adventists; with 4 Jewish mothers and 1 who said no religion); and the data also suggest that all but a handful were reared in religious households. But as noted earlier, even if they maintain persistent religious beliefs, because they may not be participating in formal church activities, they are likely to call themselves somewhat religious. In turn, as also discussed earlier, although they have religious beliefs that contribute to the acceptance of death, many respondents cannot evoke these beliefs while engaged in caregiving and concerned with leaving the care of their offspring to others. The lack of association, however, does not explain why each contributes to subjective well-being.

Apparently, those who can consider themselves to be very religious have a greater sense of continuity with their past, which enhances well-being. And those who can use their religious beliefs for acceptance of death will also have greater subjective well-being. These, of course, are conjectures that must be substantiated with richer data than we have at hand.

TRANSCENDENCE AND SUBJECTIVE WELL-BEING

Of the three mothers over eighty with transcendental SCT *Death is . . .* stem completions, as noted earlier, two had high LSRs and were able to perceive their life task of caregiving as completed.

Mrs. Green at eighty-three has a 63-year-old daughter Margie who has severe disability from cerebral palsy. Widowed for twenty years, she has relied successfully on a case manager to find a group home for Margie after she dies. She completed the SCT stem with "Don't know what to say about that. Death is something you enter into to overcome your worldly thoughts." Then to the next question she said, "I don't mind dying. You'll be in a wonderful atmosphere." The interviewer's assessment was that she was very religious, could die in peace and was not afraid of death. Her LSR was 24, of a possible highest rating of 25.

Mrs. Brown, a 89-year-old widow of forty-nine years duration has a severely retarded daughter aged fifty-three who is living at home. Another daughter also lives with them in their trailer on the grounds of a church-related retirement community. Although her LSR is not as high as Mrs. Green's, at 19, it is relatively high. The reason for not being rated higher relates to her somewhat flat, matter-of-fact approach to life and not to feelings of inadequacy in caring for her severely retarded daughter or to her daughter's future. Saying she is very religious, she simply completed the SCT *Death is* . . . stem with "Going to heaven." To the next question she answered "No," communicating that having a mentally retarded offspring did not change her attitude toward death.

Mrs. Taylor, who is eighty-one and lives an isolated life with her 57-year-old daughter, is still mourning the death of her husband two years ago. Her LSR is a very low 7. She completed the SCT *Death is* . . . stem with "You go to a world beyond." Yet she said she was only somewhat religious. Death may contain a welcomed hereafter but, depressed and apathetic following her husband's death, she is unable to think about where her daughter will live after she dies. The interviewer noted that she fears death and cannot die in peace.

THE OLDEST OLD

Four mothers were over ninety, several years beyond the eighty-five years of age now considered to demarcate entry into the cohort of the oldest old. Their interview data suggest not only several characteristics attributed to the oldest old, which includes the subgroup of centenarians, but also a determination not to give into death. Although this resolve may be inferred also in interviews with visual artists, who are akin to the mothers in that they have unfinished business, the determination not to give in to death has not been attributed to the oldest old cohort by investigators.

My conceptualization of the psychology of the oldest old (1991; in press) begins with the shift in perception from no longer just being "older" or "elderly" but now having become "old," that is, having become irreversibly near the end of the life course. Processes noted earlier that are characteristic of normative aging continue: The task to preserve the self is accomplished by blending the past and present in maintaining the self-picture: and the past is dramatized (or, if you will, mythicized) to make it vivid to oneself. Death becomes acceptable. Well-being is reflected in satisfaction with the congruence between expected and achieved life goals, and is enhanced by religious beliefs.

Beard (1991), in emphasizing the diversity among centenarians as well as how they reflect their cohort in espousing the work ethic and the importance of mastery, adds an orientation to the near future and a commitment to life, to sustaining an interest and investment in those activities that are most meaningful to sustaining and enhancing the self. The wish is to carry on these activities until the last breath but without a fear of death. Bould, Sanbourn and Reif (1989), in their exposition on those eighty-five and over, echo Beard in emphasizing how personal resources, how interdependencies, facilitate adaptation. But the most penetrating analyses comes from Johnson and her group, who are studying the 85-and-over group. Johnson and Barer (1990) begin with Antonovsky's (1987) sense of coherence, which has three components: comprehensibility, manageability and meaningfulness. To manage everyday life, the oldest old adapt to their environment by accepting limitations of functioning while resisting giving in to deficits. Using the phrase "outliving conventional concerns," they describe how their respondents ignore bothersome events and minimize worrying. Few view death with trepidation.

Mrs. Kane, one of the four mothers over ninety, does view death with trepidation and exudes a quality of refusing to give in to death.

A college graduate and former teacher, Mrs. Kane is 91 and lives with Suzie, her 46-year-old severely retarded daughter. She has no other living relatives; her husband died fifteen years ago and her sister five years ago. Although she can only manage getting about with difficulty, she considers herself to be in late middle age and refuses to acknowledge having become "old." She makes the comment, "My body gets old but I could be a youngster." And, "I'm getting old. My sight and strength is less but I do well for an old gal." Mrs. Kane's whole life is centered on her daughter. "My child is my life." Insular in their existence, she says, "She helps me and I help her." For her *Death is* . . . "the end." Only later does she comment, "Death is surrendering my life to God. A long rest. Going to another level of my life." But she also recognizes her unfinished business: "I am more concerned about my death because I leave someone behind who I love and who needs me." Although she is declining physically and aware that plans should be made for Suzie's future, she is determined to resist change. About service providers who could help her make permanency plans, she says, "Don't tell us how to live. We know best ourselves. I guess they know what they're doing, but I don't need them." The future is introduced by Mrs. Kane. "She," referring to Suzie, "is a kind and thoughtful child forever. Mental retardation is God's way of testing our love." Later she says that rearing a handicapped child "has made me see life as it is. I know the essence of life and not its trappings." Regarding Suzie's future, she says, "My greatest concern is how she will live without me. No person can love her as I do. I cannot see her separated." Indeed, Mrs. Kane, a bright and articulate woman, refuses to acknowledge a separation that will come with her death. She will resist the final separation and death itself as mightily as she can.

The other three mothers over ninety are similar in their resistance to death and determined to persist despite physical deterioration. All three acknowledge that their capacity for self-care is diminishing. Like Mrs. Kane, they take care of each other. Although aware that death will separate them, they are not yet ready to die. Possibly, also, like Mrs. Kane, they believe in a hereafter but are unable to complete the SCT *Death is* . . . stem by introducing this belief because of how thoughts of death are intimately associated with separation from their offspring.

Mrs. Angel at ninety-six says about her severely retarded daughter Amy (who is 50), "She is still a child." Although she considers herself a very religious convert to Catholicism, the SCT *Death is* . . . stem was completed with "I don't know. I never went through it or thought about it. There is nothing I can say about it.'' She is also not ready to think about future plans: ''I'll think about that *in due time.*'' The interviewer wrote, ''She is very busy performing as much as she can until she can no longer do so.'' She is now having trouble doing so because she can neither bathe nor dress herself, broke a hip two years ago and now uses a cane, and has a pacemaker. Although she has begun to feel ''old,'' she says that she is still in late middle-age.

When is ''due time'' for Mrs. Angel? She certainly will not accept that now is ''due time''—even though she is ninety-six and has age-associated health problems and difficulties in activities of daily living. With a determination that the interviewer describes as ''feisty,'' Mrs. Angel resists death which will sever a lifetime of caring. Whereas these 90-plus year old women are similarly religious to all but a few in our sample, they do not plead to God to outlive their dependent offspring. Rather, it appears that their continued survival is energized by an indomitable, highly personal will to survive that is uncharacteristic of the majority of elderly persons among the current cohort of the oldest old.

A SYNTHESIS

Three aspects of religiosity warrant synthesizing. First, these mothers are likely to use prayer for coping; second, they are likely to introduce God when talking about birthing and rearing an offspring with mental retardation; and third, although they have religious beliefs inculcated early in life that are particularly useful in normative aging, they have difficulty using these beliefs.

All three aspects reflect the intrinsic religiosity of the mothers. Prayer is used particularly to request the health and strength to continue to care at home for their offspring. As one mother said, ''Everyday I ask God to stay on earth so I can help him.'' For most of these mothers, their offspring are ''God's special gift'' to them, but for some, ''It is a cross I must bear.'' Note that ''bearing a cross'' is a religious referent. Then, they share the religious beliefs of their normative peers, but, as the qualitative data illustrated, they have difficulty using beliefs in God's blessings.

The blessing most focused upon in this chapter is one's heavenly reward. Only a handful of our mothers could talk favorably of a hereafter, specifically those mothers who had made future plans for their offspring with which they were comfortable. Recall Mrs. Green at eighty-three who could say, ''I don't mind dying. You'll be in a wonderful atmosphere,'' because she felt that adequate plans had been made for her 63-year-old daughter's future. So too had Mrs. Brown at eighty-nine who, because she had made plans for her 53-year-old daughter to live with another daughter in their trailer on the grounds of a church-related retirement community, could say that death is ''going to heaven.'' Most, however, were not comfortable with plans they had made, and many could not even allow themselves to make plans. Mrs. Kane commented, ''Death is surrendering my life to God. A long rest. Going to another level of my life.'' But at ninety-one she is not yet willing to surrender her life to God "because I leave someone behind who I love and needs me."

Another blessing, a long life as a divine reward for service, gives little comfort because it is not enough to live to seventy. Living to ninety, on the other hand, gives religious people a sense of being personally blessed by God. The wish is to outlive their offspring, even if they are ninety-six, as is Mrs. Angel, who would welcome death if she could outlive her fifty-year-old daughter of whom she says, "She is still a child."

Of interest is that a typical third belief, that a merciful God will relieve us from unendurable suffering, is relatively absent in our data, which is sensible because the mothers tolerate physical suffering very well. Indeed, some tolerate physical suffering too well and become physically dependent on their offspring for daily care. This blessing too cannot be used when the fear is of a final separation from their offspring: A mother who did say that death would be a "relief" also said, "I want to be here forever to give care." In normative aging, however, this belief in God's blessing of relief from unendurable suffering causes many older persons much anguish when God does not relieve them from their suffering. It is not uncommon, for example, for religious elderly individuals in nursing homes who are in intractable pain to question why their merciful God has not yet taken them to their heavenly reward. Many are confused because their God persists in letting them suffer while some even consider blaspheming God for not doing so.

Yet, there is a fourth religious belief in evidence among these women who cannot discuss reunions in the hereafter because the reunion they wish is with their offspring with mental retardation who will outlive them. Asked how her retarded offspring has affected her attitude toward death, one mother pointed to a solution offered in the Bible: "Perhaps Armageddon will come and I will not have to worry." She will not have to worry about her offspring's future as they both enter death together, even if the only way to do so is through the end of their current world.

REFERENCES

Antonovsky, A. 1987. *Unravelling the mystery of health.* San Francisco: Jossey-Bass.

Baroff, G. S. 1986. *Mental retardation: Nature, cause and management.* 2d ed. Washington, DC: Hemisphere Publishing Co.

Beard, B. B. 1991. *Centenarians: The new generation.* Westport, CT: Greenwood Press.

Bearon, L. B., and H. G. Koenig. 1990. Religious cognitions and use of prayer in health and illness. *The Gerontologist* 30, 249–53.

Bolt, M. 1977. Religious orientation and death fears. *Review of Religious Research* 19, 73–76.

Bould, S., B. Sanbourn, and L. Reif. 1989. *Eighty-five plus: The oldest old.* Belmont, CA: Wadsworth Publishing.

Cicero. [44 B.C.] 1982. Cato the elder on old age. In M. Grant, trans., *Cicero: Selected works,* 214–15. Hammondsworth: Penguin Books.

Diggory, J., and D. Z. Rothman. 1961. Values destroyed by death. *Journal of Abnormal and Social Psychology* 30, 11–17.

Erikson, E. H. 1950. *Childhood and society*. New York: W. W. Norton.

———. 1982. *The life cycle completed*. New York: W. W. Norton.

Gallup, G., Jr., and J. Castelli. 1989. *The people's religion: American faith in the 90's*. New York: Macmillan.

Hall, G. S. 1896. Study of fears. *American Journal of Psychology* 8, 147–249.

———. 1915. Thanatophobia and immortality. *American Journal of Psychology* 26, 550–613.

Jennings, J. 1987. Elderly parents as caregivers of their adult dependent children. *Social Work* 32, 430–33.

Johnson, C. L., and B. Barer. 1990. Adaptive strategies in late life. Paper presented at the annual meeting of the Gerontological Society of America, November, Boston, MA.

Kahoe, R. D., and R. F. Dunn. 1975. The fear of death and religious attitudes and behavior. *Journal for the Scientific Study of Religion* 14, 379–82.

Kalish, R. A., and D. K. Reynolds. 1976. *Death and ethnicity: A psychocultural study*. Los Angeles: Ethel Percy Andrews Gerontology Center, University of Southern California.

Kastenbaum, R. 1966. On the meaning of time in later life. *Journal of Genetic Psychology* 10, 9–25.

Keller, R. D., D. Sherry, and C. Piotrowski. 1984. Perspectives on death: A developmental study. *Journal of Psychology* 116, 137–42.

Kierkegaard, S. 1844/1957. *The concept of dread*. Translated by Walter Louri. Princeton, NJ: Princeton University Press.

Klenow, D. J., and R. C. Bolin. 1989. Belief in an afterlife: A national survey. *Omega* 20, 63–74.

Kulys, R., and S. S. Tobin. 1980–81. Interpreting the lack of future concern among the elderly. *International Journal of Aging and Human Development* 11, 31–46.

Lecky, P. 1945. A theory of personality. New York: Island Press.

Levin, J., and S. S. Tobin. In press. Religion and well-being. In M. A. Kimble, S. H. McFadden, J. W. Ellor, and J. J. Seebor, eds., *Handbook on Religion, Spirituality and Aging*. Minneapolis: Fortress.

Lieberman, M. A., and S. S. Tobin. 1982. *The experience of old age*. New York: Basic Books.

Lifton, R. J., and E. Olson. 1974. *Living and dying*. New York: Praeger.

Munnichs, J. M. 1966. *Old age and finitude*. New York: Karger.

Neugarten, B. L., R. J. Havighurst, and S. S. Tobin. 1961. The measurement of life satisfaction. *Journal of Gerontology* 16, 134–43.

Powers, C. B., P. A. Wisocki, and S. K. Whitbourne. 1992. Age differences and correlates of worrying in young and elderly adults. *The Gerontologist* 32, 82–88.

Scott, C. A. 1896. Old age and death. *American Journal of Psychology* 8, 67–122.

Seltzer, M. M., M. W. Krauss, and T. Heller. 1991. Family caregiving over the life course. In M. P. Janicki and M. M. Seltzer, eds., Proceedings of the 1990 Boston roundtable on research issues and applications in aging and developmental disabilities. Unpublished report.

Thomas, L., and K. O. Chambers. 1989. Phenomenology of life satisfaction among

elderly men: Quantitative and qualitative view. *Psychology and Aging* 4, 284–
   89.
Thorson, J. A. 1991. Afterlife constructs, death anxiety and life reviewing: The importance of religion as a moderating variable. *Journal of Psychology and Theology*
   19, 278–84.
Thorson, J. A., and F. C. Powell. 1988. Elements of death anxiety and meanings of
   death. *Journal of Clinical Psychology* 44, 691–701.
———. 1990. Meanings of death and intrinsic religiosity. *Journal of Clinical Psychology*
   46, 379–91.
Tobin, S. S. In press. The normative psychology of those now old. In S. J. Greenspan
   and G. H. Pollock, eds., *The course of life: The elderly,* vol. 7. New York:
   International Universities Press.
———. 1991. *Personhood in advanced old age: Implications for practice.* New York:
   Springer Publishing.
Tobin, S. S., and M. A. Lieberman. 1976. *Last home for the aged.* San Francisco:
   Jossey-Bass.

13 Gero-Transcendence: A Theoretical and Empirical Exploration

Lars Tornstam

With points of departure from our own studies, as well as from theories and observations of others (Jung 1930; Gutman 1976; Erikson 1950, 1982; Peck 1968; Chinen 1985, 1986, 1989a, 1989b; Chapman 1988; Grotjahn 1982; Holliday & Chandler 1986; Kramer & Woodruff 1986; Rosenmayr 1987; Storr 1988), we suggest that human aging, the very process of living into old age, encompasses a general potential toward gero-transcendence. Simply put, gero-transcendence is a shift in meta-perspective, from a materialistic and rational vision to a more cosmic and transcendent one, normally followed by an increase in life satisfaction. Depending on the definition of ''religion,'' the theory of gero-transcendence may or may be not regarded as a theory of religious development. In a study of terminal patients Nystrom & Andersson-Segesten (1990) found a peace of mind in some patients that is in many ways close to our concept of gero-transcendence. They did not find any correlation, however, between this peace of mind and the existence of a religious belief or religious practice in the patients.

Gero-transcendence is defined as qualitatively different from both Erikson's (1950) ''ego-integrity'' and Cumming and Henry's (1961) ''disengagement,'' since it implies a shift in meta-perspective. It is closer to Gutmann's (1976) concept of ''passive and magical mastery,'' although it does not have any connotation of an ''adaptive'' change. As in Jung's (1930) theory of the individuation process, gero-transcendence is regarded as the final stage in a natural process toward maturation and wisdom. It defines a reality somewhat different from the normal midlife reality which gerontologists tend to project onto old age. According to the theory, the gero-transcendent individual experiences a new feeling of cosmic communion with the spirit of the universe, a redefinition of time, space, life and death, and a redefinition of the self. This individual might also experience a decreased interest in material things and a greater need for solitary "meditation."

The concept of gero-transcendence offers a new theoretical understanding of a pattern previously identified as a defensive adaptive process, and sometimes mistaken for disengagement. The theory of gero-transcendence suggests that we run a risk of misinterpreting the effects of a normally increasing transcendence in personality as a negative disengagement, caused by a social breakdown process (Zusman 1966; Kuypers & Bengtson 1973) rather than as an intrinsic drive, as originally described in the theory of disengagement (Cumming et al. 1960; Cumming & Henry 1961). When defeating the old disengagement theory, gerontologists went back to the dubious assumption that old age is mostly the continuation of midlife patterns and values, rather than a development into something qualitatively different, as described by Jung (1930) more than sixty years ago. This might have led to overemphasis on the importance of continuity and "activity," both in theory and practice. In Western society there are no roles compatible with the gero-transcendent condition, which further strengthens the impression of the "introverted" aged person who prefers "withdrawal." The impression is of a negative disengagement, or breakdown, syndrome, and of a person in need of "activating" rather than engaged in positive development toward new perspectives and wisdom.

It may quite possibly be that we force upon some elderly people a positivist paradigm that they themselves no longer inhabit. Starting from the predominating ontological assumptions within gerontology, we may carry out research work and care that, in certain cases, is incompatible with the meta-theoretical paradigm that defines reality for those individuals who have come farthest in their individuation process—who have, in short, approached a condition of gero-transcendence. This paper will examine assumptions of both the disengagement theory and its counter theories, and contrast them with the proposed meta-theoretical paradigm of gero-transcendence. Finally, data from a national survey will be examined for empirical support for the gero-transcendence theory.

ORIGIN OF THE THEORY

When Cumming et al. (1960) first published their tentative theory of aging, elaborating on it the year after, the theoretical discussions turned into something like a riot. The theory suggested that there was an intrinsic tendency to disengage and withdraw when one grew old; this was supposed to go hand in hand with the tendency of society to reject aging individuals.

This theory not only ran counter to the widely accepted theory of activity, but also challenged the personal values held by many gerontologists and their views of what reality ought to be like. Since many gerontologists enter the field with a mixture of humanism and scientific assumptions, feeling that old people are treated badly and wanting to study this scientifically, it is not surprising that the theory of disengagement was perceived as threatening and unacceptable. Thus a series of modifying or alternative explanations to the empirically observable pattern of disengagement was offered. Finally, social gerontology was provided with a new model which completely reduced the disengagement pattern to social psychology. Kuypers & Bengtson (1973) took their point of departure from a model formulated by Zusman (1966) and introduced the concept of a social breakdown syndrome. Zusman's model described the process in which the individual's social environment interacts with his or her self-perception in the production of a negative spiral—a social breakdown. Kuypers & Bengtson transferred the model to social gerontology and presented at the same time a model of social reconstruction that described how the negative disengagement pattern could be broken. The original disengagement theory had now been given the coup de grâce. After this, the disengagement theory was referred to almost with disdain.

The theory of gero-transcendence was born of the feeling that something was lost when the old theory of disengagement was refuted. This feeling was sustained by other indicators suggesting that certain aspects of the disengagement theory might have an overlooked theoretical strength. An "unscientific" indicator was a personal conversation with the now-deceased Polish gerontologist Jerzy Piotrowski, with whom the author had the pleasure of collaborating during a research period in Warsaw in 1975. I discussed with him the disengagement theory and its counter theories. We were both of the opinion that the disengagement theory was incorrect. Our discussion was renewed at the Eleventh International Congress of Gerontology in Tokyo in 1978. On this occasion Jerzy Piotrowski suggested that the disengagement theory perhaps had some theoretical strength after all. When asked what new evidence could be presented to support this opinion, Jerzy stated: "The evidence comes from within myself."

Other subjective reports from staff working with old people point to some hidden theoretical strength in the disengagement theory. On several occasions staff have reported that their feelings are very mixed when trying to "activate" certain old people. They believe that activity is good, but they nevertheless have the feeling that they are doing something wrong when they try to drag some old people to various forms of social activity or activity therapy. They feel that they are trespassing on something they rather ought to respect and leave alone.

Even more "solid" indicators have, in an irritating way, pointed to the notion that the disengagement theory might have an overlooked theoretical strength. In our study of experiences of loneliness among Swedish inhabitants aged fifteen to eighty (Tornstam 1989), it was shown that, contrary to our everyday beliefs, the degree of loneliness decreased with every consecutive age group, despite role and other losses. It was the young respondents, not the old ones, who

reported the highest degrees of loneliness. It was also shown that interaction
with other people as a remedy for loneliness decreased for every consecutive
age group. Both these observations directed our thoughts toward the disengagement theory.

THE SCIENTIFIC PARADIGM OF SOCIAL GERONTOLOGY

Although the disengagement theory and its counter theories seem to be very
different, they flourish within the same meta-theoretical framework. This framework is the common positivist one, in which the individual is regarded as an
object directed by internal and external forces and the researcher is mainly
interested in the behavior of the individual.

What is needed to uncover the hidden strength in the disengagement theory
is the concept of a meta-theoretical shift. A few gerontologists have in fact
approached this shift. One of them is Hochschild (1976), who argues that the
patterns of engagement or disengagement must be phenomenologically understood. What is lacking is an understanding of the meaning the individual imparts
to engagement or disengagement—not the meaning the gerontologist attributes
to the engagement or disengagement. Gutmann (1976) has moved toward such
a phenomenological description of the disengagement pattern. In a cross-cultural
study of Navajo Indians, lowland and highland Maya Indians, and the Druze,
TAT protocols of young and old men were compared. Gutmann found a common
pattern in all societies: young men demonstrated what is called "active mastery"
in their projections of the TAT pictures, while the old men demonstrated "passive
mastery," or "magical mastery." For example, young men projected more fight
and aggressiveness into the pictures, while old men projected more solidarity
and understanding. At the same time as Gutmann observed this cross-cultural
tendency toward "passive mastery" and "magical mastery" in old men, he also
observed that this tendency is related to social activity for the Druze but not for
the American sample. Among the Druze the tendency toward "passive mastery"
and "magical mastery" is connected with religious activity and engagement. In
the American sample these tendencies are connected with social inactivity. In
conclusion Gutmann summarizes:

The movement toward passive and magical mastery appears to be universal, not the
movement toward disengagement. It now appears that the inner, subjective shift is general
and transcultural, but it does not necessarily lead to disengagement." (Gutmann 1976,
p. 108)

Gutmann is moving toward a paradigm shift but ultimately stops himself by
creating a dichotomy between disengagement and the universal tendencies of
passive and magical mastery. His perspective remains traditional, for the behavior
of the individual becomes a functional instrument for mastering a new situation.

To reach a new understanding of the disengagement theory we have to accept quite another kind of meta-theoretical paradigm.

AN ALTERNATIVE META-THEORETICAL PARADIGM

To reach a new meta-theoretical paradigm we shall have to leave our normal positivist way of thinking. It is instructive to contrast our picture of the world with that a Zen Buddhist would probably have. The Zen Buddhist lives within a cosmic world paradigm where many borders are diffuse and permeable. In this world much of the difference between subject and object is erased. The statements made by a Zen Buddhist are often difficult to understand from the point of view of our meta-theoretical paradigm—for example, that you and I not are separate objects but parts of the same entirety. Likewise, past, present and future are not separate but exist simultaneously.

It should be mentioned that this way of thinking is not totally foreign to Western philosophy, even if it is almost nonexistent within gerontology. In his psychological theory, C. G. Jung (1960) described the collective unconscious, referring to the fact that in our minds we have inherited structures that are reflections of the experiences of earlier generations. The collective unconscious embraces structures that unify generations and individuals. There are no borders between individuals, generations or places.

Now, suppose that we, without thinking about it, become more and more like the Zen Buddhist, figuratively speaking, when we age. Suppose that we reach a certain degree of transcendence. Some of us might even reach a high degree of transcendence, entering a new meta-world with new definitions of reality; definitions that might be much more cosmic than the ''normal'' definitions held by social gerontologists. Then we would end up with a remarkable situation in which researchers with one paradigm try to study individuals who are living according to another paradigm.

The theory of gero-transcendence suggests that aging, or rather living, implies a process during which the degree of transcendence increases. We believe that this process is intrinsic and culture-free but modified by specific cultural patterns. At the same time, we believe that this process is generated by normal living. The very process of living an everyday life and an intrinsic drive toward transcendence are only different sides of the same coin.

In principle, we believe that the process toward gero-transcendenc: is a continuous one. In practice, however, this process can be obstructed or accelerated. The process toward gero-transcendence might, for example, be accelerated by a life crisis, after which the individual totally restructures his or her meta-world, instead of resigning to the former one. This accelerated restructuring of the meta-world has been described in the case of young individuals facing death. It should be emphasized that this, in our theory of gero-transcendence, is not the same as a defense mechanism, which always functions within the former meta-world. As we see it, the classic defense mechanisms and the processes of coping take place within our ordinary meta-theoretical framework, while gero-transcendence refers to a radical shift from this framework.

The process toward gero-transcendence can also be impeded; it is most probable that elements in our culture hinder this process. Social gerontologists may also contribute to its obstruction. We shall return to this question later. However, if we accept the idea that the process toward gero-transcendence can be either obstructed or accelerated, we would expect to find many different degrees of gero-transcendence in old people; not everyone will automatically reach a high degree of gero-transcendence with age. Rather, it is a process which, in optimum circumstances, ends with a new cosmic perspective.

The idea of a life process which optimally ends with gero-transcendence recalls the developmental model formulated by Erik H. Erikson (1950, 1982). In this model the individual develops through seven stages and, if all goes well, ends up in an eighth stage, which Erikson calls "ego-integrity." In this stage the individual reaches a fundamental acceptance of his or her own life, regardless of how good or bad it has been. The individual looks back and feels satisfied with the past.

If the individual, according to Erikson's theory, does not reach the eighth stage of ego-integrity, he or she experiences despair and fear of death. One's personality strength during this eighth stage is wisdom, and its negative opposite is disgust and contempt. Erikson is, however, rather vague when describing what the wisdom in this eighth stage really constitutes. It may be that Erikson, as have others who talk vaguely about wisdom, intuitively has come close to what we here refer to as gero-transcendence, without understanding the meta-theoretical shift of paradigm that one must understand to fully comprehend the meaning of gero-transcendence. An important difference between Erikson's eighth stage and gero-transcendence is that in Erikson's theory the individual is looking back at the life lived, from within the same old paradigm, while gero-transcendence implies a looking forward and outward, with a new view of the self and the world.

SIGNS OF GERO-TRANSCENDENCE

We are now ready to tentatively describe some signs of gero-transcendence. The increasing degree of gero-transcendence, which, at very best, accompanies the process of aging can be described as a shift in meta-perspective—from a materialistic and rational perspective to a more cosmic and transcendent one, normally followed by an increase in life satisfaction. The shift in meta-perspective toward gero-transcendence can include the following:

- an increasing feeling of a cosmic communion with the spirit of the universe
- a redefinition of the perception of time, space and objects
- a redefinition of the perception of life and death and a decrease in the fear of death

- an increased feeling of affinity with past and coming generations
- a decrease in the interest in superfluous social interaction
- a decrease in the interest in material things
- a decrease in self-centeredness
- an increase in time spent in "meditation"

The increasing feeling of a cosmic communion with the spirit of the universe can be experienced as being a part of a flow of energy which is coursing through the universe. Feelings of communion with the oceans, nature and the starry sky are aspects of this cosmic communion.

The perception of time can change from our normal linear view. Not only the perception of the velocity of time, but also the perception of past, present and future can change. Specifically the past, even back to the old Greeks, may come alive in a way never experienced before.

The change in the perception of objects can include an elimination of the borders between self and others. An impression of being One all together appears instead. As a consequence of this, the degree of self-centeredness will decrease. To a certain extent the enclosed self is disaggregated and substituted with a cosmic self. Individuals no longer look upon themselves as especially important. Maybe they perceive themselves as part of a cosmic flow of energy, where the flow of energy, not its individual parts, is the important thing. This also involves a redefinition of the perception of life and death. It is not individual life, but rather the total flow of life that is important. With such changes in the definitions of the meta-world, it is understandable that the fear of death decreases and that the feeling of affinity with past, present and coming generations increases. Erikson (1950, 1982) describes this as typical for those who have reached the eighth and last stage of his developmental model.

With all these changes in the definitions of the meta-world, from a restricted perspective to what we have termed a gero-transcendent perspective, it is easy to understand the decreasing interest in superfluous social relations and material goods. The individual who has experienced these changes may look with pity on many younger people who are overinvested in "social engagement," seeing this as a neurotic focusing on social contacts. Instead, time is spent on what is more important, from the superior perspective of gero-transcendence. That is, after having experienced communion with the spirit of the universe and the great cosmic flow of energy within and through oneself. This does not necessarily imply a social withdrawal, although that may prove to be the case in our society, since no norms or roles conforming to gero-transcendence are provided.

It is interesting that Chinen (1985, 1986, and Chapter 6 in this volume), in an analysis of fairy tales which include older protagonists, found that the central motif in these tales is transcendence. Chinen's idea is that the fairy tales represent a guideline for the developmental sequence of old age, which reflects a process of religious, social and psychological transcendence. The fairy tales analyzed were mostly of Eastern origin, but some fairy tales from Slavic countries were also included. After reviewing over 2,500 fairy tales, Chinen found very few from Western societies that have an older protagonist. Instead, the Western fairy tales had a striking emphasis on young protagonists. In Eastern countries (and some Slavic) there seem to be normative fairy tales supporting the process toward gero-transcendence, while in the Western countries no such support from fairy tales exists. On the contrary, the stress on youth in the Western fairy tales may obstruct any evidence of gero-transcendence.

Seemingly, people in Western society find it difficult to withstand our cultural norms, which define old age as the mere continuation of the values, definitions and patterns of youth and midlife. Already in 1930 Jung observed this, and regarded it as a tragedy. According to Jung (1930), the meaning and tasks of old age are quite different from the meaning and tasks of midlife. In the first part of life, the task is getting acquainted with and socialized to society, whereas the task in old age is getting acquainted with one's self and with what Jung called the collective unconscious. Clinging to the tasks of the first part of life and not realizing the tasks of old age results in despair and meeting one's death as a half person.

GERO-TRANSCENDENCE WITH OBSTRUCTIONS

In Western culture you risk being regarded as odd, asocial, mentally disturbed or—disengaged—if you change your perceptions of the world so that they are in accordance with gero-transcendence. In our culture we have no roles or arenas where such a view of reality fits. The situation was otherwise with the Druze (Gutmann 1976), as the religious ceremonies provided a social arena for the wisdom of gero-transcendence.

Everyone in Western culture "knows" that it is social activity, ego-strength and a realistic view of the world that counts. By claiming this as "fact," we are making a moral judgment; as a result, we may impede the process toward gero-transcendence by making the individual feel guilty about his or her new view of life. Supported by well-meaning gerontologists, staff and relatives of old people obstruct the natural progression toward gero-transcendence. The attitude is that old people who are "turning inward," withdrawing to something we don't understand, must be activated. Old people themselves participate in this obstruction. Like everyone else, the elderly recognize that it is activity and engagement that count in our society. We should therefore not be surprised if we find many old people who feel guilt in connection with their own development toward gero-transcendence; they may even apologize for having a different view of life and living.

Indirect evidence for our claim that gero-transcendence is part of a normal process is suggested by Peck (1968). In a study of some thousand businessmen he focused on developmental crises during middle and old age. There are certain points where things go right or wrong, which Peck does not explain; he just describes what he has found. But Peck's description implies a right or good way. As in all other gerontological research, there is a hidden moral judgment.

According to Peck, the following crises occur in old age:

1. *Ego differentiation or job preoccupation.* Some people seem to be able to reorient their lives in such a way that their identity is no longer dependent on their previous job. Many other things assume the importance the job had earlier in relation to perception of the self. Others seem unable to let go of their earlier work career. Ego differentiation is the normal and healthy solution to this development crisis, but something prevents certain people from reaching this stage.

2. *Body transcendence or body preoccupation.* Some old people become increasingly preoccupied with their bodies. They register every little new ailment and make it a major problem in life. Others seem to transcend the body in the sense that they know all about their physical condition and they take proper care of their bodies, but they never let life orbit around this. Peck states indirectly that body transcendence is the natural way of development, which is thwarted for many people.

3. *Ego transcendence or ego preoccupation.* In the same way as the body, the ego should be transcended in old age. Peck claims that the knowledge of one's own aging and the inevitability of death should prompt a reorganization of the ego, where life is lived in a generous and unselfish way. This should induce an acceptance of death. For various reasons many people seem unable to reach such a stage. They develop the type of ego preoccupation and fear of death that Erikson referred to.

When Peck uses the term "transcendence" he means something like to "overcome" the pains of the body or futurity (Kalish 1976). But our interpretation is, again, that what Peck found were aspects of the general process toward gero-transcendence, a process which in our society is obstructed by our value patterns and notions of how life in old age should be lived.

EMPIRICAL QUESTIONS IMPLIED BY GERO-TRANSCENDENCE

The tentative theory of gero-transcendence prompts some questions which can be addressed by the quantitative study. The remainder of this chapter is devoted to a preliminary study, which focuses on the following questions:

1. *The question of recognition* focuses on whether old people actually recognize the various changes suggested by the theory of gero-transcendence.

2. *The question of distribution* assumes that gero-transcendence is a variable, where some individuals demonstrate high degrees of gero-transcendence, others low degrees. How should we define these groups?

3. *The question of gero-transcendence and social activity* focuses on a difference, which distinguishes this theory from the disengagement theory. The theory of gero-transcendence does not necessarily imply social withdrawal.

4. *The question of gero-transcendence and coping patterns* is related to the

previous question. How do individuals with high degrees of gero-transcendence cope with problems in life? If gero-transcendence were the same as disengagement, we would predict a passive or defensive coping style. But since the theory regards gero-transcendence as the most mature state of development, approaching wisdom, we expect more mature coping patterns, even the use of several different coping strategies at the same time.

5. *The question of gero-transcendence and life satisfaction* builds on the theory's assumption that the development toward gero-transcendence is a normal developmental process, which is followed by an increase in satisfaction. People who do not reach gero-transcendence would be expected to score lower on life satisfaction.

6. *The question of accelerating or retarding the process of gero-transcendence* builds on the theory's assumption that certain life crises can accelerate the process, as for example when severe illness forces an individual to redefine reality. Traditionally such changes are looked upon as defense mechanisms, but the theory of gero-transcendence regards such changes as real changes of the meta-structure, not as defense mechanisms. The theory also assumes that individuals who are not hindered by restrictive norms or values inflicted on them, or who have enough personal resources to withstand such pressure, more easily reach gero-transcendence.

7. *The question of gero-transcendence as possibly related to confoundings like mental illness and consumption of psychotropics.* At seminars, when the tentative theory has been presented, critics have suggested that the state of gero-transcendence could be a reaction to or correlated with depression and mental illness, since its "symptoms" show some similarities. Also, critics suggest that consumption of various psychotropics might cause the same "symptoms." Our hypothesis is, rather, that gero-transcendence is negatively correlated with depression, mental disturbances and consumption of psychotropics. Again, this follows from the theory's assumption that the development toward gero-transcendence is a normal and positive developmental process, which is followed by contentment, satisfaction and reduced need of psychotropics.

METHOD

Sample. The present study was based on a mail survey of 912 individuals remaining from a panel of 1.261 representative noninstitutionalized Danish men and women, participating in a longitudinal study with data collections in 1986 and 1990. Details of the sampling and data collection procedures are described elsewhere (Holstein et al. 1990).

In 1990, when the questions related to gero-transcendence were asked, the mean age of the 912 respondents was seventy-nine years, ranging between 74 and 100 years. The distribution of men and women was, of course, uneven, with 64 percent women and 36 percent men. This corresponds identically with the total distribution of men and woman 74 and older in the whole of Denmark.

Also, the age distribution within the age range of the respondents is very close to the corresponding age distribution in the whole of Denmark. Among the men, the age distribution is identical. Among the women, the younger ones are overrepresented by 2 percent, and the older ones correspondingly underrepresented.

Major measures. The degree of *gero-transcendence* was measured by a series of ten items derived from the theory and after a selection procedure, which included qualitative interviews and tests on old people not included in this study (Table 13.1). The following question was asked: "We now want to ask you whether your view of life and existence is different today, compared to when you were 50 years of age. Please read the following, and decide what you think of the statements below." For each of the statements the respondent had two response alternatives: yes (I do recognize myself in the statement) or no (I do not recognize myself in the statement).

Since the theory of gero-transcendence suggests different types of changes which may reflect different dimensions of gero-transcendence, the answers to the ten items were analyzed with an exploratory factor analysis, that is, a principal component analysis with varimax rotation. The factor analysis identified two dimensions of gero-transcendence. The first factor, consisting of six items, has been labeled *cosmic transcendence,* since it clearly defines a type of transcendence connected with changes in the perception or definition of time, space, life and death. The second factor, containing the remaining six items, has been labeled *ego transcendence,* since it is connected with changes in the perception of the self and relations to other people. It should be noted that these two dimensions of gero-transcendence correspond with the two different tasks of old age, as described by Jung (1930), and in our interpretation, knowing about the universe and knowing about the self.

For the measurement of the two types of gero-transcendence, two standardized additive indexes based on the items in each dimension were constructed, utilizing Galtung's (1969) recommendations. Essentially this procedure involves a uniform trichotomization of each item before adding the response values to an index. This procedure is done in order to reach an approximate rank-order Likert scale. The Cronbach's alpha for the six items in the cosmic transcendence scale is .81, and for the ego transcendence scale .75, which is satisfactory (Bohrnstedt & Knoke 1982).

Social activity was measured by an additive index summing up the frequency of visits to other people in their homes, visits by other people in the home of the respondent, contacts with relatives (other than children and grandchildren), contacts with other friends, and leisure activities outside the home. The reason for excluding the contacts with children and grandchildren from this index was that only those social activities where the older people themselves had more of a choice in initiating the contact were utilized. Earlier research has shown that contact between old people and their children and grandchildren tends to be made on the initiative of the latter (Hill et al. 1979; Teeland 1978).

Life satisfaction was measured by a single item, where the respondent on a

Table 13.1
Dimensions of Gero-Transcendence

Factors	Percent Recognizing Content of Item	Factor Loading
Cosmic Transcendence		
Today I feel that the border between life and death is less striking compared to when I was 50 years of age	60	.75
Today I feel to a higher degree, how unimportant an individual life is, in comparison to the continuing life as such	55	.72
Today I feel a greater mutual connection with the universe, compared to when I was 50 years of age	32	.68
Today I more often experience a close presence of persons, even when they are physically elsewhere	36	.67
Today I feel that the distance between past and present disappears	42	.64
Today I feel a greater state of belonging with both earlier and coming generations	49	.61
Ego Transcendence		
Today I take myself less seriously than earlier	60	.77
Today material things mean less, compared to when I was 50	74	.76
Today I am less interested in superficial social contacts	53	.59
Today I have more delight in my inner world, i.e., thinking and pondering, compared to when I was 50	57	.54

five-point scale stated how satisfied or dissatisfied he or she was with the overall life at present.

An *old-age depression scale* was constructed on the basis of five items, where the respondents were asked to agree or disagree (on a three-point scale) with the statement that they: feel lonely, find the time passing slowly, have a feeling of being forgotten, have a feeling of being superfluous, or feel old. The Cronbach's alpha of this scale is .77.

Psychological strain was assessed by an index adding the number of present symptoms in the following list: sense of fatigue without any cause, insomnia, nervousness, anxiety and depression.

A special *coping pattern* typology was based on four items, where the respondents on a four-point scale had to agree or disagree on what they do when they have problems or worries. The behaviors in question were: "Trying to forget and pretend that nothing has happened," "Doing something to chase the worrying thoughts away," "Discussing with persons who are close to me how to solve a problem," and "Concentrating completely on how to solve a problem." An exploratory factor analysis indicated that these four items form two dimensions. The first two items form a dimension of defensive coping, while the latter two form a dimension of offensive coping. These two dimensions are not negatively but positively correlated (eta = .33 p < .001). This means that we do not find any support for the assumption that people have either an offensive or a defensive coping style. Rather, we find that different combinations of offensive and defensive coping are utilized. For this reason we have constructed a coping pattern typology based on the two dimensions. *Low copers* (32 percent) are those who are below average on both the offensive and the defensive coping dimensions. *Multi-copers* (28 percent) are those who are above average on both dimensions. *Defensive copers* (14 percent) are high on the defensive coping dimension, but low on the offensive. *Offensive copers* (26 percent) are high on the offensive coping dimension but low on the defensive.

The respondents in this survey were also asked whether they had had to cope with specific listed problems during the last twelve months preceding the measurement in 1990. In this analysis we are using the answers to whether the respondents had experienced the loss of a person close to them or not, and if so, whether this trauma could be dealt with or not. On a four-point scale those respondents who had experienced the loss of a close person were asked about the degree to which they themselves could solve the problems connected with the loss. The response alternatives ranged from "such problems cannot be solved" to "I could do a lot myself to solve the problems."

RESULTS

The results are organized in relation to the empirical questions stated earlier. Please note that when not specifically stated as 1986 data, the analysis refers to a cross-sectional analysis of the 1990 data.

Recognition. As to the initial question of recognition of increased gero-transcendence with age, it was found that quite high proportions of the respondents recognize in themselves the qualities of gero-transcendence indicated by the various statements. It is interesting that 42 percent recognize in themselves such a "strange" phenomenon as the disappearance of the distance between past and present. This fact can be regarded as a preliminary validity check of the measurement for the gero-transcendence concept. The question of validity is quite tricky in a study like this, when we are working with the development of a new concept. Later, when the results from the qualitative study are reported, the question will be further addressed. At the present stage, the concept of gero-transcendence remains tentative, and cannot be said to be finally defined. For this reason, we cannot expect extremely high correlations or patterns in the analysis, but rather more modest tendencies, showing if we are working in the right direction or not.

Distribution. The theory would suggest that the degree of gero-transcendence would increase with increasing age. In this study, however, neither cosmic transcendence nor ego transcendence shows any correlation with the age of the respondent. Nor are there any gender differences in these respects. Controlling for both sex and age at the same time shows the same result. In this material there are no sex or age differences in the degree of cosmic or ego transcendence.

The lack of age differences can partly be understood as a result of the study population and the methodology we have used. The sample is quite homogeneous, with all respondents above the age of seventy-four. The methodology implies a retrospective technique, where the respondents compare the present situation with their situation at age fifty. Those who have experienced developments in the direction of gero-transcendence might well have done so before the age of seventy-four.

There is also another, more theoretical way of understanding the lack of correlation between chronological age and the degree of gero-transcendence. Progress toward gero-transcendence is not necessarily dependent on age per se, because it is a developmental process primarily connected with living, having various experiences in and learning from life. Such a process will only be loosely connected with chronological age, even if the highest degrees of gero-transcendence will only be found in the old.

Gero-transcendence and social activity. On the question of social activity and gero-transcendence we find a positive correlation between cosmic transcendence and social activity (eta = .17 p < .001), and a positive but not statistically significant correlation between ego transcendence and social activity. These correlations are not in themselves overwhelming, but they are theoretically interesting. If changes toward gero-transcendence were in fact aspects of social withdrawal and disengagement, we would expect to find a negative correlation with social activities. Since we do not find such correlation, but rather the opposite, we have an indication that the concept of gero-transcendence is something different from the old concept of disengagement or part of a breakdown syndrome.

Coping patterns. Further, if gero-transcendence were the same as disengagement or part of a breakdown syndrome, the predicted coping patterns would be that with increasing gero-transcendence there would be an increasing proportion of low copers and defensive copers. In our data we find the opposite to be the case. With increasing degrees of cosmic and ego transcendence, we find increasing proportions of offensive copers and multi-copers. The correlation between the degree of cosmic transcendence and the coping pattern is eta = .16, p < .001. The correlation between the degree of ego transcendence and the coping pattern is eta = .13, p < .05.

Two differences between respondents with high and low degrees of cosmic transcendence are especially interesting. First, the proportion of low copers is considerably higher among the respondents with a low degree of cosmic transcendence (41 percent) in comparison with the respondents with a high degree of cosmic transcendence (26 percent). Second, the proportion of multi-copers is considerably higher among the respondents with a high degree of cosmic transcendence (33 percent) in comparison with respondents with a low degree of cosmic transcendence (22 percent). The same type of differences are found when we compare respondents with high and low degrees of ego transcendence, even if the differences in this case are not as pronounced. These findings contradict the assumption that gero-transcendence is the same as or part of what is usually defined as negative disengagement or a breakdown syndrome. Instead, we find a pattern in which high degrees of gero-transcendence are combined with a more mature coping pattern, including higher levels of coping and more multi-coping.

Also, we find that one of the gero-transcendence dimensions, cosmic transcendence, is related to the degree to which the respondents have a positive attitude toward the possibility of solving problems connected with the trauma of losing a person close to them. Among the respondents who had experienced such a loss during the last twelve months preceding the measurement in 1990, respondents with the higher degrees of cosmic transcendence had a more positive outlook (eta = .21, p < .05). No such relationship was found with ego transcendence, however.

Life satisfaction. The data show positive correlations between life satisfaction and the degree of both cosmic (eta = .16 p < .001) and ego transcendence (eta = .12 p < .05). The higher the degree of transcendence, the higher the life satisfaction. These correlations are modified, however, when the degree of social activity is taken into consideration. The extent of social activity correlates with life satisfaction (eta = .36 p < .001). Furthermore, when both the amount of social activity and the degree of cosmic transcendence are introduced as independent variables in a multiple classification analysis (MCA) based on analysis of variance (ANOVA), with life satisfaction as the dependent variable, the explanatory power of cosmic transcendence decreases somewhat (from eta = .16 to beta = .12), while the explanatory power of social activity decreases from eta = .36 to beta = .28. When ego transcendence is introduced as an independent variable, together with social activity, the explanatory power of ego transcendence remains constant (eta = .12, beta = .12), as does the explanatory power of social activity (eta = .30, beta = .30). From this we can conclude

Table 13.2
**Correlations between Social Interaction and Life Satisfaction in Subgroups with
Different Degrees of Cosmic and Ego Transcendence**

	Spearman's Rho	n
Cosmic Transcendence		
0 (lowest)	.40 ***	154
1	.33 ***	98
2	.29 **	104
3	.30 ***	139
4	.24 **	114
5	.13 ns	73
6 (highest)	.31 **	104
Ego Transcendence		
0 (lowest)	.44 ***	86
1	.37 ***	124
2	.24 **	160
3	.28 ***	185
4 (highest)	.33 ***	111

*** p< .001   ** p< .01   ns not significant

that both types of gero-transcendence show an independent correlation with life
satisfaction. This also applies when the degree of social activity is controlled
for, even if social activity is more important as a predictor of life satisfaction.

The intercorrelations between social activity, gero-transcendence and life satisfaction can however be illustrated in a theoretically more interesting way. Table
13.2 shows how the original correlation between the level of social activity and
life satisfaction is modified when the degree of gero-transcendence is taken into
consideration.

Overall, it will be noted that the higher the degree of cosmic transcendence,
the weaker the correlation between social activity and life satisfaction. In other
words, *the more transcendent the respondent is, the less essential social activity
is for life satisfaction.* Among the respondents with the lowest degree of cosmic
transcendence, the correlation between social activity and life satisfaction is quite
high (Spearman's Rho = .40), but this correlation decreases almost systematically with increasing degrees of cosmic transcendence, with the class formed
by the respondents with the highest degree of cosmic transcendence being the
one exception to this pattern. The modifying effect of ego transcendence on the
correlation between social activity and life satisfaction shows the same tendency,
though it is not as obvious.

Also, when *satisfaction* with social activity was analyzed in relation to the
degree of social activity, gero-transcendence was found to have the same modifying effect—the more transcendent the respondent, the weaker the correlation
between the degree of social activity and the satisfaction with social activity.
Again, this is especially pronounced when the degree of cosmic transcendence

Table 13.3
Changes in Life Satisfaction as Related to Cosmic and Ego Transcendence

	Degrees of Transcendence					
Change in Life Satisfaction	Cosmic (1)			Ego (2)		
	Low	Med	High	Low	Med	High
Decrease	30	24	18	32	22	19
No Change	50	60	63	51	57	66
Increase	20	16	19	17	21	15
	100%	100%	100%	100%	100%	100%
n =	244	239	282	207	233	225

(1) eta = .13 p< .01   (2) eta = .12 p< .01

is controlled for. Among the respondents with the lowest degree of cosmic transcendence, the Spearman Rho correlation between the degree of social activity and the satisfaction with social activity is .49 (p < .001). Among the respondents with the highest degree of cosmic transcendence, the corresponding correlation is .31 (p < .01).

In summary, we find a new pattern, in which a high degree of transcendence—especially cosmic transcendence—is related to a higher degree of both life satisfaction and satisfaction with social activity, at the same time as the degree of social activity in itself becomes less essential for the satisfaction at the higher levels of gero-transcendence.

From the longitudinal perspective we also find correlations between the developmental patterns of life satisfaction and the degree of gero-transcendence. It is more common for respondents with low degrees of gero-transcendence to find that their life satisfaction decreased between 1986 and 1990. As expected, most respondents report the same degree of life satisfaction at both points of measurement. When changes occurred, however, they were correlated to the degrees of both cosmic and ego transcendence. Table 13.3 summarizes these observations. Here we have regarded the degrees of cosmic and ego transcendence as independent variables, and life satisfaction as dependent.

Table 13.3 shows that the degrees of gero-transcendence might predict *decreases* in life satisfaction, but not increases. The proportion of respondents who have increased their life satisfaction is roughly the same if respondents have low, medium or high degrees of cosmic or ego transcendence. The proportion of respondents who have decreased their life satisfaction differs, however, for the differing levels of gero-transcendence. While, for example, 18 percent of the respondents with a high degree of cosmic transcendence have decreased their life satisfaction during the period between the two measurements, the corre-

Table 13.4
Correlations between Accelerating and Facilitating Factors and Gero-Transcendence

	Cosmic Transcendence	Ego Transcendence
Death of Close Person	.11 **	.04 ns
Type of Network before Retirement	.15 **	.08 ns
Social Class	.12 *	.09 ns

Coefficients are eta correlations
  ** p< .01   * p< .05   ns not significant

sponding percentage among respondents with a low degree of cosmic transcendence is 30 percent.

The causal interpretation of this finding is somewhat difficult, since the level of gero-transcendence was measured only in 1990, while the longitudinal changes in life satisfaction refer to the changes between 1986 and 1990. If, however, the measure of the two types of gero-transcendence is tapping a developmental process starting before both measurement periods (as implied by the phrasing of the items), one causal interpretation could be the following: the reason that we find a correlation in the cross-sectional analysis between gero-transcendence and life satisfaction is not that a high degree of gero-transcendence produces a higher life satisfaction, but rather that, to a certain extent, it prevents decreases in life satisfaction.

Accelerating or retarding the process. The process of gero-transcendence can, according to the theory, be accelerated or retarded in different ways. One assumption was that major crises in life might accelerate the restructuring of the definition of one's reality. One such crisis, used as a test variable in this context, is the death of a spouse or another close person. In this sample 203 respondents (22 percent) had experienced such a loss during the twelve months preceding the data collection in 1990. When the respondents who had experienced such a loss are compared with the ones who had not, we find the degree of cosmic transcendence to be higher among the former group. Table 13.4 shows that the differences correspond to a statistically significant correlation of eta = .11.

No such differences were found as to the degree of ego transcendence. It seems reasonable to assume that it was the crisis of losing a close person that caused an increase in the degree of cosmic transcendence.

Table 13.4 also shows that the degree of cosmic transcendence is correlated with the type of work the respondent had before retirement, and with social class. Respondents who had white-collar jobs or were metropolitan entrepreneurs have higher degrees of cosmic transcendence than others. Also, the degree of cosmic transcendence is higher among the respondents in the higher social

Table 13.5
Correlations between Gero-Transcendence and "Confoundings"

	Cosmic Transcendence	Ego Transcendence
Old Age Depression Scale (1986)	.06 ns	.02 ns
Feeling Lonely (1990)	.03 ns	.06 ns
Feeling Old (1990)	.04 ns	.01 ns
Psychological Strain Scale (1990)	.01 ns	.03 ns
Use of Sedatives or Hypnotics (1986)	.02 ns	.01 ns
Use of Psychopharmacas (1986)	-.07 *	-.10 **

** p< .01   * p< .05   ns not significant

classes. The common denominator in these observations might be that the respondents with the higher degrees of cosmic transcendence have led less restricted lives, with higher degrees of personal freedom. Their personal development has been less hindered by limiting rules or values.

This interpretation is in line with the reasoning of Chinen (1989a), who analyzed the scientific works of Ludwig Wittgenstein and Alfred North Whitehead, and found that their orientation became more qualitative and "transcendent" in their later years. Chinen chose to focus on these famous scientists in his analysis because individuals like these have had the greatest freedom to let life develop in its own way. They were less restricted by prohibiting norms or rules, and had greater capacity than others to break such rules for original thought. To Chinen's observation it could be added that there are other examples of well-known scientists who have developed in a similar way, such as Sigmund Freud, Carl Jung, Albert Einstein and Niels Bohr.

In summary, we do find some evidence in support of the theoretical formulation that the degree of gero-transcendence can be affected by both life crises and other facilitating or restricting factors. It should be observed, however, that this statement is only valid for cosmic transcendence.

Mental illness, depression and use of psychotropics. The last question to be answered by our data is whether the state of gero-transcendence might be related to, confused with or caused by mental illness, depression or consumption of psychotropics. Table 13.5 summarizes our tests of this hypothesis.

The old-age depression scale does not correlate with either cosmic transcendence or ego transcendence. That the complete set of items in this scale was used only at the 1986 measurement poses a methodological problem. Hence, the correlation refers to the depression value in 1986 and the gero-transcendence values in 1990. Two of the specific items in the old-age depression scale were used, however, in 1990. Neither of these (feeling lonely, feeling old) were found to correlate with the gero-transcendence scales. It therefore seems reasonable to suggest that gero-transcendence is not to be seen as a depression correlate or defense reaction caused by old-age depression. The same conclusion holds concerning psychological strain—the psychological strain scale does not correlate with either of the gero-transcendence scales.

Nor is the assumption that the use of psychotropics is related to gero-transcendence supported by our data. The only statistically significant correlation in this respect is the correlation between the use of psychopharmacas[1] and the gero-transcendence scales. In both cases, however, the correlation indicates that respondents who used psychopharmacas in 1986 have lower degrees of both cosmic and ego transcendence in 1990. If any causal conclusion should be drawn from this, it should be that the consumption of psychopharmacas is a hindrance to achieving gero-transcendence.

DISCUSSION

This chapter suggests the concept of gero-transcendence as a new key concept for understanding the developmental process of aging. Thus, we have to prove that the concept of gero-transcendence is a new concept with relevance for the understanding of aging, and not just a reflection of well-known gerontological concepts.

From the answers to the items included in the gero-transcendence measures it can be concluded that the items touch upon something which is recognized by the respondents, whatever it is. Significant proportions of the respondents recognize in themselves the changes expressed by the items. From the initial description of the theory it should be obvious that the points of departure for the theory of gero-transcendence are quite different from the interactionist theories and the "activity theory" derived from such sources. But is gero-transcendence something new and different from the old concept of disengagement? Several results in this study indicate that it is.

First, the very content of the statements forming the gero-transcendence scales is different from the disengagement concept. While "disengagement" only implies a turning inwards, "gero-transcendence" implies a new definition of reality.

Second, while disengagement is connected with social withdrawal, our data show gero-transcendence to be positively correlated with social activity, at the same time as a greater need for solitary "philosophizing" is experienced. But, and most important, the social activities positively correlated with gero-transcendence are activities where more of the initiative for activity rests with the individual.

Third, the coping patterns of the respondents with high degrees of gero-transcendence certainly do not correspond to what would be predicted by the theory of disengagement; nor is there any support for the assumption that gero-transcendence is an aspect of a social breakdown syndrome. Instead of reporting passive or defensive coping strategies, we find that respondents with high degrees of gero-transcendence make greater use of "offensive" and multi-coping patterns.

Fourth, we have found a new pattern in which a high degree of cosmic transcendence is related to a higher degree of both life satisfaction and satisfaction with social activity, at the same time that the degree of social activity becomes less essential for the satisfaction at the higher levels of gero-transcendence. All this leads us to the conclusion that the concept of gero-transcendence is clearly different from both the concept of the social breakdown syndrome and from the old concept of disengagement.

The concept of gero-transcendence is more closely related to Gutmann's concept of "passive and magical mastery." Gutmann, however, regards this shift toward passive and magical mastery to be an adaptation by the individual, made necessary by individual and social changes in the aging process. Hereby the changes described become effects of the impact of social aging. Strained to a fine point, the changes toward passive and magical mastery become for Gutmann defense mechanisms. In this respect, the theory of gero-transcendence is very different, both from the pure theoretical perspective and from the empirical one.

Theoretically, the process of gero-transcendence is regarded as a normal developmental process which has little to do with defense mechanisms. Empirically, results from this study suggest that negative longitudinal changes in life satisfaction may be prevented by gero-transcendence. There is no evidence that an increase in gero-transcendence (as a defense reaction) is caused by decreases in life satisfaction.

There is, finally, some resemblance between the concept of gero-transcendence and Erikson's (1950, 1982) model of ego development. In both cases the process of aging is regarded as a developmental process which, in cases of optimal development, ends with a higher state of maturity: in Erikson's case, ego-integrity; in ours, gero-transcendence. In both cases the mature state also includes a new level of contentment and a new feeling of affinity with past generations. But in Erikson's theory, the integration primarily refers to an integration of the elements in life that has passed. The individual reaches a fundamental acceptance of the life lived, regardless of how good or bad it might seem from outside. In this way ego-integrity described by Erikson becomes more of a backward integration process within a fixed definition of the world, whereas the process of gero-transcendence implies more of a forward or outward direction, including a redefinition of reality.

To conclude, then, we maintain that gero-transcendence is a new concept, different from other well-known theoretical concepts in gerontology. According to the response patterns found in our data, it is seemingly also relevant for the personal experiences of older people. Furthermore, it may prove to be a theoretically fruitful concept since it focuses on new types of developmental patterns and combinations, for example, suggesting interesting interrelationships of gero-transcendence with social activity, multi-coping and life satisfaction. Whereas in earlier theorizing such concepts have been formulated in terms of either/or, the theory of gero-transcendence offers a both/and.

NOTE

1. Psychopharmacas are distinguished by their potency from such milder psychotropics as sedatives, which are used to combat insomnia and anxiety. The more potent psychopharmacas would more likely be employed to control neuroses and psychoses.

REFERENCES

Bohrnstedt, G. W., and D. Knoke. 1982. *Statistics for social data analysis*. Itasca, Ill.: F. E. Peacock Publishers.

Chapman, M. 1988. Contextuality and directionality of cognitive development. *Human Development* 31, 92–106.

Chinen, A.B. 1985. Fairy tales and transpersonal development in later life. *The Journal of Transpersonal Psychology* 17, 99–122.

———. 1986. Elder tales revisited: Forms of transcendence in later life. *The Journal of Transpersonal Psychology* 26, 171–92.

———. 1989a. From quantitative to qualitative reasoning: A developmental perspective. In L. E. Thomas, ed., *Research on adulthood and aging: The human science approach*. Albany: State University of New York Press.

———. 1989b. *In the ever after: Fairy tales and the second half of life*. Wilmette, Ill.: Chiron Publications.

Cumming, E., L. R. Dean, D. S. Newell, and I. McCaffrey. 1960. Disengagement: A tentative theory of aging. *Sociometry* 23, 23–35.

Cumming, E., and W. E. Henry. 1961. *Growing old: The process of disengagement*. New York: Basic Books.

Erikson, E. H. 1950. *Childhood and society*. New York: Norton.

Erikson, E. H. 1982. *The life cycle completed: A review*. New York: Norton.

Galtung, J. 1969. *Theory and methods of social research*. Oslo: Universitetsfrlaget.

Grotjahn, M. 1982. The day I got old. *Psychiatric Clinics of North America* 5, 233–34.

Gutmann, D. 1976. Alternatives to disengagement: The old men of the Highland Druze. In J. F. Gubrium, ed., *Time, roles and self in old age*. New York: Human Sciences.

Hill, R. et al. 1979. *Family development in three generations: A longitudinal study of changing family patterns of planning and achievement*. Cambridge, Mass.: Schenkman.

Hochschild, A. R. 1976. Disengagement theory: A logical, empirical, and phenomenological critique. In J. F. Gubrium, ed., *Time, roles and self in old age*. New York: Human Sciences.

Holliday, S. G., and M. J. Chandler. 1986. Wisdom: Explorations in adult competence. *Contributions to Human Development*, vol. 17. Basel: Karger.

Holstein, B. E., G. Almind, P. Due, and E. Holst. 1990. Aeldres selvrapporterede helbred og laegemiddelforbrug. *Ugeskrift for laegere* 152(6), 386–91.

Jung, C. G. (1930). Die lebenswende. Vol. 8 of *Gesamt werke*. Olten: Walter-Verlag.

———. 1960. *Det ubeviste*. Kopenhamn: Gyldendal.

Kalish, R. A. 1976. Death and dying in a social context. In Binstock, R. H., and E. Shanas, eds., *Handbook of aging and the social sciences*. New York: Van Nostrand.

Kramer, D. A., and D. S. Woodruff. 1986. Relativistic and dialectical thought in three adult age groups. *Human Development* 29, 280–90.

Kuypers, J. A., and V. L. Bengtson. 1973. Social breakdown and competence. A model of normal aging. *Human Development* 16, 181–201.

Nystrom, A., and K. Andersson-Segesten. 1990. Peace of mind as an important aspect of old people's health. *Scandinavian Journal of Caring Sciences* 4, 55–62.

Peck, R. 1968. Psychological development in the second half of life. In B. L. Neugarten, ed., *Middle age and aging: A reader in social psychology*. Chicago: University of Chicago Press.

Rosenmayr, L. 1987. Sociological dimensions of gerontology. In M. Bergner, ed., *Psychogeriatrics: An international handbook*. New York: Springer.

Storr, A. 1988. *Solitude*. Glasgow: William Collins Sons.

Teeland, L. 1978. Keeping in touch: The relation between old people and their adult children. *Monograph* 16. Gothenbourg: Dept. of Sociology.

Tornstam, L. 1989. Gero-transcendence: A meta-theoretical reformulation of the disengagement theory. *Aging: Clinical and Experimental Research* (Milano) 1(1), 55–63.

———. 1992. The Quo Vadis of gerontology: On the gerontological research paradigm. *The Gerontologist* 32(3), 318–26.

Zusman, J. 1966. Some explanations of the changing appearance of psychotic patients: Antecedents of the social breakdown syndrome concept. *The Millbank Memorial Fund Quarterly* 64(1–2).

For Further Reading

Alexander, C. N., and E. J. Langer. 1990. *Higher stages of human development*. New York: Oxford.

Blech, B. 1977. Judaism and gerontology. *Tradition* 16, 62–78.

Bianchi, E. C. 1982. *Aging as a spiritual journey*. New York: Crossroad.

Birren, J. 1990. Spiritual maturity in psychological development. *Journal of Religious Gerontology* 7, 41–54.

Blidstein, G. 1975. *Honor thy father and thy mother: Filial responsibility in Jewish law and ethics*. New York: KTAV.

Bolen, B. J. 1978. *Personal maturity: The existential dimension*. New York: Seabury.

Butler, R. N. 1963. The life review: An interpretation of reminiscence in old age. *Psychiatry* 26, 65–76.

Chinen, A. 1989. *In the ever after: Fairy tales and the second half of life*. Wilmette, IL: Chiron.

Gutmann, D. 1987. *Reclaimed powers: Toward a new psychology of men and women in later life*. New York: Basic.

Harris, J. G. 1987. *Biblical perspectives on aging*. Philadelphia: Fortress Press.

Isenberg, S. 1992. Aging in Judaism: "Crown of glory" and "days of sorrow." In T. R. Cole, D. D. Van Tassel, and R. Kastenbaum, *Handbook of the humanities and aging*, 147–74. New York: Springer.

Jung, C. J. 1961. *Memories, dreams and reflections*. New York: Vintage.

Kegan, R. 1980. There the dance is: Religious dimensions of a developmental framework. In C. Brusselmans and J. A. O'Donohue, eds., *Toward moral and spiritual maturity*, 404–40. Morristown, NJ: Silver Burdett.

Kimble, M. A., J. W. Ellor, S. H. McFadden, and J. J. Seeber, eds. In press. *Handbook of religion, spirituality and aging*. Minneapolis: Fortress Press.

Lefevre, C., and P. Lefevere, eds. 1985. *Aging and the human spirit: A reader in religion and gerontology*. Chicago: Exploration Press.

Meredith, W. 1987. His plans for old age. In *Partial accounts: New and selected poems*. New York: Knopf.

Moberg, D. O. 1990. Spiritual maturity and wholeness in later years. *Journal of Religious Gerontology* 7, 5–24.

Moody, H. R. 1986. The meaning of life in old age. In T. R. Cole and S. A. Gadow, eds., *What does it mean to grow old?* Durham, NC: Duke University Press.

———. In press. Mysticism and aging. In M. A. Kimble, J. W. Ellor, S. H. McFadden, and J. J. Seeber, eds., *Handbook of religion, spirituality and aging*. Minneapolis: Fortress Press.

Myerhoff, B. 1978. *Number our days*. New York: Simon & Schuster.

Post, S. G. 1992. Aging and meaning: The Christian tradition. In T. R. Cole, D. D. Van Tassell, and R. Kastenbaum, *Handbook of the humanities and aging*, 127–46. New York: Springer.

Reviv, H. 1989. *The elders of ancient Israel: The study of a biblical institution*. Jerusalem: Magnes Press.

Sapp, S. 1987. *Full of years: Aging and the elderly in the Bible and today*. Nashville, TN: Abingdon.

Seeber, J. J., ed. 1990. *Spiritual maturity in the later years*. Binghamton, NY: Haworth Press.

Staude, J. R., ed. 1981. *Wisdom and age: The adventure of later life*. Berkeley, CA: Ross Books.

Sternberg, R. J., ed. 1990. *Wisdom: Its nature, origins, and development*. New York: Cambridge University Press.

Thomas, L. E. In press. Cognitive development and transcendence: An emerging transpersonal paradigm of consciousness. In S. N. Alexander, M. Miller, and S. R. Cook-Greuter, eds., *Transcendence and mature thought in adulthood*. Lanham, MD: Rowman & Littlefield.

Thomas, L. E. 1991. Dialogues with three religious renunciates and reflections on wisdom and maturity. *International Journal of Aging and Human Development* 32, 211–27.

Thomas, L. E., S. J. Brewer, P. A. Kraus, and B. L. Rosen. 1993. Two patterns of transcendence: An empirical investigation of Wilber and Washburn's theories. *Journal of Humanistic Psychology* 33, 64–79.

Thursby, G. R. 1992. Islamic, Hindu, and Buddhist conceptions of aging. In T. R. Cole, D. D. Van Tassell, and R. Kastenbaum, *Handbook of the humanities and aging*, 175–96. New York: Springer.

Tilak, S. 1989. *Religion and aging in the Indian tradition*. Albany: State University of New York Press.

Vogel, L. J. 1984. *The Religious education of older adults*. Birmingham, AL: Religious Education Press.

———. 1991. *Teaching and learning in communities of faith*. San Francisco: Jossey-Bass.

Weibust, P. S., and L. E. Thomas. In press. Learning and spirituality in adulthood. In

J. D. Sinnott, ed., *Handbook of adult lifespan learning*. Westport, CT: Greenwood.

Wilber, K. 1983. *A sociable God: A brief introduction to a transcendental sociology*. New York: New Press.

Index

About the Contributors

W. ANDREW ACHENBAUM is professor of history at the University of Michigan and deputy director of the Institute of Gerontology. His publications include *Old Age in the New Land: The American Experience Since 1790, Social Security: Visions and Revisions,* several edited volumes, and numerous book chapters. He is currently completing a book on the emergence of gerontology as a scientific field of inquiry in the twentieth century.

STEPHEN BERTMAN is professor of classical studies at the University of Windsor, Windsor, Ontario. His books include *Doorways Through Time: The Romance of Archaeology, The Conflict of Generations in Ancient Greece and Rome,* and *The Power of Now* (forthcoming). His essays appear in Falkner and de Luce, *Old Age in Greek and Latin Literature;* and Perry Rogers, *Aspects of Western Civilization,* Vol. 2.

ALLAN B. CHINEN is associate clinical professor of psychiatry at the University of California, San Francisco. He is the author of *In the Ever After: Fairy Tales and the Second Half of Life; Once Upon a Midlife,* which discusses the spiritual aspects of aging; and most recently, *Dancing on the King's Grave,* which focuses on men's development.

SUSAN A. EISENHANDLER is assistant professor of sociology at the University of Connecticut. A former Administration on Aging trainee, she conducts research on the social construction of identity in old age. She has studied the relationship between driving and identity in old age, and her current research focuses on life transitions and the construction of meaning in the lives of the elderly.

ELISE M. FULLMER is assistant professor of social work at the University of North Carolina at Charlotte. Her research interests include aging and alternative family forms and intergenerational issues as they relate to communities. Recent publications and research cover topics related to older caregivers of adults with mental retardation and aging in the lesbian/gay community.

RICHARD B. GRIFFIN, in his second career, works as a writer, educator and gerontological consultant. He also appears regularly on public television in Boston discussing religious and ethical issues. Earlier in his professional life he was a Jesuit priest, finishing that career as Roman Catholic Chaplain at Harvard University. Subsequently he served as director of Elder Services for the City of Cambridge, Massachusetts.

J. GORDON HARRIS is professor of Old Testament and vice president for Academic Affairs at the North American Baptist Seminary, Sioux Falls, South Dakota. He is the author of *Biblical Perspectives on Aging: God and the Elderly*. He teaches graduate courses on "Ministry and the Aging Adult" and "Ethical Issues and Aging," and has conducted seminars on aging for professional and lay audiences.

SUSAN H. McFADDEN is associate professor of psychology at the University of Wisconsin, Oshkosh. She is an editor of *Aging, Spirituality, and Religion: A Handbook*. Her research interests include examining sources of meaning in long-term care and the motivational/emotional dynamics of spirituality.

HARRY R. MOODY is deputy director for academic affairs at Brookdale Center on Aging of Hunter College in New York. A philosopher, he is interested in reminiscence, late styles in art, and education and public policy for older people. His publications include *The Abundance of Life: Human Development Policies for an Aging Society,* plus numerous articles and book chapters.

BARBARA PITTARD PAYNE is professor emeritae of sociology and former director of the Gerontology Center, Georgia State University, Atlanta. She has conducted research and published extensively on religion and aging. Her most recent publications include two edited volumes on gerontology in theological education, and chapters and articles related to religiosity and spirituality among older adults. Her current research and writing is on gender differences in spirituality and faith development.

EDWARD J. QUINNAN is a Roman Catholic priest and a marriage and family therapist. His ongoing research focuses on the life experience of religious celibates, in which he makes use of qualitative research methodology. He was a fellow in gerontology with the Travelers Center on Aging at the University of Connecticut, and now teaches Family Studies at Loyola University in Chicago.

ROBERT L. RUBINSTEIN, a cultural anthropologist, is director of research at the Philadelphia Geriatric Center. His publications include *Singular Paths: Old Men Living Alone,* several edited works and numerous chapters and articles. He has conducted research in the United States and in Vanuatu in the South Pacific. His areas of interest include older men, environments and aging, childless elders, and health and aging.

DENA SHENK is professor of anthropology and coordinator of the Interdisciplinary Program in Gerontology at the University of North Carolina at Charlotte. She has completed research and published on rural older women in the United States and Denmark. Her research interests include social support systems, aging in cultural context and the use of visual methodologies in aging research.

GREGORY C. SMITH is assistant professor in the Department of Human Development at the University of Maryland, College Park. He is currently working on an edited book, *Enabling Aging Families: Directions for Practice and Policy.* His research publications have focused on various psychosocial aspects of aging from an applied perspective.

L. EUGENE THOMAS is professor of human development and family relations at the University of Connecticut. As a Fulbright Research Fellow, he conducted research on life satisfaction and spirituality of elderly in India and England. The results of this research are summarized in the book he edited, *Research on Adulthood and Aging: The Human Science Perspective.* He is presently studying life transitions and meaning construction among elderly born in this country and Russian elderly who recently immigrated to this country.

SHELDON S. TOBIN is professor of welfare and research associate of the Ringel Institute of Gerontology at the University of Albany, SUNY. A former editor-in-chief of *The Gerontologist,* he most recently authored *Personhood in Advanced Old Age: Implications for Practice.* He has published extensively on normative aging, encompassing church and religion, adaptation to stress in aging, and services for the elderly.

LARS TORNSTAM is professor of sociology at the University of Upsala, Sweden, where he specializes in social gerontology. He has been the leader of the Swedish nationwide cross-faculty research program, "Elderly in Society—Past, Present and in the Future." His current research interests include intergenerational relationships, lifestyles and aging, formal and informal caregiving, abuse of elderly, loneliness, and aging and psychological development.